DADA BUDAPEST

John Olson

Black Widow Press is an imprint of Commonwealth Books, Inc., Boston, MA. Distributed to the trade by NBN (National Book Network) throughout North America, Canada, and the U.K. All Black Widow Press books are printed on acid-free paper, and glued into bindings. Black Widow Press and its logo are registered trademarks of Commonwealth Books, Inc.

Joseph S. Phillips and Susan J. Wood, Ph.D., Publishers
www.blackwidowpress.com

Design & production: Kerrie L. Kemperman

Collage images: The Whirlpool Galaxy (Spiral Galaxy M51, NGC 5194), a classic spiral galaxy located in the Canes Venatici constellation, and its companion NGC 5195. Balloon illustration from: B. Faujas de Saint-Fond: *Descrizione delle esperienze della macchina aerostatica dei Signori di Montgolfier. Traduzione dal Francese*, Venice, Graziosi, 1784. Author image provided by John Olson.

ISBN-13: 978-0-9971725-6-0

Printed in the United States
10 9 8 7 6 5 4 3 2 1

For Roberta

ACKNOWLEDGMENTS

The author would like to express his gratitude to the following publications in which some of these works have previously appeared: *Alligatorzine, Cloud Rodeo, House Organ, Make It True: Poetry from Cascadia, The Meadow Wobbler, New American Writing, Nouveau's Midnight Sun, The Pip Anthology of World Poetry of the 21st Century (Volume 10),* and *Word Swell.*

TABLE OF CONTENTS

AFTERNOON OF AN AUTUMN AUTONOMY

The autonomy of a monotonous mood rolled by with a sigh. It crashed into an abandoned pile of socialism. A crow arrived and furnished the bruised autonomy with glasses. The glasses were French ocher and veined with absent-minded rivers. The autonomy hurried to wear them, but stopped to paint an exhibit of alcoholic ice skates. The clatter of naked peculiarities produced by the creative fervor of the short-sighted but determined autonomy worried a nearby elephant, a female from Sri Lanka named Sathyanga who sparkled with telepathic alphabets and blew aromatic furloughs from her oracular trunk. Autumn writhed and flickered on the ground in an ecstasy of pumpkins and evergreens. This received an ovation from the forehead of a hawk, and a fine, warm, brisk operetta simmering with fecundity in the heart of a taproot. The autonomy, full of speed bumps and Phillips-head screws, jerked forward carrying a conclusion for this story, which can only be deciphered by a gentle vitamin purged of seaplanes.

THE ORIGIN OF LANGUAGE

How do you do my name is Luigi and I am the Duke of Abruzzi. I love bubbles, strawberries, and extortion.

What can I say?

I grew up in Minneapolis. I grow obscure 50 feet above the ground, where I can shuffle metaphors around and make sandwiches out of clouds.

That's my last Duchess on the wall, the one with the hairdo that looks like a shoe.

I know all the sorrows of the jukebox. Sometimes I feel like a cloud of opium. And sometimes I'm more like a hat, or elevator.

Do you hear? There is a song in the ink, a pool of words dangling from a genital of ceiling fans. Life is an endless struggle, it sings, and death is a long sweet rest. Let's not fuss over little things. What matters is reinforced concrete.

I would have to agree. But I would add hydraulic lifts, boom cylinders and swingdrives to the list. If you let the world in, you have to let it back out. It may be heavy as a truck tire, so be careful. There are times when the division between the organic and non-organic ceases to exist. Dry yourself by the fire and mull it over. The division among things is blurry, but complementary, like a continental breakfast at a roadside motel.

What holds atoms together? Consonants shining in the curve of a spoon. Impulse. A dream in the fold of night. Form and color. Max Jacob dangling from a balloon.

It is in the origins of things that we discover tides of fortune on the sifted sand. Baubles, bubbles, birds. Skates, oysters, adjectives.

The origin of language is hectic with adjectives. Preposterous moss. Inscrutable rocks. Invisible powers. All of which go to feed that complex organism called a poem, that thing of words and meaty convolutions, grits of irritating sand and the occasional pearl.

The poem is a contraption, a flirtation with gloves. It is pure sorcery. Last night I saw my face floating on a license plate. And then a bunch of predicates set the universe on fire. Everyone flinched to see themselves on TV, and then went bowling, which made the sound of thunder, and revealed the truth of Plato's Republic, which is everywhere, and indicates heliotrope, and emotion, and that the world is swarming with government.

The U.S. government is run by a man in Williston, North Dakota. When there are no women around he gets angry. He gets drunk and irrational. He filters the world through plums. He turns social security into credit default swaps, and formulates flippers for jaywalking.

One thing he cannot do is stop growing old. Getting old is a process. Getting old is an education. What can you learn from growing old? The cat swims through his fur with red hot veins tangential to consciousness. Shoes have soles and ships have hulls. Courtrooms are a frequent cause of headaches. And if you shake a bottle filled with earthquakes, it will erupt into Christmas bulbs.

HIPPOPOTAMUS

Why do I do this? Why do I feel compelled to put words down on paper? Will it fill stadiums with people waving smartphones? Will it keep me from dying? Will it make me immortal? Is it any fun to be immortal when you're dead?

It's the very futility of the thing that draws me in, the subversive energy of making something of no possible use, a document of hedonistic glowworms, a subjective tortilla, a cabbage of vertical consciousness that sways me into sewing words of clay and hunger, an embroidery of dusky migration.

This thing which is wallets to a dada bulb. This sound of letters in a drop of heart. This chemistry of sensation, this extension of shadows. The whole thing shakes like an ocean detonating glands of kaleidoscopic light in a Budapest of humming narration. If a mouth opens a fugue balloons into Bach. Comparisons create more differences than similarities and so lengthen into sequoias of canopy and choir. My lady's lips are like the west coast of Ireland and must serve their purposeless purpose in a Kantian flood of emergent fire.

Bob Dylan on a horse.

Nothing pleases me more than mustard. The skin of night telling consonants of seashore, ravenous vowels mushrooming in a slop of intermediary rain. The elbow slams its grease on a wrinkle of steam and militates against stubble. This confers chewing and art and instinctively becomes a postmark slamming its door on a glistening abstraction. If I flop on the couch at 8:00 p.m. enfoldments of reverie recoil into catwalks and I can feel what pleasure there is in being an invention, an emotion so big it mirrors reality, a dream of slate and exotic biology. If there is a giant version of myself elsewhere in the universe let it be spectral and wear my eyes like a paper incubus. Let it stir into subtlety. Let it become a strain, a culture aloud on a spoon.

If I feel sticky at the airport let me flop and flap my way to a hole of wind and disappear into history like a simulacrum squirting headlights at the night.

Picture a gold box containing a stillborn opera, something that would delight Joseph Cornell. Think of a smear of significance flirting with formulas for beaverboard on my forehead. Swerve it into accordions. Park it near a loaf of pumpernickel. Engorge it with prose. Let it ricochet during an argument. Lean into letters amid the oarlocks of a foggy description.

The reason I do this is simple: it makes me happy. I can throw a vibration at a thread of elevator and watch it emulsify into euphoria. Operas in rockets, trumpets in books.

I don't sneer at ears. No sir. Nor will I ever fully understand the personality I drag around. Death falls through a preposition and finds life attracting a crowd of astronauts. So be it. Bleeding is all about long-hand, and the problems of the sidewalk sparkle with therapy. My wool is caused by syntax. And if we unite one another in writing our muscles will serve us taproots and the delicacy of dachsunds will glue itself to the water and bounce into parallels where the brocade turns pink and hippopotamus.

RADICAL TAPIOCA

"All philosophy," observed Paul Valéry, "is born knowingly from illusions which are illusions of language." Illusion is the joker of human existence. It's the original placebo, the sweetest anodyne around. Illusion can get you through a dark night of the soul but in the morning the eyes and ears are better served when they're open. Otherwise, chances are good you'll get hit by a car.

Words are the best illusions. Words are everywhere, books in brooks and sermons in stones. They comfort our mortality. They give us the illusion of meaning. "And so, from hour to hour, we ripe and ripe, / And then, from hour to hour, we rot and rot; And thereby hangs a tale."

Words are the music of time and wave.

Hyper-objects, such as government, are particularly interesting: government has no reality, there is nothing tangible about government, government is a concept; and yet government is quite real. We pay taxes to it, elect officials to it, expect it to provide us with streets and libraries. Government is a product of language. Language creates laws, breaks laws, tells stories of outlaws. Language is the ultimate outlaw.

Unicorns, dragons, and brigadier generals all lay equal claim to being and reality. A single word, such as the pronoun "I," can serve as the nucleus for a range of experience including peacocks, doors, and pumpkins. In the realm of illusion, I is an other: its reality is called into being by talking.

"I," "We," "They," and "You" are all propositions, all can be spoken, tasted, squeezed, pressed, ironed, nailed, packed or crushed into a sentence and made to do service as a person.

Are you real?

"Language is a reality," Valéry further observed, "a usage of indeterminate coefficients." A coefficient is a multiplicative factor in any term of a polynomial, a series or any expression. As soon as two or more words are brought into combination they multiply their associative power. Syntax is fundamentally a solder. A spoon is a consolidation.

The poet works at the frontier of nonsense. This is a rare ability, but one which can be developed. The greater the semantic distance among a group of words, the brighter the illumination.

Everything is up for grabs. Words inspire me to be a better addict. I agree with Baudelaire: one should always be drunk. Drunk on words, drunk on wine, drunk on virtue, drunk on poetry. Drunk on illusion. Drunk on reality. Drunk on the illusion of reality. Drunk on the reality of illusion. But drunk. Be drunk. However you choose.

WAGGLE DANCE

We inherit in our elder years the decisions we made in our 20s. My inheritance, then, is simply this: poetry. Poetry, however, doesn't provide food or shelter. Emily Dickinson baked bread in a big Victorian house. That's one solution.

Another might be drunkenness, à la Charles Bukowski.

No question, poetry is a divine madness. Nobody would adopt this life unless they were slightly crazy.

The two most famous examples, William Carlos Williams and Wallace Stevens, are misleading. Yeah, ok, you can do a profession and write poetry simultaneously if you're crafty enough and disciplined about balancing your time, though this is going to be at the expense of your family, should you decide to have a family. If you can get by with it, though, more power to you. Dash into your office and type a couple of lines between patients. Study a hemorrhoid, then get back to your laptop to work out a heptameter. Or close the office door and write a few lines when no one is looking. There are ways to adapt. Poetry is eminently adaptable, albeit with more than a trace of rebellion. I wouldn't recommend these strategies for Starbucks or WalMart.

Until the 80s life was affordable. You could work a demeaning entry level shit job and still make the rent. Can't do that now. I don't know what I'd do if I were in my 20s now. The job market sucks. College burdens you with debt. Rents are astronomical.

What happened?

Kent State happened. Disco and MTV happened. Aids happened. Chernobyl happened. Cocaine happened. Ronald Reagan happened. Margaret Thatcher happened. NAFTA happened. Beanie Babies and SUVs happened. Wall Street and bailouts happened.

Poetry is an antidote to those things. It's just the living part you need to work out. Enough pay for an apartment or house big enough to house your books.

Language gets over everything. Empires, seminars, conversations. The luster of association. Cubism. Elephants eating acacia trees. Memories.

Memories are weird, you know? Like some sort of theater.

Books are another matter. It's important to keep them on paper, in print. Between covers. With a spine. The spine is everything.

Digital books are sent over a wireless network. A controlling company can make them vanish in an instant. Censorship is invisible.

Publishing houses that produce books as physical objects are also subject to control due to pressure from a government or vagaries such as market censorship in which only writing that is plainly marketable gets published and more obscure or difficult writing is rejected, at least by the mainstream presses, which come increasingly under the domination of myopic, profit-driven corporations. This, coupled with the near-extinction of independent bookstores, endangers free thought and quality writing. Nevertheless, it's still much harder to control a physical rather than a virtual reality.

The magic (and it is real magic) is to bring something into the world that hasn't existed before. Paul Eluard's surrealist line "The world is blue as an orange" serves an example of the kind of journeys words are capable of creating. Words like 'universe,' 'soul,' or 'thought' have a profundity and charge that are automatic in expression but in reality are no different than the words 'pencil,' 'bread,' or 'worm.' Their values differ in our imagination. This is where thought acquires the sorcery of music.

Take César Vallejo. This guy is amazing. His poetry is wild, full of stunningly imaginative lines like "when on the fraudulent scales of someone's breasts / I weigh and weep for a fragile Creation," or "what does not burn burns and even / pain doubles up dead with laughter."

Words are propositions. "Of" and "above" and "fast" and "slowly" and "them" and "you" are all propositions.

Words vibrate with witness. Ideas that explode and rain down as stars. It would take a bizarre form of acrobatics, a kind of Japanese butoh, to express the inner realms of our being.

Take two hydrogen atoms and add to them an atom of oxygen and you have water. Compress a mass of hydrogen atoms at great temperature and pressure so that they fuse to form atoms of helium and in the process you will create a big ball of heat and light called a sun. Put a noun and a predicate together and you'll get something wet and large like Great Britain.

The mind sips words and discovers desks. Nihilism feels pinched like a museum. Prophesy doesn't come cheap. But who wants to prophesy? I recommend truffles.

Poets, writes Duncan, hear languages like the murmuring of bees. They swarm in the head where the honey is stored. He speaks of an instinct for words where — like bees dancing — there is a communication below the threshold of language, a clairvoyance of wiggle and buzz.

At home, I become greatly intrigued with that communication below the threshold of language that Duncan mentions, and Jacque Lacan's statement that the unconscious is structured like a language. What in the world does he mean by that? My mind is still stuck on the goo of wax and honey in Duncan's image of a hive. Like bees dancing, he says.

Bees do, indeed, dance. They do a dance called the waggle dance, which is a figure-eight dance in which information about the direction and distance to patches of flowers yielding nectar and pollen can be found, to water sources, or to new housing locations. For instance, a figure-eight shaped waggle dance of the honeybee (*Apis mellifera*) oriented to 45° to the right of 'up' on the vertical comb indicates a food source 45° to the right of the direction of the sun outside the hive.

And so it begins: language. The mouth shapes the air into pneuma, the spirit as air. Opium eyes opium thumbs. Carnivals, friendly dogs, and cleavage. But remember. Always remember what it is that clouds do. You can disguise your feelings with fictions and equivocations, or give them fangs and wings and let them loose.

THE SENTENCE AS A FORM OF CROCHET

What else can I do with this abstract ice, this jingle of bells, but be silent and enjoy it. A tall pink tower sparkles below these words. Whispers of cumbersome chronology help grease the gears of the elevator. I sometimes imagine the dead are trying to pull us into their realm. Could it be that Rome is even more wonderfully imperfect than at first imagined? I can feel something hopping around in my heart. Snakes and rapiers are more like axioms than gumdrops. But what is it that awakens the syllables of a warm farm crowded with shapes as the afternoon begins to lift itself into the air and a totem of vowels chatters its story of frogs and whales? Is it a big man doing delicate things, or a shiny Pythagorean pain? There is a meaning that seeps through these words and it would explain everything if I could only find it. I do know I prefer the sheets tucked in at the end of the bed but that doesn't help explain the powers that are invisible to us, the splashes of divinity sweeping over our oars. Form is the beginning of consciousness. Touch is optional. Gnawing is acoustical. Conquest is rudimentary. The vast unfolding of a consummate ache renders one's fingers more personal, more nimble of themselves as soon as one realizes that that inner pain, that inner hunger is riding a train through Texas. I'm totally into dumbbells. If my tongue is encumbered by a rabbit I accommodate its being and wrestle my incentives to the ground. I get up. I look around. And if the sun is still there I cheer the light and approve the playground slide. Raw essential being urges conference with a rhinoceros. I create holes in the air to escape from war. This causes art and stimulation. Darkness dangles like bats in a mouth of cabbage. I call this necromancy. But it doesn't work. No dead people appear. Just Bob Dylan on a horse. Tinfoil is emotional. I feel its attractions whenever I smell a catalogue rotting in somebody's garage. Maybe it's best to leave the dead alone. I'll be joining them one day, but for the meanwhile I'll continue my cartwheels and sexy indiscriminate perceptions of singing. I saw Finland once, in a dream, which is the true geographic location of Finland. I saw the face of its deliverance, and huge fuzzy eyebrows on the faces of the men, and women so flashy and beautiful that my eyes unraveled in gold. It's then that I realized that the universe is bigger than I initially thought and may be applied to the principles of the accordion, which goes in an out as one squeezes it, producing melodies and dilations of spirit. I can secrete anything I want. Ramification is something else. For that, we'll need an engine and a large comfortable armchair. It's time that we included our elbows in something. One can accomplish miracles in bas-relief. Opera stirs the senses. It's here that we begin to feel a heavy fire in the growling air and let the sidewalk do its thing, just lay itself out in all that concrete, allowing us to abandon our oars and luxuriate in the sweetness of incantation.

HOT BUTTER IN AN EMBARRASSED WORLD

The paragraph rolls on rails. A paper sun flames revelation. Words translate grass. Any bundle that can talk is interwoven. We forged an orbit by gambling on a planet. Drifting must therefore write a doctrine occasionally jingled in circumlocution. The strength of the tray is that an enigma amuses pain. Attitude is pulled from the ocean. There are horses in me that stitch ghostly horizons together. I languish in the emotion of the immaterial. Opium craves the opinion of the stars. I go prospecting for roots, for essences, for pencils and nouns. Language is a hallucination. This means that it is mentally viable but not quite what anyone expected. Portugal lifts itself into the sky and so affirms the metaphysics of denim. The eyes are crazed with veins. The mind explodes into indigo. Eyebrows forest the forehead. The painter ponders space, ripping an old hole into a papier collé tiara. Pain scours the nerves for meaning. Feeling a feeling is a feeling evocative of everything. Which is why I can't do this for money. I do it for slobber. I do it for noise. I do it for recital and cracks. I texture in immediacy. There are adjectives for this but I'm not sure they're ready for the spirit of the wind, which is romantic as mustard. Exasperation inspires crawling. Know what I mean? The harlequin hangs from a peg in the kitchen. Action swarms with cotton. Images arrive in baskets. Clothing drools from the drawers. I am a twang. The wind is the wind. When I hear the sound of machinery I confuse idealism with pragmatism and salt the strain with exercise. The sound of an odor called coconut. I feel dispersed, raw and unrehearsed. My T-shirt is gray. I'm developing a wattle. It's disturbing. Is it because I didn't expect to get this old or because I expected to get this old without actually getting old? I need a haircut. I know that. There are so many things to learn. Time disperses the syllables of history and the dragon of myth spreads his wings. I carry my mouth to the dentist and hope for a good cleaning in which I'm not left in the dental chair with a People magazine. Is there a color for consciousness? Would it be brown or blue? Shouldn't I be able to answer that for myself? And wouldn't everyone's color be different? Maybe there's no color involved at all. It's just waves. My skin, like all skin, is its parchment and scripture. Is there anything goofier than a reproductive organ? The sky leans over the horizon conferring light and water. When the river drops from a cliff it becomes a waterfall. The roar of it is stupendous. The hunchback of Notre Dame walks among these words, a silhouette of pathos swinging maniacally on a bell. I study the motion of blood in my veins and experience science as a serendipitous prose apprehended as a mortar in its prescription and shape, a pestle and bowl for the grinding of pills. Silk on silk imposes the milk of postulation. This is called brocade. Details fill with light as hot butter in an embarrassed world. The semantic fabric spreads into the weather of absorption, a door banging in the wind, a daub of raw sienna on the thumb. Memory is a form of willing, or threshold. And when the rain comes it will dream it's a sunset over the Columbia River gorge as Bob Dylan sings "I Shall Be Released" and there are horses in me that want expression on the hills.

WHY I WRITE

The mind dilates in language. Knock knock. Who's there? Moonlight.
Moonlight who?
Moonlight on the Susquehanna.
I have to let it in. Everything gets wet. The ceiling falls up into itself.
The exudations relax into Ping-Pong. Bells clang. Hysterias resolve.
The moonlight turns obsidian. The Susquehanna flaunts a China rose.
I love speculation. I love the reach of headlights on moonless nights
on the prairie. I love to describe sensations. Everything is thought. A
mouth opens to let it all out. And when the Susquehanna gets up and
leaves I feel a conversation between myself and the world has become
Mesozoic.
There is a man in Cameroun who talks to birds. And the birds talk
to the man. The man's words all sound like birds. The air is rippled by
rattles and chants. Ecstasies and shadows. And there it is. There is
writing.
What happens if I let myself go completely?
The question implies that there is a part of me which is chronically
subject to restraint. I have no restraint. Not really. Restraints are
imagined. Restraints are a form of social programming. There are no
restraints in the arena of writing.
It is in the reality of everyday life that the Other appears to us, and
its affections and objectivity are humid and tangled. It is a greenhouse
of the mind.
Does it hurt? No. Not at all. Because pain always comes to us
naked, and must be adorned with food. Olives, eggs, spaghetti. This is
especially true if I am pierced by a predicament called Being which
must bicycle around the room like a cranberry.
Like Apollinaire eating a hot dog.
Like the weather from a burning log.
I scrounge for thunder in the long gray day. The mythology of rou-
tine is chiseled into stone. Hints of another world are buried in stories.

The ensuing process is wrinkly, like the consciousness of consciousness which is one with the consciousness of which it is conscious.

And that's why I write. We can hear the floorboards creak. Georges Braque is making scrambled eggs in the kitchen on a wood stove. Each sensation has value, each feeling has heft and art. The good moods arrive unannounced. They slip in and out quietly. The good moods are like a wad of pharmaceutical cotton. They don't knock. They move through us blatant, blessed, and taffeta. Words strung together like beads in a kitchen door.

THE SQUIRREL THAT ATE CINCINNATI

If tuna is immediate and scratched, is salt rational? Each time I construct a moment of sand I produce a sensation not unlike a context. Words, pushed out of the mouth and into somebody's ears, will resemble semen.

A mosquito, meanwhile, removes blood from a thumb. I collapse from too many scruples and crawl into the Rio Tinto Zinc Mine to get subversive. The drug that brought me here is orange. It inhabits me like a new experience. We can be caviar together and create metaphors for the holes in our heads.

Please forgive me. My tongue is an afternoon.

Just now I saw a woman pass the library with the skinniest two legs I've ever seen. There are truths so intractable they have to be tilted. This proves my theory about ecstasy.

A face is more like a moon than a noun. It has nowhere else to go except the fact of its own existence.

A cloud flaps out of a word and fills the air with thought. Which changes into a crease. Which changes into a golf club. Which changes into an abalone. Which changes into a mustache. Which changes into a squirrel. Which eats Cincinnati. All of it, including the Harriet Beecher Stowe House and most of William Howard Taft Road.

I'm sorry this happened. Sometimes these poems get out of control. Nothing remains the same. They have to rub themselves up against everything. Some of us inhabit bodies for the sole purpose of reproduction and good jobs and cable TV, while others surrender themselves to the moss. Solitude does the rest.

WHAT 68 YEARS ON PLANET EARTH HAVE TAUGHT ME

Revolt agrees with me. I cut cotton into wings and fill areas of conversation with humidity and kerosene. I dissolve in amber, culture pearls, light Colorado with my limestone piano. Structure collapses on the moon. My emotions smell of language. I feel extraverted and tangible. Life is not always quixotic. It can be rough. It can incandesce like a spinal cord. I can feel the medication kick in. Most of the carrying is sullen. Redemption will sometimes shake you to your core. Decisions are sharp and hard and riding the rails is full of thrust and steel. It's better to bounce around in the United States like Neal Cassady than it is to arrive in a flying saucer. The mine is haunted but the gold is particular, like the legs of a tarantula. I must do some wash. There is always wash. Dishes, clothes, windows, chairs. The world is full of bananas and numerous subtleties of salt and dogs. The allegories take care of themselves. They reveal themselves in dreams. I'm dry now. People like to sing in church. I begin to think about eating. I think eating is silk. I salute my blood. I wave to my digestion system. Hello down there. How's it going? I'm old now and have developed a wattle, much like the one my dad had, and his dad before him, and his dad before him, and so on. Grandmothers too. They all had wattles. It was Aldous Huxley that introduced me to the idea of a door and what a door is all about. Perception, you know? Like when a clock radio goes off and you hear a Bach cantata on KING FM and words fall through your mind in strings and you open one blood red eye and see a ceiling doing push-ups on your forehead. That's what getting old is about. The brain reflects on its own reflections. And you feel like a rag on a shelf in somebody's garage. And the garage smells of paint and turpentine and car grease. And that's when it hits you: existence is soapier than death and money is lousy with symbols. But the funniest things in the world aren't pimples, they're fingernails.

A SHADOW CLIMBING A CORNSTALK

Sense experience has once again become an adventure for me. A bell, a syntax, a grandeur. Empiricism emptied it of mystery, but then I saw a sentence have sex with a predicate, and the world dilated. I won't say language is necessarily implicit in sense experience, but I will say that a bazaar is full of people and objects, and many amphibians have a mucus layer covering their skin. Touching things is one way to progress and discover the texture of a pathos or bubble in terms of how it is connected to the raw material from which it is made without focusing on the surface. This is called conceptual analysis and is a form of listening and cracking when the object in question howls its symptoms up and down a spinal cord.

Between touching and feeling experience establishes a difference which is sensible and hypnotic. It attracts the attention to a supermarket where one's reflections sway with contrary perspectives. A sharp cry is no more no less than a green thumb. Neither is a body in repose the same thing as a body in which opposing forces are in equilibrium. Faith fulfills the destiny of hair and gravity provides a tire.

Reality is already inhabited by signification which gives it humidity and skin. Sense experience invests the quality of this word with enough thunder to power a forklift. If I can feel it, I can condemn it. The problem is to understand the strange relationships between things and make something of them, a moral or a pair of moccasins. Sense experience is, essentially, a vital communication with the world which renders it present and immediate and dripping with medication. One must be supple and full of the steam of capacity to play with the many parts that comprise the machinery of marriage. It cannot be said that a reality is analogical when it spouts fresh cream. It only dribbles. It does not moan.

The first philosophical act appears to be to return to the world of actual experience a little of the enamel which is anterior to the objective world, and endure the ensuing calypso. The drill is only as good as its bit. It is by way of experience that we can restore to subjectivity its inherence in stucco. The phenomenal field is not an inner world. Nothing is more difficult than to know precisely what we see. Cotton turns Technicolor when it crawls toward its realization in shirts and towels.

The tacit thesis of perception is that at each instant one can feel the exultation of existence. There is something brass about it, and wire and bonbons. One must learn how to kill time. Get a facelift. Leak information. Fulminate. Garden the mind. Existence is creative, and intersubjective. What we see is not always what we get. That which is indeterminate can become a wrinkle, a carp, a handful of coals softly glowing in a hibachi on a balcony in Alabama. Definition is assembled by mimicry and hardware. Knowledge is realized in the thing itself when perception bumps against the brain, and a thought pops out, a notion of wool, or a shadow climbing a cornstalk.

A HAPPY DISORDER

Nature has given us the use of language. But why? What for? I have
made a thesis of this. And glue. Syntax is the glue of words. Secretion is
how our bodies communicate with the outer world. Corduroy makes
excellent pants and the moon just hangs around all day. The wind is the
wind. Clothing, meanwhile, drools from our drawers, listless and hungry
for use. Syllables chisel redemption from the air. Am I a fiasco, we some-
times ask ourselves, or just another convolution of skin and anguish? My
dream is to one day utter a sentence so long and complicated that our
little village will levitate and jingle when I walk. Each day has its own
excuse. Today's excuse is late summer, lightly peppered with eyes and
hinges and a dash of idealism. When Mick Jagger asked me to join the
Rolling Stones I had to say no. Why, he asked. Well, I said, I don't know
how to play a musical instrument. I hear the sound of machinery and
want to replicate it like Keith does on his mighty guitar, but I can't do it
with spoons or strings, I have to use my mouth, I have to form words
with my mouth, and let them drip into the world like Delaware, like
analgesics from heaven. I am hectic with tin, Mick, and I want to join
the Rolling Stones, but I must go it alone, yes sir, just like Samuel Beck-
ett when he stood on top of a hill and shook his fist and berated the
earth for its miseries and mud. We all have a need to escape ourselves.
There are often miscarriages, but in the end it is the politics of the
potato that must remind us how malleable behavior can be, how
remarkably like henna as a dye and how, during summer, words smell of
rum. Proximity is a form of approximation. This we know. But the bur-
den of being human attracts totalitarianism if it isn't watched closely.
Insecurities do this. Insecurities cause insult and statues. The sublime
makes its demands, I know, but it doesn't hurt to drop a nail occasion-
ally while you're building a new salon and play with perception as if it
were shapes of crystal and elevated our existence from our habituated
empires and saw space for truly what it is, an autumn in the bones, a
roller coaster full of screaming teenagers, a break in the sky from which
thunder rolls, and rain, and the darkness of night when the horizon
drags itself out of the sun and into the sugar of a happy disorder.

HALIBUT TODAY WITH A CHANCE OF BUBBLES

A find sucks Scotland. I feel planets and scrub. The weather appears
halibut. A steep relation chirps invisible black participles. Civilization's
stars exult in churning perspective. Severity is air and how it becomes
spectral. Driving is diving is tears when there is sheer form and velocity
hangs in the mind like a raw geometry of vapor. The Parisian snow
articulates clothing. Parabolas of taproot attitude statements are
singing and clouds are mouths of heavy ships and rope. There is a
grease for the propeller and strolling and axles and subtleties of abstract
garage. Words in a sentence protecting things like grammar and
baptisms of combinatorial arms carrying popcorn and metaphors. I
like your touch. I don't mean to seek approval, but the elegance of your
feeling is just like saws or powwows. Get wet in the city dude. I mean
babble. Bubble. Click together like spatulas. Presence tastes of heat.
Ice cubes melt into experience. Lucidity floats in my head like a world.
Hospitable trapeze tubs for quitting bad habits and mitigating dye.
The water is a dime that indulges the eyes in a parable of metal and
little bronze hats for the elves. French ocher impact kings playing at
a swamp. I want to know more about you. Can you send me your
name, number, and a sample of your wings? I like being abstract, you
know, and writing things that bare themselves with an automatic
awkwardness. Language cuts the air and unfolds by finger and aching
desire. Winter is everything cabbage. This is how we fold ourselves.
Cogitation is just a fancy word for consciousness. Description prowls
behind the painting in blue tennis shoes and eight years in Ethiopia.
Bob Dylan pays a visit. He's old now. He owns his snakes and shivers
from so much poetry that the beauty and grace of Italy compels my
tongue to speak in time and twigs and arouses the good sense of fire
when it's sleeping to get up and walk around in a dusky migration of
age and semantic mustard. Nothing pleases me more than knobs and a
great many words so many words that silence eventually ensues and
curtains and brushwork and incongruity. Can you imitate a box? All I

need now is a little dynamite. All the letters do is excite my personality. But what can you do? If morning drops my heart I know the night will pick it up and carry it somewhere good.

SEASON OF A DREAM

This is the season of a dream. It has chairs and pleasure and smells of dwelling. Every dynamic possibility opens its arms and accepts our excursion, as if circumstance dripped with silk and incision. Sensation is humored by clouds. But this is more like reminiscence. Pain is often sexual. The lumber is alive, though the antennas are French. There is a despair that is blonde and geographic but this is not the despair of life, which comes to us jingling in the guise of King Lear's jester. The tea of incident is distilled in valor. Injuries of the spur make the sentence hungry for meaning. Concrete carries its subtleties to an extreme of Euclidean geometry, and we fall asleep, bathed in amber. This is why nature has given us the use of legs, and arms, so that we can go for walks on the moon and fashion our morality according to the etiquette of outer space, where even the stars seem to burst out of themselves with effortless panache, much like the sidewalks of Paris. I have no particular feelings about machinery, but there is a little village in my head that makes me think that the prairie is a more suitable context for my ghostly rants. I've lost buttons before, but nothing that couldn't be replaced, not like this dream of the prairie in which the sunset seems squeezed from a tube of Vandyke red and a purposeless wind glides over the grass causing it to whisper like a pituitary gland in a fever of promiscuity. History is like an elevator whose doors open on the wrong floor. Is it any wonder I feel totally alienated from society? I have the temperature of an elk and the inclinations of a bear. This is why I wear pullovers, and not hills and glue. I'm not just another balloon in a comic strip. My skin tells a story of oboes and waves. I'm easily aroused by England. The ceremony of words floats obscurities of thought. I feel plunged into water. Hunger is a notable symptom of eternal life, but don't ask how. Just try languishing in Euclid. Watch the waves splash against the rocks. Decorate your brain with bathtubs and hookers. Contraptions like raspberries. You know? Name your favorite emotion, then mimic the snow as it falls on the river. It takes a big man to do delicate things.

Perception is a process involving adjectives and cork. This is why I like to tuck the sheets in at the end of the bed. It makes me feel pertinent to sleep. Once I get the light bulb changed I can attend to the fireworks. And sometimes when I think of kelp it helps to move my fingers. I find that consciousness often causes itself by fattening on words and rupturing from fatalism in a semantic convulsion of money and deer. I'm not from Harlan County, no, but I know a postmark when I see one. The muffin dreams it's an appliance and eventually grows dials and rinse cycles in its abstraction. Such things have been known to happen, followed by the clapping of hands and the architecture of doubt. It reminds me of the thrashing of science when all logic has failed and culminates in dots, like Dagwood and Blondie. Money is ultimately too sophisticated for me and so I turn to poetry, which is where all the magic is, and as surely as an artery carries blood to the heart, the words go on expressing something reachable and large.

THE SUNLIGHT OF THE MIND

Believe me when I say art is powerfully stiffened by olives, the chopped intentions of the poetry anthology, the literal significance of any boat stew cooked into literature. This is where I nudge the meaning of the eyeball home to its skull. It would be a labor to suggest that sugar is involved. But it is. Sugar sprints to my elbows and jumps into the chemistry of my oaths. I swear at everything, swear to everything, swear about everything. I mean, what else can you do with existence but live it? Wear it? Fly it around the room pleading for understanding? This is how things are. Lobsters become postmarks. Participles flavor abstraction with the boiling scenery of the mind. Let us ruminate on the reality of clothing. It gets cold here on earth. I see a Viking wandering around Norway with a flashlight. I see the breath of the deer. I can feel a nude woman squeezing a sponge against her leg. The flop and flap of a sentence liberates the spirit of malleability. Simulacrums that contain stillborn operas, ancient dilations, the congeniality of significance falling over itself. My forehead is ready for the trumpets in books. Let's explore consciousness, shall we? Put on a hat of quarks. Ride palominos. Swerve into thought like a lunatic caboose. Let me offer you the smell of a splendid worry, the deification of trout, the music of pain. There is providence in the fall of a sparrow and dissonance in the rain. The secrets of the heart get splattered on the driveway gravel. Syllables abound for the puzzles of sound. Bulbs and neckties and process are everywhere, delicate as paths. The death of a hair floats in the air. There is the hint of a sexual squeeze. The leaning of a lazy breeze. Definitions unravel. Solitude swallows the ripples of time. The nerves are birds that guide us to feeling the loop and lift of reverie. That's where the treasure is. The shine of acceleration. The sunlight of the mind.

RESORT

I smell Plato. Wherever I go I smell Plato. My inner fire blazes with a higher reality. I fold it up and put it in a drawer. I go on my way. My sternum is as severe as a winter sky. I live in a skull of sugar which is placed on my shoulders like a story of labor and pain. Hair comes out of it. A goodly amount of it. Why, I don't know why. If Great Britain takes umbrage with Amazon, who can blame them? This is why I've decided to go through life with a warehouse in my back pocket. Various personal injuries decorate my heart. I expand into eyes. I deposit pretzels in the Bank of Pretzels, as I was advised, by the King of Pretzels. I drift across a piece of paper leaving words behind my pen. The words get up and walk around. Nothing in life is ever truly incongruous. Therefore be glad and culminate in dots. Evade predictions. There is more to a chair than a chair. There are gnarls of wood and grain and shapes that snake through Tuesday bundled in glue and nails. So many subtleties are distinguished in dishwashing. There is a certain glamour in grammar. Red fingernails growing in reckless abandon. I'm held together by buttons and shoes. It helps to point these things out. Utopia wasn't built in a day. By that I mean popcorn and cymbals. What is the harm in harmony? If I sound like a piano, will the diversities of life go on squeezing my lingerie? Identity is just another antagonism to appease. By this I mean babble, sparkle, and yearn. Really, just like reading. Open a book and there they are: words. Pronouns walking around dressed in adjectives. Does it worry you that silver is Italian? Buy a bathtub. You'll see. Water is drunk with being water. Is that a door in your head, or just another eyebrow? The dime shines on the sidewalk calling out in miracles of bas-relief. I sense another reality clutching the trees and shaking them around. Some might call that wind. I call it the drool of twilight. When one journey ends another begins. The insects scatter and desire moves into the light awkward and romantic. The railroad is stunning. I long to hang from your lips discussing the monsters of late night TV. And no, I'm not a tuna. I dig the warm earth of Cubism. My intestines are pretty and fold around in the various colors of a sloppy but sensible convolution. The ghost of a dream inhabits my bassoon. It bangs around like a coat hanger because the escalator is thirsty. It prowls around the shopping mall dropping salads of sound and step by step transcends the floor. This is how it's done, baby. The raw umber of being alive fattens the rodents and stipples the petition of sense in a cloud of nothingness. The result is a refrigerator in G minor, infrared pickles and a gallon of cross-eyed skim milk. I won't deny the material world, no, but let's face it: consolidating blisters in a pencil factory is just so much punctuation. It ain't Chicago, dude. I have, however, changed my mind about chutney. Nobody's odor should get in the way of sweating. Imagine Joan Baez in a T-shirt. Roll into a bistro whistling a zygodactyl ditty. Order some coffee. Sit down. Lift your cup and smell it. Smell the coffee. This is how things are done in the material world. The firmament lies down in the fog and nurtures a fertile anonymity, a lovely monotony, a kind of purity mixed with cocoa. Infinity dripping with hope. This is what I meant to say all along. I'm sad, not bitter. Just down a quart. All I ever wanted was to get out of this world. And here I sit: wandering around in my head like a ski resort.

SAGA OF THE SUGAR ANTS

They're persistent, I'll give them that. They keep coming. And coming and coming. Their little black bodies. Legs like little black hairs. Most of them are dead. But some continue to move, to wriggle, to persevere, to struggle, to labor forward in the quest for food. These few, these happy few, these bands of brothers, are less than exuberant. The spirit is there, but not the capacity. Their movements are slow and sluggish, their direction uncertain, their agitations vain and absurd. It astonishes us how they manage to penetrate the thick, gooey Maginot line of dish soap and powdered cinnamon that we've applied between the metallic trim of the carpet and the tiles of the kitchen floor. It suggests a power of will that towers above my own. We're confronted with an alien intelligence, a formidable aporia.

I imagine a labyrinth of tunnels under the floor, of galleries and corridors snaking through the sandy soil, each passage teeming with ants in busy, fervent endeavor: unwearying, unwavering. inexorable. We spend hours on our hands and knees searching for little black dots, the convulsions of a miniscule being in its death throes, a tiny life with a gargantuan appetite in a desultory funk, going in circles, giving up the ghost. It amazes us that they persist. Where is the logic? Rarely do we see one trotting its way merrily across the floor in mindless triumph. The scouts make their way to the surface and die. Or so we think. So we hope.

We study their behavior. We search for patterns. For cracks and fissures, ports of entry. It isn't amusing. Maybe a little amusing. Amusing in a curious way. Amusing in the way that a pain or a disquiet can simultaneously keep one company while also burdening and fatiguing one's spirit.

Whose planet is this, anyway? The sun shines equally on all things great and small. This does not, however, ameliorate sentiments of estrangement. One finds comfort, sometimes, in the peripheries. It's in the margins that life feels less argumentative. At least until hunger and desire take hold. It is this dialectic that we share with the ants. Desire is universal. Hunger is unavoidable. Sooner or later even the most ascetic among us must emerge from the shadows and find some form of nourishment, reproductive gratification, or redemption from the crazy, distant stars.

I add a little more soap to a crack in one of the tiles beside the stove. Do ants have eyes? Yes, two compound eyes and three ocelli (simple eyes) on the top of their heads which can distinguish intensities of light and polarization. Eyesight is poor. They mostly rely on their sense of smell, on pheromones by which they make their trails when a source of nourishment is discovered.

Aren't these sentences a form of trail as well? What is thought if not a catastrophe of words laid carefully in a path of hungry meaning? There is sense in sensation. Words with little legs. Words with hungry black bodies. Words in perpetual quest. In quest of what? Transcendence? Order? I don't know. But there goes another ant. Just barely making it out of a line of goo.

THE BIRTHDAY JUMP

I remember the first & only time I parachuted it was 1964 my 16th birthday a rite of passage if you will from the old man an aerospace engineer & former WWII B24 bomber pilot I practice-jumped from oil barrels taught how to fall back then when the time came & the plane got fired up & took us up high in the sky over Snohomish county mostly pretty farm country I got the signal & stood out on the little step & took hold of the wing strut with both hands wind blasting into my face & racketing my clothes & waited for the signal to let go the instructor inside a genial guy in his 30s counted down with his hand & shouted now! & I let go & tumbled crazily didn't remember anything I'd been taught I was senseless with terror then the chute opened I felt some-thing scrape my neck & jerked like a puppet into air with the canvas ballooning over my head & realized there was something wrong with the left pull cord it was missing the men on the ground kept yelling at me from a little transistor radio pull your left cord! pull your left cord! & I kept yelling back I have no left cord! I have no left cord! I can't turn! I can't turn! but of course they couldn't hear me it was a one-way radio they no doubt wondered what the hell I was thinking they stopped yelling they must've just figured something was wrong with the radio I stopped yelling the silence was weird I'd never heard such silence birds went sailing by it surprised me I didn't think birds flew that high it was really nice floating in the sky but then as I neared the ground I worried over some high wires I barely cleared those then began drifting to a big field of freshly furrowed black dirt as a farmer in his tractor looked up watched me go over I was told not to look at the ground but I did I couldn't help it then wham my legs hit the ground a knee hit my jaw they warned me that might happen bite my tongue off but I stood up & was ok.

INVOCATION

I flow into the invocation enigmatic pungency. This is called interacting. We ripen in snow. Cram it with ermine. Möbius blue sputtering the truth of rain. Bump a monument under the air. The kinetic boat glue opened by pliers. Clutter and luxuriate in our pockets. My dab at flab deforms the wiggle with skin. The hymn sends us jumping into a hammerhead's hat brimming with Germany. My arms pause in mutation. It anchors a painted red and a white and blue seclusion, darkness and sympathy. My stick bumps the heart and the fragrances, beggars, groans, dampness hook into this existence and there is a consequent conviviality and the light is a form of gasoline that weighs as much as a buttonhole. Plurality shows thought. Do you believe in singing? The sky is totally eczema. Below the authorization structure invites provocation. Moreover the form of a farm is in its livelihood. This is punches to a dirigible. Zip to a propagation. I came into this life riding on a comet. There is a quicker way to begin to be hectic. Reality is a shiver and a sweat and we lengthen the volume of thumbs. Radio is watched hugging one another. The hoist suspends the pipes in solid resilience. Let's explore consciousness by spreading cowslip. Or swing it with a pendulum. The yardstick of the eye stirs handsprings. The stick stirs paint. I find a screw in the sawdust of sound and appetite. Redeem the profligacy of singing with a coiffure and an angle. The ooze swims with cockeyed worms. Representation obstructs its chains. We remain unconvinced. What can we do? We burn a colloquy and powder it and dangle. The Mediterranean is peppered with sticks. Circles of Apollinaire. The Cinnamon King whose earrings whisper artemesia. Powder blue ovals accelerate the noise of my skin. What does this say about pulse? The air reeks of wonder. Dictionaries are engines of thought. Intent and a lip in a system for reflection. A thunder that is snappy and bright, a biology like a jellyfish, a drink of coffee that crackles when the wind blows and the piano sweats and anything horizontal rattles in some way that we can share. The carp are riding the rails. The tie helps us to understand granite. The glimmer of goose bumps are instruments for making bourbon. The flop of extrusion in a mind of ice tastes of oblivion. Atmospheric pressure equiped with socks. Pain is the deformation of information. Glue is the adhesion of tin. The rain is a medication. I spit prescription. Power shouts adjectives and butter. A bird in a bottle and a stab of grammar petitions the adverbs to cohere into a concept. This is called spinning, or solving the mystery of glass with an ugly towel.

CONFESSIONS OF AN IMPERSONAL SPECTATOR

Another way of understanding khaki is in terms of mesmerism. The human brain is divided into competing philosophies which are connected at the center of the cerebral cavity by a tissue of moonlight. When I tell my friends that I have a brain, they tell me that they have one as well. I have no reason to doubt this. These people are engaged in extremely interesting adventures. We all wonder about what the universe is made of, how it works, what we're doing in it and wherever it is it's going, if it's going anywhere at all. Imagine a city made entirely of bricks. If we substitute 'universe' for 'city' and 'particle' for 'brick,' the narration becomes gelatinous and cork.

Inside an elevator, however, the evaluation of our situation is very different. We have different explanations for the phenomena in the elevator. X calls it a process. Y calls it a ripple in time. Z pockets an ensemble of biases then abandons them many years later. There is no method to prove who is right. What we do know is that light is energy and energy has mass. There is no excuse for seaweed. If the wings are simple and the blood is ardent a smile can be explained by innocent inertia.

There are eight types of mass, which means that there are eight manners of speaking. The first is trash. Rags, cardboard, empty bottles and cans. The second is bathrobes. The third is eucalyptus. The fourth is apple blossom. The fifth is sweat. The sixth is dust. The seventh is concrete and the eighth is hairspray.

Gravitational mass is the raison d'être of a bag of potato chips and inertial mass is a school of soluble fish lit up by lightning.

Expulsions: Brutality and Complexity in the Global Economy is a book by Saskia Sassen about populations of people displaced, exiled, and imprisoned by the predatory practices of neo-liberal capitalism. This explains little as to why a feather and a cannonball fall with equal velocity within a vacuum and even less to say about the miracle of pancakes, but it does have much to suggest about why poets like Lorine Niedecker live in poverty to do their art, or Bartleby the Scrivener perished in The Tombs.

The point is that objects within the solar system do not move by some mysterious force exerted upon them from a distance but by the nature of the neighborhood through which they are moving. I can carve a fire out of a bar of soap but I cannot make it blink like a waiter at the Café de la Mairie near Saint-Sulpice in Paris. That requires the existential magic of a Jean-Paul Sartre.

This is why I've decided to assign myself a position in life similar to that of Stuart Sutcliffe with the Beatles. A sunglassed Impersonal Spectator, marginal, insignificant, and transcendental, struggling to do what I can on the bass.

Unless I prefer not to.

OUR BOOKS OF POETRY

Detail is cesarean. Denim dollars of the music twig. My despair, on the other hand, comes furnished with sandstone. Each worry has a personality and conveys shape and motion. I spin faster and faster among the stars. Breakfast is powder blue ovals accelerating the noise of my skin. Processes of hair emerge from my head as Albert Einstein plays the accordion. Assumptions of gravity are implicit in a Martian's ear. I feel monstrous, blessed, and useful. Each sentence gives birth to itself on the tongue of a moment. Life causes description, which is effervescent, and smells of evergreen. I don't like broccoli. But I can lift a thought into utility with a little straw and glue. Reading is complementary. A few people continue to read and think while the rest of civilization unravels in dead ideologies. My arms continue the idea of my shoulders to the tips of my fingers. I hold a book in my hands that says that substance is literal and paradise is dreamy and soft. The mind is a soup of pharmaceuticals and syntax guides us to feeling. Those of us with a taste for oblivion endure waves of personal water. Our wings are ourselves. We gather abstractions in baskets of kerosene and light them on fire. The spectacle swims with the veins of purity. I study the flow of blood. I carve a life out of the mountain. A strand of blue rag dribbles down the bathtub mirror. The amoebae moan. Television jingles and twitches in unexpected snow. Television is a box that acts like Technicolor. Our books of poetry tell us something different. Our books of poetry tell us that pronouns are forceps for the illusion of identity and that prophecies of flight amplify the engines of inspiration. Our books of poetry smell of railroads and creosote. Our books of poetry offer properties of meaning that glow in consciousness like incidents of rib and rhubarb. Writing is not always paper. Sometimes it's vermilion and cries like an anguish suckling a headlight of words. Semantic fiber. Autonomous ornamentation. Anthologies of throat. Whipped cream in a red mug. The experience of spars beneath the stars.

THE LONELY GAZE OF MEN IN NIGHTCLUBS

A silken air bends the greenery in a tangled mind. That would be the mind of the earth, which is a splash of calculus on the face of eternity. Which is chronology when chronology occurs and the lonely gaze of men in nightclubs. It's the naked rupture of excursion when an excursion is called for and the personification of prayer in a radio vibrating with the definition of eyes. The eye is a ball of jelly. The human eye is an organ that reacts to light and allows vision and colors. It does delicate things and lives in the head. It liberates form. It does not completely answer why there is something instead of nothing but it does a good job drinking a canvas by Cézanne. Two eyes are better than one. Three is the optimal number. A third eye in the forehead drags winter behind it. A third eye in the head pushes the impact of an olive into the sag of time. Sometimes all it takes is a little concentration to discover sewing, or infinity, or a sale on light bulbs at the drugstore. Quarts of philosophy may be transacted by semantic obstetrics. Gravity thickens as we approach a planet or a headlight made of words. You must act like a cloth when the wrinkles of local emotion jerk forward churning in abstraction. This is the time to play a sublime accordion. This is the time to construct a symptom of rain. To open a suitcase in Wisconsin. To feel the planets ride their orbits in tranquil velvet space.

THE STUDY OF OAK

Study oak, I tell myself. Press your nose against it. Smell it. Touch it. Feel it. There is a god inside.

Beatitude is the steel of well-being. Which is itself fragile as an antique cut crystal English condiment set. Don't wiggle this sentence. Everything depends on it. Including the sounds of Rome. The opacity of light in a dusty old caboose. Words twinkling and swarming around an hallucination of gravity salt.

The myriad narrations of life are polymers of being. Protein chains in serum albumin. This is called a residue. It's a residue of thought. My body is engorged with the enigma of the stars. And I felt compelled to write that down. And now it's an arabesque of gold and rattlesnake blood fluttering in the thorny truth of raspberries.

If a plate breaks in Africa, I can hear it in China.

The mountain pulls itself into a thought with a serenade of cedar and pine. I walk to the end of a promontory and look out over the valley. A song of thread pulses in a violet sky. Death is a glissando of snow falling on the river. Life is a cartoon drawn by creosote and grace.

I wonder what's the best way to experience a philodendron, grip a revolver, or put something down on paper that will shine and spurt. I like things that spurt. The last bit of mustard from a plastic bottle. Water after you twist the nozzle and all that pressure gushes out onto the driveway where little incipient weeds twist their way through the cracks in the concrete.

Life makes me dizzy. There's so much of it. So much possibility. So many choices. I'm always indecisive. Don't know which way to go, what to do for the cat, best way to get to the bank, which bank, and what's money anyway but a form of language: this paper means I spent X amount of time laboring for humanity, this is my share, my portion in the struggle to attain well-being, which is what we're all after, all trying to achieve, all trying to figure out the best way to go about it, there are no maps for the future.

Sometimes money just falls into people's laps. There's no pattern or predictability to it whatsoever. Hence, the popularity of casinos.

So many fragrances in the air this time of year. Things blossom at different times. It begins in May, and by July I'll start getting nose-bleeds from all the pollen. Fine ocher dust collecting on the paprika red of our Subaru.

Don't get me going on clouds. Endless fascination there. I'll get a crook in my neck from staring up at the sky all the time.

My absorptions spin and shine. I'm haunted by antiquities of gold and granite. There's no wave whose form and direction is entirely predictable. The wind can adjust things in less than a second. I feel the universe spread its wings. If I speak in metaphors it's because the intimacy of the moment has become pink with affability. Even the cement solicits a reciprocity of spirit.

A SWEET PREPARATION

Experience tastes like chicken. Even chicken tastes like chicken. But this isn't about chicken. This is about experience. Right now I'm experiencing ramification. Paper, architecture, space. You name it, I will experience it. All it takes is a little physiology. Bones, blood, skin. Nerves. Medulla oblongata. Sulcus of corpus callosum. Legs, arms, fingers.

Let's talk about fingers.

Fingers fascinate me. I have two handfuls of them. And two thumbs. Thumbs are the senators of the hand. That is to say, thumbs are pivotal to the enactment of fingers, which is to grip, to hold, to curl around knobs and open doors. That sort of thing.

Few adjectives are required to experience dinner. It is only afterwards that adjectives are required to describe things like coleslaw and potato chips.

Mirrors are good for the face. You can put your face in a mirror and open a door in your head. This is called memory. If you see any wrinkles it means you've been around for a long time. Maybe longer than you expected. Nobody really expects to be an old person. At first, old people seem like a different species. Like they came from outer space or something. Then you realize old people were once young people. And so one's experience of the aging process becomes navigable. One begins to feel the hills of distance, whole highways of vanishing perspective. The horizon is composed of gold. And suddenly experience turns sexual as a dashboard. Knobs and nipples and rock 'n roll.

Bohemia, rumination, Ted Berrigan's sonnets.

The experience of puddles is both light and dark and full of contingency.

Ethiopia is where Rimbaud went when he had his fill of snobbery and mediocrity. Which is why I have chosen to endorse introspection. No experience is fully experienced until it is experienced as an exploration of consciousness. In other words, candy.

Candy is serious. It's why people tend to suck on it. Candy can be anything that is sweet, superfluous, and vivid. Leaving the house and going for a walk can be sweet, superfluous, and vivid.

I lean into walking and let the sidewalk emerge as an experience of symmetry and cement. One thumb is an airplane. The other is a violin concerto in B minor by Bela Bartok. I've got the sparkle of music in my head. I remember the first time I heard Jimi Hendrix. The song was "Purple Haze." The place was a bedroom in a Victorian house with high ceilings and ornate molding near downtown San José. It blew my mind. My emotions rolled across the floor like earrings whispering hair. I was stunned. It was then that I discovered experience is enhanced by description. But that happens later, after the experience is experienced and the next song begins.

THESE WORDS

These words are dripping Delaware and these words are eating your eyes. These words are unpredictable and these words are clouds on Mars. These words are vomiting one another and these words are bouncing around in a palace of salt. These words have been harvested from the edge of night and these words smell of rum. These words are sticky and these words are cradled in philosophy. These words have one large blood red eye and these words have rails for the locomotive that is your blood. Blood is a word and so is locomotive. I'm looking for a good radio in which to put these words and golf my way through Switzerland drooling language like a locomotive full of blood. These words are grease marks and these words are looking for something to do. These words are vertical and these words are plunged in thought like a brass bell in a courtroom. These words are delicate as calculus and these words are twinkling in savory misunderstanding. I have harnessed some goldfish to these words as the Notre Dame walks through this paragraph plunged in verbal apprehension of itself. There is a headlight on these words and an ecstasy on Jim Morrison's blue bus, which is eternal and photogenic, like a secretion. When I think about words I use words to think about words. These are those words. And when the words go their own way I tend to follow. I'm happy and lavender and follow them to the end of the world where proximity is an approximation and the planet rolls through its diversions, purposeless and prodigal as a dragon of dreadful lucidity spreads her gorgeous banjo wings and the empire of space carries a large red mouth in a small green jar.

THE DIVIDENDS OF DESIRE

Go ahead. Pepper the potato and sparkle. Let the kerosene slosh around in the can. The thermometer is compelling and voracious for oars. The temperatures this year are gloomy and mild, sliding through the veins like envy. I'm going to paint the kitchen sink and frame it in a galaxy of oak. The stabbed ghost of my childhood wanders in a herd of caribou. Even the paper upon which I write ejaculates words in the exigencies of the moment, which are uncannily public. Thereby I'm going to glue my throat to the river and speak in the language of bark. I'm going to accommodate beauty. We will boil cabbage and admire beautiful things. The bold suppleness of my passion fulminates in an agitated journey of hospitals and horseshoes. If I spend a dime and let it flourish like a dime and circulate like a dime the dime will return to me as a dime and shine like a dime and enter my pocket like a dime and slip like a dime and slide like a dime and drop like a dime.

Bend your thoughts to the infrared. Let conception sway in your brain. I will give you an odyssey of lobsters and elves. Deliver opinion to the hunger for cypress. Include the growth of crystal. There are arms for this. I love coffee and the color red. There's a certain red that flutters its wings in an academy of black. The black of coffee. The black of night and angels and mirrors and meteors and messiahs. O spirit of paste allow me to embody cardboard in an ambience of pique. Let my tongue extend beyond the spoons of pleading. Let me explore the invisible. Let me wade through the surf singing of chivalry and formaldehyde.

My intestines operate according to the laws of digestion. This is proved by biochemistry. There's a hammer in the lobster boat that will confirm the weight of my dreams. Increase your fingers with a smear of rose. The crabs are on strike. Heaven's arms descend like steep cliffs. The highway twists over a geology of divine elocution. The road toward paradise crashes through the ribcage. Erupts from the throat in a blaze of glory. The development of history proves more and more apocalyptic. It's easy to see where this is going. Picasso has splashed my words with the sexual fluids of his muse. You can see it in the glimmering of the mouth. The warm flailing of the tongue. The passion to explain the inexplicable.

Corot's magic oars flourish beyond the compote. A wall of spices secures the vagaries of an ancient religion. A timeless anthology of whispers suits the grain of the table. We endure the persistence of hope. An antenna emerges from the great tugging body of expectation and wiggles around looking for scarabs. The groaning of pipes extrudes from a phonograph. I ponder nutmeg with an armload of clay to embolden my reckonings of fire. We like to wear bronze as we pour ourselves into our hands. Grammar parodies the gymnastics of thought. My acceptance of acupuncture arrives as a revelation. In the end it's the suppleness of the ghosts in us that neutralize the pain of existence. The heart is sterling that weighs the dividends of desire.

MY SECRET VALET

I opened the closet door and there stood Eugène Ionesco lost among our clothes. I removed my coat and gave it to him and he kindly hung it up. Thank you, I said. Don't mention it, he said. Can we talk about sadness, I asked. What do you think of sadness? I think sadness is awkward and desire is French, he answered. Sometimes a hat is necessary, and sometimes it's not. You must always bring little rubbery outlines to an orgy and verify the naturalness of the new airplane. The brain smells of algorithms, or until I get dressed. Finally! Pants that really fit. Go now, and avenge the zip codes.

I DON'T BELIEVE IN WATER

I don't believe in water. I experience water. I dive. I swim. I float. I drink the stuff. Please be cooperative. Read these words as you enter the water. That is to say, be daylight. Be infinity. Sound like a piano. But walk like a poet in Paris. Birthdays are filigreed. Sparkle and flail. Be beads. Be a spatula. Don't look for approval. Age into wrinkles with lightning and atmosphere. Emotion is only dilation. Puddles and puzzles. Epiphanies of the harmonica. Socks for elves. We consign ourselves to reality too readily. Think of a kiss engraved in copper. Ride a comet into a hall of mirrors. The railroad shoots into Texas enlivening the frogs. Dumbbells embody impact. Endurance and coffee, which juggle the nerves. It is astoundingly inaccurate to crawl through a fish. The autonomy of snow has a warm earth beneath to confirm the postulates of Cubism, which are multiple perspectives distilled into thirst. Since the advent of medicine the world has become a bashful texture of heartwood and sleep. We feel pretty among ourselves and heft arguments into the conversation of life. We wade by kiss and greet by hammer. I stitch my troubles behind the studio and cast a long shadow crawling with thread. I pin my vividness to the world and it runs on the gasoline of love. It is intriguing to stroll through the frictions of life feeling massively pink and peppered with light. The crustaceans whisper among themselves and sound like the surf. Perhaps it is the surf and not the crustaceans. But I prefer to think that henna is more than just a color. I pull myself into adaptation and when I clank I seek the liberty of mind and space. I'm beside myself with excursion. I turn guide and explore the stars. My opinions are feathers. Power is only clutter. I forge, instead, the delectation of a moment and paint the stepladder green. If this should strike you as focused, it's not. It is contusion and glue. My aching heart dripping with implication. The universe convulses in its architecture of trigonometry and calculus and sparkles just how Leibnitz described it. I've written this sentence not so much to alarm anyone as to float more boats, houses in

Louisiana, and bang against the shore in a dream of earth, cotton among the lobsters, wide-eyed and gloves wherever the space is a napkin I can fold. For poetry is not the same as talking, and Ted Berrigan's sonnets savor of sense and water.

THE URGE TO CREATE

The urge to create is explicit. It's prodigal and incendiary. Words are forged in a furnace of snow. Clouds boil with purple. The sand turns crimson. My mind fills with reflections. I become voracious for gold. For liberty. For a life lived among horses. My sternum is made of syllables. I can abandon nothing. I'm invested in everything.

The urge to create is pure energy. The music of amphetamines. I want to touch everything. Water, bones, mud. An insect cupped in my hand spreads its wings. The wings are transparent and veined.

The mind isn't matter but pure energy. Waves. Electrical impulses. The charm of language clarifies this fact. We laugh, we sing, we eat, we sleep. I'm captivated by the organization of bees. The production of honey. The electrical energy of all those insects combining to produce a liquid gold.

The heat of my breath fills a word. Desire opens the world. A storm of sound is assembled on the neck of a guitar. Adjectives swarm over a sentence fueled by predication. Almonds on a blue plate. Time uncoiling in a proverb. A maturing sun. A lake gone mad with the sparkle of diamonds.

A robe of silk hangs on a tin skeleton. We name him Falstaff. The café goes about its business as usual, serving ham and scrambled eggs and pancakes smothered with blueberry syrup. The tide begins to rise. The mind fills with thought. A fan twirls on a tablespoon. Art creates new perceptions, the silk of listening, the appeasement of anger, a tiger gliding through the liquid of the eye.

What is morality? Wine in a crystal glass. A still life by Jean-Baptiste-Siméon Chardin. The caress of warm water on the skin. The value of friendship. A mountain climbing through your hands.

Eggplant is an agreeable form. Gold is an agreeable metal. It doesn't belong to the world. It belongs to a supernatural beauty. Parables help us discover what is gold and what is not gold. The entrance to the cave is blocked. Some of us see shadows. Some of us see fire.

Jellyfish wash ashore, iridescent and beautiful. New perceptions infuse old memories. Experience feeds on experience. It's a never-ending tautology. The way out is through words incarnating the tangle of the mind. A grebe falls from the sky and plunges into the water. A ghostly necessity falls through a hole in my personality. I can feel the weight of your eyes reading these words. They're not my words. They're not your words. They don't belong to anybody. That's what makes them words. The weight of your voice putting breath and motion into the words. They exist for your breath. For my breath. For the breath of the unborn. For the breath of the dying. For the breath of cougars and lightning in the distance.

I love the odor of a freshly painted canvas. The construction of snow. The depiction of trees in a shock of wind. Cold and rain. Totems in the fog.

Each thing has a presence. Napkins, sidewalks, forests. Old barns smelling of horse piss and hay. A bag of freshly bought hardware nails. Gargoyles atop the walls of Sainte-Chapelle. The charm of development. Words propagating like waves where ideas float.

Ideas are hyper-objects, like Nebraska. They're composed of thought and paper. Wolves and abandoned farmhouses. Spiders and squirrels. Sawdust. A wrinkled old face. Man or woman. Makes no difference when you reach a certain age. Descriptions get smaller. Ideas get larger. Biology becomes unpredictable. Life gets crazy. Intentions get lost in their own manipulations. A corpse falls out of a closet. A rag on a window sill saturates with water. The whole idea of representation is strange. Writing is not a contact sport.

How is it possible to be in a crowd of beings similar to ourselves and yet feel unique? That our own personal narrative is singular and gallant? Is vanity a good thing or a bad thing? Why bad? Why good? Isn't the good sometimes bad and the bad sometimes good?

The components of sleep glow in a swimming pool. Chiaroscuro is indispensable. Dissonance makes life tolerable.

Impulse is great but you have to learn to accept the bite of remorse.

Me, I like umbrellas. I rejoice in begonias. I kiss the moon. I can hear my heart beat. The parliament is in session. I hear a siren. The cat coughs up a fur ball. I tear off a paper towel and wipe up the vomit. It's still warm from his body. Outside, the willows sway. Space goes on being space. What was space before there was space? Can gravity be bottled and sold to those who are tired of floating? What would the dead tell us if they were able to return? Do they come to us in dreams? Or are dreams just dreams and nothing else? If time cold be folded and put in a suitcase, which hours would I choose to bring with me?

I like two o'clock. Always have. And midnight. Midnight is the rupture of rapture in an invisible ear. Sleep and rain in perfect conjunction. The affiliation of thought with the warrant of the sky.

The afternoon lifted itself into my eyes and said hi, it's two o'clock. Midnight stopped by later and we drank until morning. I awoke feeling strangely beautiful. I became a glissando. Snow fell on the river. My lips danced on syllables until my tongue got drunk. I bought tickets for Paris.

I need the lucidity of water. It inspires me. Rain, rivers, puddles, oceans, lakes, ponds. It assumes so many forms. But it is finally the currents of the Seine in January that fascinate me, that make me want to write something. The turbulence is exciting and menacing. Even if, weeks later, I end the day by doing the dishes. Something was said. Something needs to be said. Something always speaks.

IMPATIENCE

I hate to wait. That's why I like to write. There's no waiting. You simply write. It's all there. Stepladders, dachshunds, Louisiana. It's just a matter of converting experience into words and words into a geography of mind. Egypt becomes a diversion of sand, an urgency of stature, a sphinx, pyramids, crowds agitating in the streets, everything in confusion and conflict, everything a display of life and spirit. I see my incendiary urges made magic in a world of glazed illusion. I shiver at the infringement of dawn. If my mood gets hooked on a drug I spit and purge myself of guilt, the sugar of ruin. A dream of earth makes the sleep of angels sublime. Ted Berrigan's sonnets are one example. Another might be walnuts, or the bubbly manifestations of the chin. Poetry is not the same as talking. It's rain on glass, the clarity of waves, the movement of the elbow when playing the violin. I ruminate on the meaning of cork. I see a kind of totem stitched at midnight dramatize the music of the spheres. There are excursions of words that feel warm as skin in the novels of Proust, though I don't care for many of the people, they're snobby aristocrats, but what does that matter when the highest elevation one can attain is pinned to the dirt in jubilant light. The eyes accommodate the dazzle of the airport as a religion hoists thought into space and the planes themselves seem like ideas that have luxuriated in our minds for so long that even the boarding pass seems garish and overblown. There is enough gravity on the sidewalk to hold the world in place. One needn't worry about time. Time is tattered and our lingering in the parlor serves the spirit of our conversation. I hurl my needs at a habit and steer into regret, as if the debris of my life were a form of endeavor and mattered together in tinsel. A ride in the mirror flies over Apollinaire and elongates into a spatula of spectacular reality. What is success? I want to know more about bugs. They obviously know something that we don't. There is an evident mystery in incentive. The drool of twilight comes to us in ribbons of light and crawls romantically forward over the hills and walls turning the bricks to gold and sitting down in a bar finally to await the night. I hang a thrilling mud from my lips and talk it into monsters. I spread the wings of my medication into narrative. Jokes wade through a reference to Queen Elizabeth. Each story is fulfilled in a bowl of astounding inaccuracy. I ride my intestines like a bus. We juggle our muscles and feel pretty among ourselves. We feel the friction of life. We hurry to get it all written down. And now that we've all become literal and scrupulously chronicled, let's catch the golden pain of resilience and blaze our way through Texas. What kind of train is it that rumbles through a paragraph distilling gloom? Beauty is a convulsion for the mythology of definition. The seashore is an open structure. There's no waiting for anything, not here, not there. It all just happens. I open a symptom and find a house. My interior is full of proverbs that want to itch out of regret and argue the ground into sexual abandon. And so I do. And so it does. And so it shall do for now and forever. Which is to say cough, sneeze, adapt this museum to the vagaries of sand and let your eyes float over me. We will join one another in words. Escape the world in words. Visit other realms in words. Words, my friend, words.

THE LEGEND OF THE GARDEN HOSE

These are my thoughts on the hose. I'm sympathetic to the hose. Let's start there. Sympathy. Sympathy with rubber. With water. With current. Anything red, or scientific, or generational. As for the potato, the potato is behaving badly. The potato is unhappy being a potato. Meaning seeps through the potato, the image of the potato, the afternoon of the potato, the postulation of the potato, and liberates its truest form, which is that of a cloud. The cloud is evidence of feeling. Feeling is vital. Feeling is un-structured, like kelp. Here is a map of my heart: mountains and valleys and rivers. Rivers of blood, of course, but also muscles and rags. Birds confirm the climate, which is sad with a developing front of prodigality. Let's crawl out of here and do something else. Ink sags with imagery. There's plenty of that to go around, and granite and headlights. Alliga-tors and prophecy. The warrior yells in battle and wields a mighty sword. I'm drawing a picture here, but it's not what you think. It's not what I think either. It's something else, something hungry and green and wiggly. It's a hose. A garden hose. The kind with a nozzle. The kind with water running through it and coming out of the other end where it feeds a bed of zinnias. Let's respect the sanctity of the zinnias by bathing in their odors. The world is an excursion through space and time. The hose is an abstraction. Not just a hose, but the idea of a hose. The idea of a tube in which the churning of thought prolongs the image of the hose as long as the hose can stand it. The hose is a symptom of horticulture. But let's not let that stand in the way of developing a bush of participles. It will be reflected in legend. It will riddle the mind with movement and nouns, swimming and running and painting and scrubbing. It will need watering. Watering is a gerund. It needs participles. It rips the rain in two and comes up with a way to inhabit Scotland. I can feel the heft of spring springing to power. When spring arrives we can dispense with the hose. We can open our suitcase and put on something else. Some-thing like languor. Severity is gaudy. Languor is soft, like silk, and culmi-nates in dots. Little ships that undertake the voyage of the century and sail into the heart propelled by electrical plums.

THE MIND IS INDIGO

An emotion floats a bus station and accommodates reading. If you slam this it will be remembered as a capillary and the odor of elephants will haunt my dreams. What this means is squirrels to me and furniture to you. A paradigm feels thick and bubbly because England has the sound of thatch. Calculus spouts a nearby forest and life grows still. We erect a bulb. Words increase by teasing their frame and the story is structural with nothing ecclesiastical for the crabs. Symbolism sips privacy from a Russian guide. Energy shines from wampum and clashes with the morality of size. The allegory calls for a kangaroo. I'm filled with premonition. The paragraph is now giving birth to a thermometer. Consciousness is brown, like singing. But what is truth? A sneeze with the naturalness of a chisel. The grebe falls suddenly from the sky in a gentle rain. The radio crinkles cod. Today is without precedent, a flicker of time. Meaning seeps through these words and is paper. The inertial mass of a single railroad car can be calculated by using the Schrödinger wave equation. Detachment expands the emotion which wrinkles the paper and juggles knives constructed out of fandango slop. What can I say? It's a living.

ACTION INACTION

Consciousness is exhausting. And so is rubber. But what is reality? That question gets asked a lot. But does anybody have an answer? A lot of people do. They're called philosophers. I like to think of reality as a blatant wind thudding through the trees, beating drums and hallucinating. It's either that or a garage door. Those creaks and springy sounds they make when they open and all those funny odors come flying out.

As you might've guessed, I like maneuvering words. It allows me to act like Technicolor. I can glow into longhand or type my way into hills of assumption. But it's this private pain that is so hard to put into words. I feel like an ocean engorged with squid. I use forceps to handle the pronouns. They're so slippery. And they smell of abstraction, like the rain. The shoulder was invented to carry the burden of the world. We also have totems, and tattoos and trumpets. These things help.

One day I hope to evoke everything in a single sentence and retire. I will learn to play the Fauve guitar and create sounds of such savage hue that the effect will feel more like a punch to the stomach than a religious belief. A song is a form of bruise and if it wrinkles it will clutter with scientific handshakes and resemble a forest of boiling taxis.

Dragons of concentration ride on streams of consciousness. The lumber is perfectly present, however imperfectly sawn, or expressed in grammar. Verticality has its shadows. But the slobber of abstraction enriches our perspective of cloth.

Pain is often sexual. Which is why it is so often a pleasure. There are adjectives available to describe this phenomenon, and bungalows in which to enact it. The sound of it gets sweet and light drips from the lamps ins scarves of delicate implication. The climate unseals itself in scripture. Silk trails across the neck. Sensations of creative liberation run along a tangent of bone and skin trembling with examples of gold. There is clutter in consciousness and proposition and meaning. This is what makes it so energetic. So impenetrable to gravity. Even the limestone swarms with its science.

Life is erratic and conversational. There is a house in New Orleans where we find this amply demonstrated in a general looseness of direction and antifreeze. Experience tastes like chicken. Experience is what happens when syllables interact with milk. The map collapses into words dripping with Delaware. We can smell tallow. Intentions are hectic with tin. A harridan rages within a leviathan RV. The TV is unpredictable. Each day has its own sounds and odors. And it drives us crazy.

When Mick Jagger asked me to join the Rolling Stones, I didn't know what to say. I jingle when I walk. And my keys are always a little sticky during the summer. I can juggle a few oranges but I refuse to bark like a dog. Language is hallucinatory. But powerful. If they can use a song writer I can use a wider desk.

The politics of the potato are a little strange, but worthwhile remarking. I can still smell the dirt. Clearly, there is a trace of Paris in the salon, and if this conversation is to continue, let's let the subtleties stir into action. The drop of a nail can sound like an epitome. And the paragraph has given birth to a turnstile. What do you say we pass through, and let Portugal overwhelm us with its haircuts and cork.

Culture is ontological. A fist of ganglions holds a pound of sugar in each skull, in each maieutic balloon. Dignity is round like a reproductive organ. My skin tells a story of labor and pain. If your mouth is in prison, you should visit more bars. There are too many referents but not enough signs. The present tense is tart as a martini olive, but the future is in vermilion, anxious and ornery like the twinkle of an incendiary noun.

For the ocean is plunged into its own diversions and when the river becomes a waterfall the hunchback of Notre Dame walks among these words murmuring something about ornaments. I sometimes imagine that the dead are trying to pull us into their realm. Heaven's parabola slams into fireworks. We need to re-enchant the world. Seethe in awakened syllables. The capacity to gaze at something, anything, is a gift. I like to watch my hand dance on the ceiling. I like to gather its shadows and squeeze them into words. Why is there something instead of nothing? All five senses insist that there is more to a goblet than pewter. The table causes itself by pressing its surface against the hands. When we walk in exhibition of ourselves we are purple. But when consciousness dissolves in sleep, the house of language opens its doors. Everyone is welcome to attend. Just do what the words suggest. Camaraderie is prodigal. The journey begins with a single ghost. This is why I smell like a suitcase. I'm not from here. I'm from elsewhere. For who hasn't felt the wind in their hair and wondered what time breakfast is served in the afterlife?

HOLDING PATTERN

Hold this poem and rub it with space. Ingest it with your eyes.
Enkindle it with needs. Drip abstraction. It just happens. Abstraction
happens. You feel alive and blaze in the snow of Iceland, a carnival of
thought and emotion with a head like a sack of helium. Blood and
lightning serve the fertility of experience. The map amplifies the dis-
connect between reality and an implied geography whose mountains
and rivers exhibit the gum of time as it occupies a schematized space.
Incidents of rubber absorb the shock of monotony. The repetitive
rhythm of walking. Headlights shining through words of granite. The
human mind is smeared with sexual metaphor, the teased agreements
of audacity and steep relation, the incentive to suck and sparkle, the
courage to pin a passion to a fold of fingers. The light is swollen. It
indulges the walls. A sharp wind hangs from a highway sign. The
grease at the center of the world allows everything to turn without
squeaking, its axle is wet as veins. And so useful it is to consult
consciousness that consciousness strains to find meaning in hockey.
Words, thumbs, glances, glass, glans, baptisms and powwows. And
sometimes we taste the heat of thought in a balloon of dizzying lucid-
ity, rising into the sky like a cabana with a checkered past. Possession
can also mean inglenook. Or mulberry. It takes a friend, naturally, to
confirm the thickening thoughts on a piece of paper, each word clear as
an ice cube and each sentence a wading pool for the eyes. Symbolism is
nothing more than a bag of groceries, items arranged by weight and
density. The lettuce goes on top, and symbolizes courage. The jelly is
upside down but if the cap is on tight it should remain true to the
image of kings. We feel the full impact of reality at the checkstand.
Here is where being water gets a little messy and hanging words
upside-down doesn't help the situation. It's better to stand there being
quiet and dream of returning to the sea as an albatross on a long glide
of delectation over dinner.

AIR LOOM

Whenever I smell the endurance of feeling I grow instinctive with reference and savor the spirit of permeability. I can do this alone or with fish, either way. I wash my seclusion with the warm earth of Cubism and as soon as Baudelaire deduces a skunk I go my merry way. I dig it when a studio comes up cheap and I can afford to sleep in it turning my head toward the sun or burying it in sleep. I feel the autonomy of snow spring from a monstrosity of verse, paper I have stowed away in a closet when I was watching a harmonica fill with music. I love the astounding inaccuracy of hope despite its evident cruelties. The railroad shoots into Mexico enlivening the frogs. The flowers have agreed to amuse us and so another day grows to another conclusion, an ending that never feels quite right, or conclusive. I could sell it as incense if there were a way to tease it into a cardboard box, something large and splashed with oranges and perforated with holes so that the embroideries of the afternoon can breathe and spread the wings of narrative into further expansions. Singing is in emission. I hang from my lips in the thrilling mud of the unconscious talking to monsters and crawling with meat. Hallucinations deepen in elegance and maturity until even the paper begins to wrinkle with effort and a funny congeniality flits through my nerves in shining alabaster and endless mirrors. These words are swollen and textured by sagas of unfocused rage. That's why I use them. My robins are pretty and deserve a better world than the one outside raining and gray and cold as a grocery checker in the middle of December. Blood should be nicer when it's acoustical. It should be like language. Desire is French. Gravity is German. But the stepladder eating pronouns, well that's completely rhetorical, you know? Like a metaphor that hasn't fully developed and hangs around the room exploding into bark and lifting itself into life. Is it any wonder we find ourselves grappling with consciousness 24/7? Touch is genial. Vision is zinc and adobe. Hearing is the unfolding of water on the sand where the highway meets the beach grass and the eyes in the depths of the ocean shine with the parable of value. This is more than a story about bugs. I'm talking rawhide.

I'm talking miracles and pearls. This is serious. It isn't so difficult to find pleasure in a ruffle or the thin playful contours of a woman's wrist, but try finding romance in a hospital with the stink of mortality everywhere and the head like a world orbiting its own digestions. This is how I've come to love the lucidity of antiques and the promise of a good pair of shoes. Throw some pills into the bargain and I'm ready for reality. Ready to build a parenthetical Arizona for all my contraptions. Consciousness is exhausting. But there is remedy in distillation, and geometry helps to articulate clothing.

THE ATHLETIC EMOTION OF BARK

I grant that the athletic emotion of bark has expanded the growth of mirrors. Tears play your spoon to an animal. Escape your head. Heat the spoon until it flowers into morning. There is a moral above passion that coordinates clowns. Neck the clatter a bump. Explain flirtation. I burst my asterisks. Contrast echoes into old English barns. It's lyrical to exhume a soubriquet from the graveyard of a ditty. There are pipes for the world and butter for the bread. Thrilling altitudes attract the assembly beside the peccadillo. We gnaw the lawn until the green is teased into cafés. I fugue my paraphernalia with pronouns and decorate the music with incense. I occur to scrounge my grow along. Punish the painter's coin. The oath bark has a calculus to say. An infrared asphalt for the monstrosity of nature. I draw the daub then absorb it into lingerie. This spins the glue to my build. A papier-collé ape has swallowed the authority. I feel the attitude of your distorted begging and endure it upside-down. The hand is peremptory that holds an iron nerve. This chemistry slashes into the electricity of a mind and causes events to quicken into reverie. We blow it into a written galaxy. This is where I wade my parody and feel how the impersonal brain can wear itself by converging on charm. What the horse jingles is precisely my point. Spirits are sifted over the extrusion. We exhibit gizzards since the charcoal floats. It is to twist the intestines into springing forward, as discrimination should. I carry a dot. The swans follow. If I appear to distill the cake of experience it is actually the frosting that navigates the milk of incident. Euclid takes out the garbage. I feel Parisian to represent a dribble. The mood is sterling that sneers in embryo. Abstraction is the potato within the chin. I have refined this milieu so that its vapor urges the use of moccasins. Motion is good for yelling. Interaction is good for impartiality. Tricky glitter changes my hat. I haunt the canvas and shake a declension. I sleep within clapboard, groan the declaration. Flip the nails into snow. Hammer an incendiary elephant into blue existence. This becomes yellow. Then we gleefully hug the aurora and meditate there until it cringes with snow in the orchard. The conception is an insect, but a big one, and it smells of resource. Luxury is no more than that. Just a root that burns into writing, and whispers reality.

Nothing escapes necessity except the necessity to escape. The world is a place of migration. The colors of the horizon are eternally alluring. It's a mood that you carry with you, like a crumpled ball of aluminum foil. Each moment is a voyage. Press a button in the elevator and see where it takes you. Mutations are normal. In fact, plans for a new kitchen are spread across the table this very day. It sings in my blood like protein. I can smell the music in an Idaho potato. The door hangs from its hinges pleading to be opened. After all, this is art. Perception is a process, not a jackknife. We're talking black pepper, marjoram, kaffir lime, aromas that are distinct on their own but send wearers on imaginary getaways and daydream rendezvous when blended with other scents.

Be kind to your legs. Let them finish what they're doing. Remember: the moon's distance from the center of the earth is 240,000 miles.

A sentence can justify so many things, including consciousness, which is a basket of light. Vermillion murmurs like an apple hanging in the brain of a blackbird.

Gravitation is mutual. For every action an equal and opposite reaction is produced. Marilyn Monroe wore nothing to bed but a few drops of Chanel No. 5. This proves that the dark is a contradiction of stones and sponges wet and sparkling, funky and fresh.

Every fundamental event in the universe can be interpreted by bringing it close to your face and sniffing it. The olfactory membrane inside the human nose has 50 million receptor cells capable of transmitting information on some 10,000 different odors and is the only part of the central nervous system that has direct contact with the external world.

This includes Wednesday, granite, and meat. It might also mean hair, or a simmering example of vanity.

Infinity climaxes as a shadow by percolating itself through a pretzel. This creates a semantic powder called seeing. The obstetrics of upheaval arrive in perception tracing a ripple of time. Repair yourself with pain. This will entail fatalism. Blood is alive with thirst and will play with secretion until a sentence is produced answering prophecy with criticism and adapting to the vagaries of digestion with exquisite conjugation.

And just like a library where you can find all the best books, the human mind starts the sexual morning with a bubbly ear and raw dancing. The riddle of malt whiskey wanders through consciousness like a swollen begonia. Contrasting cries for help grow into prose with literal terra-cotta sideburns. The floorboards creak. Even the accordion over there in the corner has something to say about Being.

Quality, whatever it may be, is revealed to us as being. This will appear obvious if the gas station is open. The car submits a headlight, a bell rings, and everything falls into place, including these words, which are tilted toward an expectation of bugs.

WHOSE DWELLING IS THE LIGHT OF SETTING SUNS

Thoughts have no substance, except whenever I go fishing in Idaho's Snake River. And since I never go fishing, my thoughts have no substance. This thought has no substance. But it's a thought. It's a thought about a thought. It's thought on thought, thought about thought, thought through thought. And that makes it a thought, but where is the incandescence? There is no amperage. That's precisely my point. Nor do I play the concertina. If I played the concertina there's a good chance I would entertain some thought about the concertina, about my playing the concertina. I might ask myself "why do I play the concertina?" Or, "is my playing of the concertina any good?" And these would be thoughts. Thoughts about the concertina cut deep from a drop of sunlight and glued to this sentence with the moral emanations of structure and language. Most thoughts are made of language, but language has no substance, unless you consider pixels or ink substance, which they are I suppose, but nothing like flour, or Colorado, or limestone. Conception is largely frustration. Is there life on Mars? Probably. But it's probably microbial, nothing to write home about, unless the microbes murmur analgesics, or certain subtleties of architecture, in which case one would have to admit that not only is there life on Mars, but microbes that can sing, and think, and jingle with analgesics, just like a TV ad. TV has never had substance, which makes it so alluring. The sidewalks of Paris are particular and sometimes fuse brilliantly with the idealism of the flâneur, who is always full of thought, and window dressing, and mannequins and suits. The Snake River does not flow through Paris, it is the Seine that flows through Paris, but if the Snake River did flow through Paris, I would be the first one to tell you about it. Behavior is malleable. I can change my behavior to suit the situation, and if thought has no substance, my behavior doesn't either, it's more like rills in the sand, waves on a lake, the smell of rum in a Spanish fable. Flowers bob their heads in agreement. Though it's the wind that makes them do that. The politics of the potato are more connected with Europe, though originally they were a gift of the Incans, and grew on the sides of mountains, the majestic Andes, where thoughts flowed over the slopes as shadows, and carried the truth of the high thin wind through the enigma of time, shaping the rock and sneezing an empire.

BENCH PRESS

Grammar is a muscle. Grammar consists of velvet and lingerie. And powwows. Popcorn and cymbals are astonishing reasons to have emotion. Resolution is like that it in that it mitigates hoping. And floors. When the north wind agrees with the ground and plays in the swamp language fills with blood. English is heavy, but not as awkward as German, or as slippery as French. English goes into wrinkled paper and when meat is constructed out of words funny things happen. Our seclusion feels sublime. We draw our opinions from dreams and shiver when diversion bangs against the spirit. Poetry is not the same as it was fifty years ago. It has turned thick and bubbly and withdraws in the rain. Events find people to fill them with testimony. It has the bones of a piano and a view of everything. I clasp the wind to my breast and rise into glory. The voyage begins to swell with vertical consciousness. One way to feel a feeling is just to feel it, however it feels. Another way is to take a drug that evokes piccolos. There are adjectives for this. This is how trumpets turn cool in truancy. There is a despair that nothing can bungle except comedy. The spirit of the wind mistakes mustard for romance. The goldfish ponder water in their house of water. What else is there to do? We watch the water and find that it resembles consciousness. I am a wrinkle in time and I am imponderable. Or so we think. Meanings spill onto the table and open the writing to process. Description widens with length when apple blossoms blossom into Boston. Hang in there. Sooner or later the swans will appear and we will have graceful implications swarming with cotton and quince and porte-cochères. Structure sparkles like an experience. Space drools obsidian and the mountains dream they are clouds. Syllables interact with milk, bringing us gooseberry and leather to our little village. Analgesics may be harvested from spider venom. But did you know that the mine is haunted? Yes, it is, and its architecture of old, creaking wooden beams canopy our murmur in the dark. Did no one think to bring a lantern? Is there life on Mars? Is there life after death? Is there death after life?

Does each and every day have to bubble in agreement with starch? The flowers bob their heads yes. Behavior is malleable. The ocean is full of eyes. Poetry is a form of resistance. But it can also be used for alchemy and simulating dirt. Animals recognize this power and keep to themselves. Bells bend the winter air. The ceremony of words turn sanguine with silence. Desires swarm with perception and cork. Is our social being ever truly the same as our more authentic being? Writing is always like this, proposing things and then vanishing into thin air, leaving behind a residue of experience and a pound of sound fossilized in abstraction. It's at times like this that I like to stretch into Nebraska and murder the syntax of salt. Colors walk among their bones jerking forward in a wooden brain. I am a fold of night, I say to myself. And then, for lack of anything better, I dream myself into time riding a theme of grammar.

HERACLITUS IN AN INNER TUBE

You have to feel what you write. What a strange thing to stay. I have an odd feeling about that statement because I write to escape feeling. What I desire most is to transcend my emotions. I don't like my emotions. Not all of them. I like feeling happy. Who doesn't like feeling happy? But happiness, which runs the gamut from intense euphoria to a mild sense of well-being, is difficult to maintain, much less invoke. A lot of books have been written on the subject but no one has yet discovered a sure fire method for inducing a state of happiness at will. There are certain drugs that might lead to a brief state of ecstasy or euphoria but when they wear off they leave one feeling much worse than before one swallowed or injected the drug. Drugs are not really a good solution.

If the rent is paid, the mortgage is amortized, there's food in the refrigerator, the water and electric bills are paid, one's work is agreeable, there is plenty of positive feedback from friends and family, one's health is good, and there's freedom to do what one wants to do whenever and however one chooses to do it, there's a strong possibility that something like happiness might be perpetuated for a respectable period of time. Days, weeks, maybe even years. But these things are no guarantee of happiness. A lot of people have such things in abundance and still feel unhappy much of the time.

Happiness is an odd and elusive animal. But it is only one among thousands of emotions, species of feeling unnamed, unrecognized that have yet to prowl one's nervous system and embed themselves in the heart. And really there is no one single emotion. All emotions are blends. I have yet to meet anyone who has felt a singularity of love without also feeling frustration, confusion, bewilderment, betrayal, perplexity, urgency, adoration, turbulence, intimidation, dread, triumph, mystery, discord, ambivalence, ambiguity, temerity, endurance, effulgence, effrontery, excitement, derangement, and lust.

What I feel most of the time is anguish. Dread, anxiety, worry, disillusion, remorse. These are not pleasant things to feel. If these were the emotions that inspired me to write I'd be in real trouble.

But the fact is they are my main inspiration to write. Because I write to get away from these feelings.

How does that work? I'm not sure. But I have some theories.

First, language is a medium without limit. As soon as I enter into the field of composition I feel an expansion, a dilation of being. I feel the joy of limitless expansion.

There is also a very satisfying feeling in seeing one's nebulous inner turmoil crystallize in the regenerative pharmacology of language. Words have a wonderful way of making one feel a little more distanced from inner discomfort. And if one is writing out of a sudden ecstasy, words make it shine back in the pellucid jewelry of linguistic abstractions. The very word 'ecstasy' is pertinent to the business of writing. Ecstasy comes from Greek *ekstasis*, "standing outside oneself."

This is precisely what writing does: it leads us outside of ourselves.

Writing is a form of pharmacology. It has healing properties. And these properties are based on a principle of combinatorial process. Diverse elements are mingled together to create a symbol, an idea, an image. Language is inherently, strongly associative. Its actions are primarily chemical in nature, drawing on a dynamic of dissolution, distillation, and sublimation. Writing is synergistic. Emotion ceases to be a static condition. Feelings flow. Vary, fluctuate, metamorphose. Heraclitus goes floating by in an inner tube.

Ultimately, what is felt in the pursuit of escaping one's feeling is another feeling. A bigger feeling. The feeling of sublimation. As one moves from a feeling of stubborn solidity to a state of vapory abstraction one feels the euphoria of displacement. Of buoyant reflection. One can feel the grip of an emotion loosen as soon as one begins to reflect on the feeling. Or out of that feeling. It's not a position of 'on' so much as a position of disposition, the consciousness of being in relation to other things.

No emotion feels the same after a deepened analysis. It becomes less substantial, less imprisoning. It becomes a pale mist of tingling sensation. It drifts in reverie. It becomes an energy, a buoyancy that leads to music. A warm immersion in water, a narcotic camaraderie in a copper California night. Equations of sugar. Quakes of anarchical joy. An ecstasy of arroyos and turquoise auroras. The glide through an ocean of words variable as waves on a sweet Pacific tongue.

BALZAC'S ALLIGATOR

I'm a mammal. I smell Plato. But I have strong affinities for Balzac, which doesn't necessarily make me French, but blazes within me reciting stories of treachery and pain. The human comedy. The syntax of emotional grammar, which expands into eyes, blends with the sultry air and becomes a hit song. The sky leans over a single blue orchid to discuss the gold of its sunset. And so a sympathy is born. A great feeling for wings and bougainvillea. Herons descend and skid into the water. Eating is a stunning necessity. Which is why mayonnaise is luminous with eggs and a hypothetical alligator splashes its way into the sentence rupturing the giant opacity of words and thrusting its way ever deeper into the ganglions where it becomes more than a perception, more than a reverie, but an entire gestalt. A sanction. A dispensation. A paradigm of Pythagorean rapture in which math is at the basis of divinity, where numbers sag through time bearing the weight of an infinite fugue of semantic mass, confusing secretion with impulse and impulse with scales, where the lumber is alive with grain and odor and grammar propels the human comedy and despair is an awakening that hatches instinct and crawling and algorithms turn primal with alligator slime. It's all in the muscle. All of it. Every inch of it. This power to flail, to twist, to growl, to wrestle and snarl. Is this what you call math? These formulas hurling themselves against the exultation of the reptile? Submarines make good examples. For instance, imagine a syntax exhibiting a swagger pound for pound, yanking a submarine out of the ocean and smoking it like a cigar. Voila! There you have it. The clatter of wiggly numbers buttering the business of thought and breaking into abstraction, an act of pleasure tinged with sandstone. Speculation is sticky. But if the clapping of hands leads to an architecture of angels and Fred Astaire sits down in a chair tapping his foot, none of the subtleties of the afternoon are lost, but grow into predictions, premonitions and vertigo. That isn't to say that Balzac is nowhere to be seen, but is quite visible, there where consciousness catches its breath, so to speak, and gargles a mountain of chronological towels. Permission is given to become a twisting, thrusting mass of bone and flesh. Who doesn't secretly entertain the idea of building an intense, parenthetical shoe into an entire dictionary? There, I said it. What it all comes down to isn't numbers, per se, but thumbs and glue and outlines. An energy like a hawk going for immediacy and form, for a difficult dye, for an epiphany in the diner and a necklace of little bronze hats.

WORD SURF

Let's say that description is created by a bas relief climbing into itself on paper. This is a sample of thought but because its behavior is somewhat larger than a harmonica it might also serve as a version of exploration. We swim in the sounds below our life. Some of these sounds emerge to the surface and get written down as the wet sheen of an octopus crawling from one tank to another in an aquarium of the mind. For the mind is a house of water and consciousness spills on the table where it breaks into the foam of stupefaction. Life is erratic and conversational. A place like New Orleans occurs when space is concentrated near a river and brocades of smooth brown water indicate the contours of the bottom. The streets and sidewalks of Paris are in better condition. But if we ask ourselves, à la the Pixies, where the mind is the answer may appear at the edge of the night shining like the rails of the Kansas City Southern as they cross the border into Mexico. My existence on paper reaches for your eyes. I salute your blood. I'm familiar with the great gift of milk. But how can anyone know if they're being ironic? Language is hallucinatory. It's hard to be sincere with one large blood red eye and a white T-shirt that says "if you've been waiting longer than 15 minutes inform the receptionist." Poetry is a form of resistance. I can smell its geography. We spin books into its shadows. Luminous emotions bathed in camaraderie inspire me to be a better addict. I'm addicted to words. I've attempted withdrawal on occasion but even my skin insists on participation, telling a story of labor and pain in a scripture of epidermal honesty. Sometimes you can't escape the traffic. You can attack the duplicity of politicians or drink their elixirs while the rest of the world performs its fusions and expands in our eyes tart as the present tense of a martini olive. It's your call. Me, I want to exercise my rights as a citizen of the sun. The sky leans over the horizon leaking light and water. Our only real duty is that of a moonlit puddle singing its silent lucidity to the indifferent stars. Wrap your pickles in incendiary nouns. Let your inner anarchy out of the proverbial bag. Whenever I feel my life hanging like a rag from the faucet of the kitchen sink I strain to excite a crisis of words plunged in their own diversions, teasing a thought or two like a single blue orchid asleep on the escritoire. Words incarnate the tangle of the mind. But once they get going even the parrots turn capricious and say things no one could've predicted. My sad green desires turn Pythagorean and yesterday's muffins languish in Euclid. I hum algebra. I crackle. I cackle. I postulate mosses and dips and eat potato chips. Shadows gather in accommodations of mood and weather. The world turns. I ride a comet like a washing machine. Churning feels romantic and pleasantly awkward, but the rinse cycle is fully discursive. And then it happens. Language simmers in its unfolding like a fist unfolds in fingers or a seashore gushes onto the land.

PYTHAGOREAN TOOLBOX TEATS

Experience is what happens when blood circulates, the heart pumps, and life pops out of the box. Everything goes Technicolor. The room glows. Pronouns assume the private pain of impulse. Various dimensions simmer in space sweetening the nerves with saffron and juxtaposition. Is there anything prettier than a jackknife? Escalators percolate in my skin causing action and growth. I ride up. I ride down. I move sideways to let people pass. I'm polite, a courteous person. This is my attempt to hold the society together. Poetry is my way to blow culture up. Smash capitalism to smithereens. This is misleading. You can't smash capitalism, but it will certainly smash you. You've got to find an antidote. Poetry is that antidote. It's useless as tits on a hammer. I love that image. A hammer with tits on it. Wrenches and screwdrivers suckling at its underside in the toolbox of life.

Movement deepens my comprehension of soup. Sparrows are brusque but powerfully themselves. I feel incidental and ghostly, but also a little like asphalt, as if I cried on the inside to be a highway joining Nevada to Arizona and poured distance and velocity into the long Nevada night. Here comes Walt Whitman driving a Nissan Stanza. He's got gravy in his beard and a twinkle in his eye. The stars awaken the thrill of a palpable yearning. It takes some time for the imagination to slide into another form of being, but once that happens, one can excel at adhesion and act like a flap in the flag at the borders of noumenal being. Punches flicker beside the anthology of contemporary poetry. The nightclub bursts into streams of consciousness. Leopold Bloom admires the cutlery. Feeling feels wintery as a paper airport for paper airplanes. Swimming is incongruous and therefore delightful. The mind is but a shadow. Speed bumps are annotations. All of my memories have been cooked in reminiscence. Baby you can drive my car. And maybe I love you. Beep beep yeah.

It's hard to build a house when the lumber is alive. But you can bungle it like comedy and find something much fuller than a house. You can take all the silence of out of a poem and put it to use as something blonde and geographic. Sprinkle adjectives on it. Jingle it. Put it in the freezer until it turns hard and pragmatic. Cold to the fingers. Like a tool.

Painting is instinctive and reckless. A pile of rags flirt with a harmonica. The plywood conveys vividness. The oak screams in the ban saw. I savor the gumption of construction. Even my nerves bubble their opinions in a slow simmer of being. Sunlight slices through the air like a knife of singing light.

I slide cinnamon into my intestine and digest the world. I accommodate seclusion well. Fingernails rely on time to grow into themselves. The black cord of the hair dryer curls in the humidity.

Sometimes I work late at night juggling giant handshakes. This is what I experience when experience turns experimental. Any language will do, but English is particularly supple. Not enough has been said about that. A mind draws parables out of life. The sound of it is sweet and seditious. Ocher is a friendly color. But yellow, well yellow is yellow. It shouts joy from the bathroom wall. I think of myself as an occurrence of meat. This feeling widens and rivals Wisconsin. A wild energy crashes through the symmetries of science resulting in the experience of birds. Dirt. Obsidian shining out of a mountain.

Is there life on Mars? André Breton arrives in a flying saucer. His eyes murmur oranges. Why is there something rather than nothing? We all wonder that. But André seems especially obsessed. His premonitions seep through the words murdering distance and chattering fictions that are actual whales. Wheels. Weather. Bakeries and postulation. A patisserie filled with maps. Lips. Promontories of frosting. Pythagorean sensations serving the fertility of experience abstractions of invisible empires, the sublime appeal of concertinas and chaos and string theory.

I like words in strings. And when the strings run out there is still a trace of Paris, kitchen lights edged with gold. And down below a kangaroo leaps over a turnstile and catches the M4 to Versaille. Daylight marries the vowels of night and the wedding is twilight and the twilight is a delicate thing. Twilight is what happens when I feel open to everything. Even meaning.

THE TONGUE IS A STRANGE MACHINE

Enigmatic Corot that a chicken thickens if a cut thrills. I strain a spoon to hit the moon. The singing sidewalk is my blossoming and bile. I smell incense below the float and start the car. I will push this idea until it crackles below the bean bang.

The performance glows and we feel its heavy steam. We assembled the stomach during the fall and luxuriated in winter feeling it work itself into rhetoric. I bald into honesty like paint. The dusty soliciting of spring became my cause and controversy. I stood there in the orchard including sense in my art and absorption.

We can maneuver the fence if the court so deems it necessary for our escape into the wilderness. Jerk a swim through the pool. If you lose yourself during the elevation you will find resurrection in the consonants strewn throughout the sentence. The proposal attends your punches. One must endure one's secretions as they become implicit in perception.

Mark this, my friend, the bowl will quicken as it fills with ice. Scribbles toss themselves into circulation. I feel the pulse of an indentation brush a babble with an admonition. Plump my draw to a collar stud. I can only answer the wonder of myriad structures since I branch into many coconuts and burn the deformation with laughing up there.

We play the trapeze and tap the wall with autonomy. We pull our excuses out of a perception of ratio and make proverbs out of silk. Our assembled logic accommodates gravity, crustaceans it to vermilion, and we go ahead and pull the rest, fastening our spoons as we go. There is cement for exploration and glass for decipherment. We clothe our echoes beneath knowledge and see what green Apollinaire wore when he flowed toward the mysteries of secretion.

It's in the streams that our reflections pin themselves to the water disturbing the graces of the heart. We linger to collect ourselves and travel into the beyond weeping over the compliments of apples. Conceit is a form of coherence. It is the mind we hope to press against when we write something. The tea is cluttered with subtleties, too many to describe as sidewalks or cloth, which have their own distinctions, and inflate with the nutmeg of desire.

We fill our anthologies with aesthetic persuasions that never quite gel into paradise. Confusion explains the larynx. We flail what we can with our theories and tumble vowels on our lips. I can't quit altitude. There is the spring to the blade of my knife and age is a palette whose colors can never adjust to the brass of trouble. Cream by violin, and use binoculars for the rest.

My feelings fight for the rub of the wave. I can do nothing without teeming. I feed my insistence the clang of the sleeve and wash the greenery with meditation. The tongue is a strange machine, though some might call it a muscle. I call it a convocation of cells and let it shape the song as it will.

UMWELT IN A BATH TOWEL

Sensation serves the fertility of experience, although the fireworks are unpredictable. The structures are oars. The pronouns delicate and sweet, like whipped cream. There is evident a splash of divinity in everything, a rub of dribble sparkling across the floor. I keep smelling parables. They appear to be everywhere. It's just a matter of learning how to read them, how to coax them into the basement where they might enlarge their capacity for enjoyment, for throwing darts, or listening to the crackle of wood in an old-fashioned stove, the kind that might've stood in the studio of Georges Braque as he continued to work out another Cubist idea, a dance of fingers bringing a touch of orange there, a little blue there, and properties of meaning shattered into reality. The heart cries out its desires and the brain turns copper, consciousness bubbling with mass just as words do. Words, after all, are a form of semantic camaraderie, a prodigal performance of fish and recognition. At least we act like it. Sometimes we sag with the transference of meaning into singing. The burden is palpable, but not so squeezed that it percolates hope like a green bandana while the rest of the gold camp rush to hear Sarah Bernhardt. Oh no. Nothing like that. More like gold itself. Those little sparkles of gold in a pan. Which is what laughter becomes during times of war and illness. I've heard that salt, under certain conditions, towers into fulfillment as a long abalone proliferating in coral, like flowers in an opium dream. And this, too, becomes fodder for romance, at least at the mouth, where the sheen of duplication takes the form of two lips, and the tongue goes to work shaping sounds on the palate of the mouth, or unites them with suction, blowing them out at the end of the day in a fountain of minivans and accordions. The airport, meanwhile, is cut in two by paradox, one half jaunty in the spring and full of wrestlers and people passionate about mushrooms, the other half sad and almond and straining to grasp the geometry of flight, obtaining an enlarged disposition in the process, a mind of swallows darting and soaring over a churchyard somewhere, an England of towers and rags and the quiet severity of hidden turmoil. Certainly nothing like France, nothing like Paris, where the emotions unbuckle in color and go to extremes, soaring out of the mouths of beggars and kings equally, immeasurably, grappling with the sheer vertigo of existence, bundled as it is in propositions, and friendly as a bath towel.

BLATANT TAFFETA

You could say that a word is empty but if it cuts the air and rides on a tongue there is an incentive to say something abstract, something wet and automatic, like rain. Blood is awkward. But desire is French. Therefore, say something consummately sincere. Say it is snowing in Asia. Say the door is pushed open and the insects are scattering into the cracks and corners. Form is the beginning of structure. It is there that the shadow pinches the light and pharmacy hugs its drugs. Push forward despite the evident virtuosity of leather. You won't regret it. Life is better than television but not as bathetic. One must learn to accept the heaviness of the traffic. Forget about the woman honking her horn behind you making you feel embarrassed because you were daydreaming when the light turned green. Engage the clutch slowly as you step on the gas. Language isn't entirely a matter of traffic lights. The heart is a dark genius. Its accessories twinkle under the weight of a transcendent sympathy. I begin with the charm of flowers and end by sitting in an attic leafing through old *National Geographics*. By the end of the Cretaceous the continents had roughly taken their current position. But why dinosaurs? Well, why not dinosaurs? There's a drug that offers miracles and if you pull it along a fire escape it will activate and talk about seeing things before you even swallow it. Next time you see me I may be wearing a necklace of little bronze hats. Before I became the philosopher king of my living room I pondered taking up plumbing. Some oil had formed on my chin and so I removed it and pasted it to the desk where it steamed and smoldered like a kerosene lamp on a humid night in Anchorage. What was it, I wondered. I figured it out later: an amalgam of words I'd forgotten about had assumed meaning and image and turned itself into a paragraph when I wasn't looking. This happens a lot. Let a dime shine and a nickel will entrance you with a parable of value. It's rather astounding. You should see the bulge in my pocket. I'm lazy about spending change. I just shove dollars at people, clerks and automobile salesmen, just to see what will happen. I now own twelve cars and a mountain in China. I feel foolish, but I'm also an authority on the symbolism of groceries, and that education wasn't cheap, brother. My advice: tailor your success according to the ancient saws. A penny earned is a penny saved, that sort of thing. Explain swimming to an extraterrestrial. Grammar is a muscle. Meaning arrives later dragging its attitudes behind it. Some things beg to be expressed as imagery and straw. This is why we name our emotions Larry, Moe, and Gravy. But if a fly could talk we wouldn't be able to understand its language. Until then I'm just energy, a pair of ears waiting to hear something from Mars, a sad sweet song about the winds blowing over the deserts, or a powwow in my pillow, scents and refinements expressing themselves in the streets of Paris. This happens every time I read Proust. I sit down and put words in a sentence in the next thing you know I'm lifting thoughts into blatant taffeta.

EACH AND EVERY WAY

Each and every way that I position my regard provides a plurality of relations and samplings from a mass of pure sensation. Each perspective insinuates its own incendiary geometry. Expectation acquires a piquant lucidity. The light penetrates the basement window. A chisel gleams. A ban saw screams like a banshee. Sawdust accumulates on the floor. It smells of pine and oak. A nearby gravel road articulates the convulsions of impeccable clouds. A furious awakening flashes on the horizon. The weight of the sky thrills the bones and unpacks its provisions in a dialogue of thunder. The light is perforated with silver. If I choose to read the world like a book it puzzles me with snow. It dazzles me with pearls. It threads the mind with correlation.

The desk emphasizes its existence in a determination of wood. I sit down and open Ulysses to page 305: "A monkey puzzle rocket burst, spluttering in darting crackles. Zrads and zrads, zrads, zrads, zrads. And Cissy and Tommy and Jacky ran out to see and Edy after with the pushcar and then Gerty beyond the curve of the rocks. Will she? Watch! Watch! See! Looked round. She smelt an onion. Darling, I saw, your. I saw all. Lord!"

Even the rain dripping from the black rungs and curls of the wrought-iron patio furniture in front of Molena's Taco Shop bear some relation to the rest of the universe. Rain collects in a river which powers the turbines of Grand Coulee Dam which feeds electricity to the arc welder welding the patio furniture. The shell on display in the window was made from proteins and minerals that were created when the planet formed and life first appeared out of a jelly-like glop of lipids and carbohydrates. The rain dripping from the patio furniture was once a wave in the ocean that made the shell that housed the snail that crawled ashore and died on a rock molded by the gusts and pounding surf of a windy shore.

    Sit, Jessica. Look how the floor of heaven / Is thick inlaid
    with patens of bright gold. / There's not the smallest orb

which thou behold'st / But in his motion like an angel sings, / Still choiring to the young-eyed cherubins. / Such harmony is in immortal souls, / But whilst this muddy vesture of decay / Doth grossly close it in, we cannot hear it.

So declares Lorenzo in *The Merchant of Venice*. That harmony that is in immortal souls is consciousness of the unity of interrelation that is the juice and savor of pure experience. But this would be an experience without the adornment of words. Words are a filtering membrane through which experience percolates before it dances on the nerves.

The urge to arrive at a pure experience is a journey of bone and skin, muscle and blood. It comes down to the body. Toes, hands, hair, eyes, knees, everything in this envelope of flesh that connects my being in the world with that world as immediate as possible. Sensation is a product of nerves. It gets to the brain in electrical impulse where it's translated into lettuce, a woman's touch, a man's voice, a slice of bread popping up in the toaster, the electric smell of the air in Kansas before a tornado droops from the clouds and begins spinning debris in a whirl of radical energy.

William James coined the phrase "radical empiricism" to describe his notion of pure experience:

I give the name of 'radical empiricism' to my *Weltanschauung*. Empiricism is known as the opposite of rationalism. Rationalism tends to emphasize universals and to make wholes prior to parts in the order of logic as well as in that of being. Empiricism, on the contrary, lays the explanatory stress upon the part, the element, the individual, and treats the whole as a collection and the universal as an abstraction. My description of things, accordingly, starts with the parts and makes of the whole a being of the second order. It is essentially a mosaic philosophy, a philosophy of plural facts, like that of Hume and his descendants, who refer these facts neither to Substances in which they inhere nor to an Absolute Mind that creates them as its objects. But it differs from the Human type of empiricism in one particular which makes me add the epithet radical.

To be radical, an empiricism must neither admit into its constructions any element that is not directly experienced, nor exclude from them any element that is directly experienced. For such a philosophy, *the relations that connect experiences must themselves be experienced relations, and any kind of relation experienced must be accounted as 'real' as anything else in the system.* Elements may indeed be redistributed, the original placing of things getting corrected, but a real place must be found for every kind of thing experienced, whether term or relation, in the final philosophic arrangement.

Now, ordinary empiricism, in spite of the fact that conjunctive and disjunctive relations present themselves as being fully co-ordinate parts of experience, has always shown a tendency to do away with the connections of things, and to insist most on the disjunctions. Berkeley's nominalism, Hume's statement that whatever things we distinguish are as 'loose and separate' as if they had 'no manner of connection.' James Mill's denial that similars have anything 'really' in common, the resolution of the causal tie into habitual sequence, John Mill's account of both physical things and selves as composed of discontinuous possibilities, and the general pulverization of all Experience by association and the mind-dust theory, are examples of what I mean.

— from *A World of Pure Experience,* 1904

The pulverization of experience occurs as soon as we begin to classify, label, identify, analyze and organize our experience according to a model that we cultivate over time to give meaning to our perceptions.

What we lose in pure experience we gain in cognition. All the sensations that comprised that experience lose their acuity but it would be wrong to say they're lost. The process is similar to the refinement of ore. A mass of unrecognizable dirt and rock becomes a dinner set or a bridge, a car or an Eiffel Tower, a surgical instrument or French horn. It's a process of metamorphosis. Of transformation. A sequence of events that never culminate in a single definitive end but keep metamorphosing in a network of balances and instabilities, attractions and repulsions.

A simple example will serve: I have a cut on the inside of my right middle finger. I got it from playing with Toby, our cat. He likes to chase a piece of ribbon, particularly that type of narrow ribbon with the little grooves in it so that you can run it over a sharp edge to make it curl. I swing it over his head, run it over the floor, hide it behind my back as he attempts to catch it with his mouth or claw. He leaps, pivots, lunges. He loves to play with this thing. He got me on the inside of my middle finger with a claw. This isn't unusual. My right hand is generally constellated with little cuts where he has bit me or nabbed me with a set of claws. They usually don't hurt. I'm often surprised to find myself bleeding. But the one on the inside of my middle finger really hurts. It feels like a paper cut. Maybe it's because the skin has greater sensitivity in this area. It also seems slower to heal. The pain has a purity that resists artful assassination by analysis. It persists in exquisite particularity. It resists the attentions of intellect. There's no meaning to it, no lesson in it, no symbolism or parable. It just hurts.

Meanwhile I use my index finger to tap the surface of the tablet that brings up the rue du Fauborg-Montmartre, no 7, Paris, France, where it is said that Isidore Ducasse, the author of *Les Chants du Maldoror*, passed away at the age of twenty-four, November 24th, 1870. I get a street view: the buildings appear to date from the nineteenth century and may be the ones in existence when he lived there. There's a restaurant at street level called La Rose de Tunis serving Pizza, Panini, Crêpes, and Grilades. Next to it, on the corner, is a shop called Minelli which features shoes and women's accessories. How much has changed since

Isidore Ducasse, a.k.a. Le comte de Lautréamont, lived there and labored at his strange, magnificent book?

I tap Pandora and get an instrumental song by Johann Johannsson titled, in Icelandic, "Ég Átti Erfiða Æsku," which appears to mean something like "I struggled in my youth." The music is simple, strings, bells, drum, a sad, wistful, languishing melody punctuated by the rhythms of bells and drums.

All pure experiences occur outside of time. They become part of time in memory and narrative. When we structure them in a lineal sequence that leads to a concluding statement, a solution, epiphany, irresolvable ambiguity or pithy vignette.

Framing an experience is a way to give meaning and produce a sense of control over one's life. We have clocks and calendars to give us a sense of structure. But pure experiences have nothing to do with clocks and calendars. They have a lot to do with expectation. This is where surprise is a constant reminder of how little actual control we have over life, including our own existence.

Pure experience, William's "radical empiricism," occurs in a simultaneity of mass and sensation. Yesterday when I was out running there was so much humidity in the air that it tingled on the skin. You couldn't quite characterize it as drizzle it was so fine. It seemed to sparkle out of the air and penetrate my clothes and make me wet in a mingling of sweat and drizzle. There was no separation between me and the world. Interior and exterior were fused. There was my breathing, my running, and a vague, unnamable sense of being unqualified by anything else than its effort to keep going.

A SUMMONING

I don't know, maybe it's just me, but if the vault is variegated my elbow clicks like drapery. I don't know where else to keep my money. I'm not entirely sure what makes money money in the first place. I do find that it's democratic to blend with reality as much as possible, but if one's illusions are compelling enough, well, why not just go ahead and walk into the mirror à la Jean Marais following Heurtibise into the under-world. It is said that if one looks long enough in the mirror one will see death. What I see is a face creased with age and eyebrows going crazy under a bad haircut. A bad haircut is a sure ticket to the underworld. You don't need gloves. All you need is love, sang the Beatles, and they were right, of course. But it's harder than one might think to go around in love with the world all the time. There are a lot of people out there that requires a supreme effort to like, much less love. It's slightly easier but less democratic to parachute through one's mind without getting tangled up in one's thoughts. Thoughts are funny things. They're like doors to other dimensions. Sometimes you can find redemption in a trumpet or hot dog. Scan the fetus and see if it smells of puddles. The fetus to which I refer is that of thought of course. Because each thought is a fetus in its infancy. And if it smells like rain or puddles in the street it's time to go bowling my friend and get out of your head. Calendars are fun too, giving names to all the shifts in temperature, draping the sullen cliffs of Arizona with amulets of sunset fire or blanketing Ireland and its ancient castles with snow. If you act like a clarinet expect quartz to appear on your chest in place of your other minerals. There is ore in the heart, gold and copper and sometimes veins of silver. Imagine it raining on a tank. The men inside playing cards. That's my definition of breath. Another is lungs. And still another is streams of air flowing out of the mouth, thoughts included, getting sculpted into words. Variables and dots, tinfoil oysters wrapped in zip code catfish skulls. That's my idea of thinking. It's a calling of things forth. A summoning. A provoca-tion. A fishing around in the depths, dangling words in the limpid pool of a cavern. The syntax of blind white fish. Wiggling. Outside in the good clean air the atomic moon becomes a highway and illumines our personal histories with the kerosene of desire and the wick of remorse. Who wouldn't want to walk through that mirror to the underworld just to retrieve a past moment, a bittersweet morsel from the vault of that ancient jukebox stuck beneath the ribs, the bump bump bump of the beating heart, blood pumped to the brain, oblivion lapping the ghostly shores of a scene enacted over and over again, behind those curtains, behind that mirror in the bathroom, the one that smiles back, and looks like you, and is you, and isn't you. The twisting you do, the voltage it takes to run a thrill up and down the spine, a trembling in the membrane of night.

THE SORCERY OF GLASS IN
AN AGE OF PHARMACEUTICALS

Glass is pure sorcery. I watched some once in its folds and colors inflate a flip of air savored in a spirit of permeability roam around a ripple of transparency. It made me feel dribbled, as if the universe bombed in a nightclub telling jokes about existence, and how existence makes no sense, there's no purpose to it, but here we are ha ha. Existing. Burning. Putting out heat and light. Fucking one another. The best way out of this nonsense is to sit down and open a book. The paper hovers above a whisper of words juggling one's nerves in a vividness of snow and monstrous temperatures of swollen idea. You know? Like fireworks. Once I watched some music flirt with a harmonica and an emotion floated through me in shiny alabaster and mirrors reflecting knives and hallucinations constructed out of words. This is what happens in a marriage between emotion and words: broadcloth. This is why I had to call the concierge and report the darkness in my room. Broadcloth. I needed to see the broadcloth. It was imaginary broadcloth but I had to see it. I had to see it in my mind, which I could do in darkness, but I wanted to see the word, the word 'broadcloth,' floating in the air of my hotel room. I could catch it with a butterfly net and bring it home and put it in a piece of writing. Eugene Ionesco stands in our closet lost among our clothes. I bring him breakfast. If language had not been invented, how would I be able to represent the sun? My skin tells a story of labor and pain. It's written in my face. But the sun is a different story. The sun is a story of nuclear fusion filling a paragraph in space with heat and light and miscreant syntax. My inner fire blazes like a forge. Out come swords and patio furniture. Tanks and andirons. The metal frame of a bed or a sneeze spinning around like a reproductive organ made of bronze alloys and specialty copper. That kind of stuff. I folded the sky and put it in a drawer. It felt like velour. Proverbs spilled out of the clouds. Bells bent the winter air. It was then that I realized what incendiary objects nouns can be, spitting themselves into the air, impelling redemption in the parabolas of despair. Nouns stick to my body like refrigerator magnets. Verbs are more difficult. You have to do them. Perform them. Gaze at mahogany. Run around the block. Describe the naked rupture of sleep by manipulating a garden hose. Argue with a forehead. Tour an escalator. Ride an elevator. Sing. Talk. Eat. Languish in Euclid. Blow glass. Blow it into vases. Blow it into bowls. Blow it into bottles. Blow it into Dublin, Ireland, then step away and admire the beautiful transparency of nouns. The sorcery of glass in an age of pharmaceuticals.

SOCK

There's a pretty density which grips a sock, makes it a sock, socks it into sockness, soaks it in the energy of sensation and parachutes it through oblivion. This is the reality of the sock. The quiet weave of the sock is its unity, a continuous union as in association and thinking. If the phenomenon of the sock is established through the form of time, then the phenomenon that is consciousness is a unifying activity. We see that the relationship between consciousness and the sock represents a transcendent, unchanging reality apart from time. The life of an individual is the development of consciousness that constitutes a sock. But which sock? For there is a left sock and a right sock. The right sock is independent of the left sock and the left sock is independent of the right sock. For when one sock is lost in the laundry the other sock loses the penetrating force of its utility and becomes a rag-like thing whose only saving feature is that it may join forces with another sock, a sock that it may or may not match imperfectly, or with enough conviction that it may pass as the other sock's true mate. There is always a certain unchanging reality at the base of the sock. This reality enlarges from day to day until it develops a hole and a toe pokes through. This is the reality of the toe in conjunction with the reality of the sock. One might wonder about its form and how it maintains itself. The form of the toe and the form of the sock form a conjunction by which the hole itself becomes an entity, a hollowness whose integrity comes from an absence of material, acrylic or cotton worn down until it is nothing, and a toe appears, that is the fundamental fact emerging from another reality. All people believe that there is a fixed, unchanging principle in the universe and that all things are established according to it. This principle is the sock that unifies consciousness. It is not possessed by mind or matter but establishes them. There, in the laundry basket, or upon one's foot, tugged into place, toe poking through, where it is an object of consciousness, a cotton or acrylic form occupying a certain time in a certain place, and may be regarded as singular, however imperfectly it matches the other sock, the other lost sock, given a place at the extremity of one's leg, joined together by linguistic signs, by words, these words, which I have offered to fill the sock, and make the sock a sock, and not just the word of the sock, but the sock itself, as I sock it to you.

CRAWL CONVOCATION

Crawl convocation a dribble a gleam a phantom oboe squirts sensation into the bumps. I am waxed and towered under bone. The velvet bistro cloth is everything I need. I navigate by fathom. We whisper Cubism to one another and carry a heavy kiss. Heartwood lends gravitas to the circus, and the travel is rank with shape.

We wade through our troubles erect and blazing. Opinion's autonomy forms my hive. The drawers jingle with habit. I smell of almond and bomb the air with French. Job my muffin if the sparkle heaves. We evade we snow we glaze. The fractious sag of our bacteria empties our supply of wire.

The meridional glass is what the peremptorily diametric tyranny grew to subvert itself. What I have written I bark and burn by significance. There is a house I am supposed to have remembered. What springs knocks a stick. I return to the club to squeeze some pretzels and think.

The bank distills our vermilion and makes us wealthy with skates. Our genre of pounds is apparitional but infinite in roots. We give it energy and math and touch the cleavage. The train excels at roaming. The ovals bang into eczema and convulse themselves into sleeping.

The pavement ambushes a sidewalk with its severity. The sidewalk simmers and spreads into delineation. I wrestle a thin incident of nails and fight to initiate some power over the hydrants. The cloth is so malleable we can savor the shells and shepherd the pain of existence. I ache to sweeten my escape with intellectual crimps.

When I apply my seclusion to writing I yell that I am full of good intentions and get swept away anyway flipping my pancakes and juggling my eggs. The dream steals what laughter I preserved in jars and makes it silver. I am on a trapeze in the raw migration of rope. Fauve your pasting. The attack fork is boxed in a salon of bulbs and its nativity is rattan, not buckskin.

Cézanne imbues us. We shiver by the waves. We roughen the bristle cylinder and walk into abstractions sobbing then swimming. We eat the waves slowly, then move forward, arms sliding in and out, elemental as mushrooms. Before I disturb you with my face I want a jaunty wrinkle to exploit my nose.

I like to shove people around with power and wealth. But outdoors is different. Outdoors the dimensions are swollen and photogenic and all I can think about are ghosts and algebra. I hit the bread with an incendiary tea-hat then shoot myself into the world pulling endeavor behind. I've tried getting used to gravity by fluttering but in the end it was nothingness that I whispered and amber that I thundered as the lost day rose into the boil above.

FOR THE RECORD

Here I sit as always clouds floating out of my head. You know those states you get into sometimes when the writing turns hornet and motorcycle? When the jewels appear, when the rubies hit patterns of elsewhere? Experience is turned into crystals. There is so much to describe. You can't keep up with it all. All you can do is jabber. Talk to the walls. Hang from the ceiling like a human chandelier. Like a chandelier chandelier. Hazel and lurking. Pamphlets on the table describing a Utopian world in which nobody works that doesn't want to work. Where work isn't work where work is more like play. Where night disintegrates into heated dancing and the strange servitude imposed on the body. The original body. The body of Adam the body of Eve. Those wonderfully innocent bodies. You see people like that sometimes in the desert. Or wandering the streets of Manhattan. Believe me, nobody wanders Manhattan, not unless there's something weird going on. Something primordial, something full of fire and fingers. It sometimes happens that a word will assume a quality similar to water. In that it will flow and float an idea. And the instincts will tickle the bones and the parodies of the blood will circulate in volumes of meat imagined as an arm or a leg or a torso. As if our thoughts were mohair, a suspension of gumbo pulled into percolation. I might get occupied by doing brushstrokes, or shooting tin cans with a .22. How do nerves work? Electrical impulses fire up the brain like lightning forking through a storm cloud. That's my image of it how about you? How do the nerves in the eyes do their thing? What did Cézanne's eyes look like? Were they blue? Green? Did his pupils dilate? Age is how we discover ourselves. As we get closer to dying we get bigger in our being. Being dilates. As being ebbs it deepens. The mind grows truant. We inhabit a permanent Saturday. There's a nakedness that happens on Saturday. That's all I know. I don't care where you're at you can be in the Antarctic without a clock or calendar within fifty miles but somehow when Saturday arrives you'll know it's Saturday. Bubbling out of the air, creaking in the snow, blazing out of the stars, funny rectangles on a floor black and ivory sprinkled with dimes. Picture Stephane Mallarmé pounding on a reluctant vending machine and you'll get the picture. There's endless support in writing these things down. Keep a record, my friend. Document it. Everything. Nothing is too thin, too thick, too audible to call mud.

SOUVENIR

Words smell of the hothouse. Orchids and moss. Light glued together with eyes. Animal eyes. Human eyes. The camaraderie of eyes that occurs in the darkness of a theatre. The ocean is full of eyes. The darkness creates its own kind of language. Something vague yet tart as a martini olive. Sensations that elude description and so enlarge the complements of snow, the words that evolve into something more than words, into click beetles and cord, gutta-percha, tragacanth, flintlock, folds of meaning still warm from the mouth. These are more like daubs of color, a canvas stippled with insistent signs. It just happens. There are presences that blossom into afternoons, wrinkles of an apparition, eyes crowded with shapes. Awakened syllables alive and blazing as they walk into a conversation and eat potato chips and marry the delicate things seized by a shiny impersonal pain. It's so easy to get lost in abstraction as soon as the words get rolling. But then you have to decide for yourself what is mere effervescence and what is a more substantial response to this anguish, this widening abyss. What's a dream and what's a recognition? Life is sticky with such semantic obstetrics. Giving birth to images upside-down, repairing our wounds with art. There is a poetry in us that acts like Technicolor once it's out of the box and making its assumptions, prophecies based on nothing but mimicry and flags. Put a skull on the table and everyone knows instantly what is meant. But this isn't language this is culture. Culture is when the crowd fondles a belief and the connections get wet with blood and semen. There is no smoke, no incense or perfume that doesn't in some way climb into itself when it's written on paper and sits there sparkling like an experience. These are the kind of images that's so easy to lose, to surrender to more abstract speculations. A window folds itself into a car and penetrates the night with its long golden beams. Two days later it has eyes and a long thin spine and drags itself along on a string of vowels looking for something to eat. The words that describe this jump into a sentence and swim for their life. It's a sloppy world. Though slightly Etruscan at times, especially when the lobster is served and the trumpets blast. What is it, this obsession with gold, this maieutic journey, this cardboard sky in which the tangle of the mind is represented as so many cherubs among the clouds? It's still with us, you know. Nobody gets out alive. But it's healthy to keep trying, don't you think? I mean, what else is poetry for? You can't get hung up in Dilbert and call it a life. There are places where the Sunday paper isn't delivered at all. Desolate places, where creation snarls and lashes out with its claws, wild and groping for something romantic to seize and wrap in a rag and show to the folks back home.

TAKEOFF

Talk had thermometers to mirror. The water to twist. Labor its jackknife by wafer. I understand the handstand by cleavage, triumph which infinity melts. Fruit and zippers in jigsaw antifreeze shows the incidental sugar of the tangerine in summary of a day's orchids. There is a fire that anneals in scope and pine to become the umbrella that minarets dirt by the plywood molecules of a ghostly dog. Infinity hangs from the lip of the jackhammer glittering with enough stars to intone an omelet into lassitude. The oboe sparkles in the delivery of its music. The lacuna that dreams it is a bench at a bus stop detours to tongue the veil of a moment and make it wax like a vegetable, which is to say tactical, Thursday, and romantic. A ripple in the broth. A twilight coughed up by a sun as it hums on the horizon like a comb in the garbage. The squid gets carried away in its rhythms and the kayaks are laminated by analysis. An intrepid zero bristles like a sore on the chicken. The mathematics of warmth gets crabby and the scarred photographer takes her picture with a piece of language called a forehead. The obelisk is lambent with doorknobs. The closet bounces through its clothes on the border of a new reality where the hangers shine in distinction of themselves and a winter coat dawdles in nirvana. You can engender a storm quite easily by getting angry and shouting. But meaning something is different. For that you have to chew particles into calculus until an apocryphal clam comes whittling its way along the beach and confuses you with its goofy handshakes. An X-ray pauses long enough to show you its bones in veneration of the flesh it has chosen to ignore in celebration of the skin of the tongue. The tongue which is near to itself in asphalt and by gargling civilization embarrasses the apocalypse by naming experiences and waffling around in daylight wherein the bleachers are calm and Norway is unnatural for a day. If any of this makes sense you must call your doctor and tell her that Mick Jagger is dancing in your bathroom. By that I mean glistening, which most of us have some familiarity with, our laws and our roads being made of energy and bricks so that horsepower will have some place to perform its paroxysms and the jet may undertake its takeoff.

CONCERTINA

Cubism plays flirtation into helium. Baffled clutters of intent fidget through morality. Metamorphosis sips the forehead. Honor sits in a cemetery. A thumb does ham and it's magically red. An indigo phonograph serious as an airplane landing in an oasis of introversion deepens the stars. Candy is an invention, a pleasure of visceral lucidity in food. My medication resuscitates its own peculiarities. Structure begs for development. The texture of a sleeve tastes of pagan stubble. Wrinkles of rawhide find their foam of a perfect moment. Finger and mouth go resonant in a concentric propinquity. The sky murmurs of a Fauvist train remembered as an engine of sound. The winches and pulleys of consciousness create a linguistic element that occurs as a wisecrack in the ice and seizes chemicals never before aired on TV and so goes about the interior of the head disguised as an arena in a flake of wax. The mathematics of this is where the squirrels come in. They leave behind a skeleton of numbers. And Cubism arrives at last in a sedan chair of nipples figured by thread. In other words, a perfect concertina. Romance galvanized by a fez, a face in the asphalt, Nikola Tesla standing in an alley in the rain squeezing it in, letting it out, so that a wheeze of music cools into a marvelous stew of shrubbery chalk.

TOMBSTONE

The bug is an abstraction. Truth flies around the room and lands on the back of a chair hungry for lies. Franz Kafka opens the refrigerator and removes a bowl of jello with the face of Bella Abzug in it.

Name one thing that isn't a metaphor and I will hang naked from the skin of the tongue.

An umbrella is simply an umbrella and if a pen travels over a sheet of paper it is not long before I just sit and laugh. Time impregnates a long sentence which is strange because I'm not wearing shoes. I never do. I have a pair of wings that unfurl into enormous metaphors as the Beach Boys sing "Don't Worry Baby" and palominos resist the erosion of human understanding.

What happens when we sleep? We journey with our eyes golden with the residue of dreams. Apple trees remember the great battles of the American civil war. But for the time being let's just live forever.

How did I ever get here?

Life is an enchantment. You betcha. You may proceed at your own risk.

Each of us creates our own story. That's the beauty of it.

Make no mistake. There is such a thing called reality. But no one has yet figured out its true dimensions. All any of us have are these five measly senses. Even the headlight has a personality.

All this happens in Tombstone.

Why Tombstone? The way it sculpts the air. Everything is possible. I open my mouth. I make things appear and disappear. Cactus, shell casings, grains of sugar scattered on a Formica tabletop.

I'm missing a molar. My gum feels odd when I put my tongue there.

It's like they say: shit happens.

But it all balances out in the end.

Sometimes it takes an allegory to sublimate pain.

For example: interesting results can be obtained by dollying out while zooming in or dollying in while zooming out so that the size of the things stays the same but the perspectives change. You can evoke everything and bump into people or open a door and leave.

The mind is an unofficial patina in which the desert is a glutton for absorption.

France hisses its absence.

I can't tell you how to live. But I can tell you how to do the locomotion.

Jump up, jump back, make a chug-a-chug-a motion like a railroad train.

LET ME TELL YOU A STORY

Let me tell you a story. I can hear the gardeners blowing leaves. They carry engines with long tubes that blow air in a great rush and send the leaves whirling forward as they advance. Fairies dance in a ring as the gardeners approach, oblivious to the whirr of their engines. The fairies are blown into the air, but the gardeners continue their advance. They are serious men. Serious about gardening. Serious about making money. Serious about raising families. Serious about everything. How's that for a story? Here's another: pain is accidental. The end result is ice and divorce. Fat sentences brushing against the warmth of someone else's skin. It's touching. A touching instance of envelopment and fat. This is a story about spoons.

Spoons.

Spoons lie spoon to spoon in a kitchen drawer, sandwiched between knives and forks. There are two grooves for the spoons. There is a groove for teaspoons and a groove for tablespoons.

There is more drama concerning knives then there is surrounding spoons.

The weather today is Cimmerian with a trace of sky.

Vertebrae and velvet.

This is a story about velvet. The great king felt for his vertebrae in a gown of velvet.

This is a story about the origin of life: tune in next week for the exciting conclusion.

This is a story about horses grazing by the side of the road.

Horses grazing by the side of the road.

Horses.

Grazing.

By the side.

Of the.

Road.

I have a photo of Paris in my wallet. Would you like to see it? That's me, and that's Nikolas Sarkozy with his arm around me, and Carla Bruni giving me a peck on the cheek.

Aren't words wonderful? You can say anything.

This is a story about language. One day, there was a synonym loose in the library. It sawed the library in half and exposed a baby's sock lying on the sidewalk.

This is a story about a baby's sock on the sidewalk.

Why is there a baby's sock on the sidewalk? There is no synonym for sock. A sock is a distinct thing, explicit as the veins in Cezanne's vivacious hands.

A flash of lightning.

Clouds, bluebells, harmonicas.

All I'm saying is that if you swing from a trapeze 50 feet above the ground, you should be able to trust the person that is going to catch you.

Propositions resemble arrows.

Or hot water squirting out from the valve when it gets turned open.

This is a story of hot water squirting out from an opened valve.

I marvel at the way facts assert themselves.

Bing cherries. A woman riding a lawnmower off Highway 17 near Moses Lake.

Wild Bill Hickok sitting at a table in a saloon holding a hand of cards.

The little bulb inside his head is crying like the soft eye of the antelope in a blaze of snow.

LIQUIDITY

On Friday, July 9th, 2009, I vacuumed the car. I threw myself into it with the rage of a hundred Vikings on the shore of the real.

I never use the same hose twice.

Or is it ten?

Did I mention that there are woods nearby? The woods abound with acorns.

The age demanded an image and so I gave it acorns.

When consciousness is cut into words, it becomes a struggle.

Hummingbirds and wine.

The poem grows legs and crawls from its surroundings. It becomes sunlight gleaming on a construction crane.

A warm body of air.

I never take the sun for granted. I never take anything for granted.

I love the way the waiter at La Palma says margarita. The r's roll off his tongue like the daughter of a German ambassador rimming a glass with salt. Though I must say margarita does not sound German. It arrives at the table with details that are entirely Hispanic.

The story goes that a bartender at the Rancho La Gloria Hotel near Tijuana named Carlos Herrera, who went by the nickname Danny, concocted the drink for a Ziegfeld dancer named Marjorie King. Spanish converts Marjorie to margarita. Consequently, the history of the margarita is forever doomed to romance.

And speculation, which is the cousin of romance.

Speculation has the clarity of the Mexican sky.

Here comes a man with a thousand hearts, and there goes a woman hemorrhaging stars on the western horizon.

One has to ask oneself: is it human to want thought? A little water tossed into the air? A transcendental hat? Mania? Sedimentation? The MGM lion tap-dancing on a treadmill?

Feeling inclines toward feeling and tequila maps our relation to the universe without any idea of why yearning is soft and blue in the lounges of Tenochtitlán.

But enough about margaritas, which I don't drink anyway.

I want to talk about neckties. Who wears them, and why.

I prefer the bolo. It slips on easily. No knot necessary. And there is a shine in the movement.

Like that of the soul.

The question of form is inextricably mingled with expression. From Latin ex, out, plus Latin pressare, to press. To press out. Expression is a pressing out.

Every day there is a new way to be liquid.

HARMONIC DISTORTION

I like crowds. I can't say why. Maybe I'm in love with profusion.

Yes. That's it. I'm in love with profusion.

Who knows, maybe one day a scab will gargle the literature of the heart and Manhattan will appear in my fingernail. Later, I can extrude it through my mouth and draw many friends to my bosom.

I like skin. Particularly on the small of a woman's back.

Also, the heat of a fire on hands numbed and stinging with cold.

Can you hear me? There is no one to do this feeling but you and I.

Which is to be nowhere and everywhere at once, like the twitch of a horse's rump.

The branches of the trees agitate in a light breeze. A ball bounces down a street in Valencia. Fisherman unload baskets of fish and crab.

Death is not what you think. What we think of as spirits are holes in the fabric of time. It's handy, like being delirious.

Today I want to avoid anything unpleasant. I often feel the urge to lie down on the floor and stare at the ceiling.

And then there's the matter of ears. This morning I awoke to the sound of words stuck in a beard like food. That's because words are hallucinations. If you don't believe me go to France.

Nothing escapes necessity except the necessity to escape.

Kerosene is a proposal, a puff of breath on a feather that illumines the campsite at night.

Only the lonely recognize atmosphere as a pragmatic heresy. Fatalism is an oversimplification, like a Texas drawl.

Lust will sometimes perch high and defiant on a finger of stone and cause descriptions to grow eyes and linger on stalks of pure electricity.

Electricity is amazing. It will provide a narrative to your life. Plug it in, and watch the ceiling come to life, feature-length movies crawling through a Persia of clairvoyance and rain.

SELF-PORTRAIT IN A CONVEX GOB

The sky is catching fire. The sun is melting into the ground. I dip my brush into some celadon green.

Have you ever opened a can of paint? Pried the lid off with a screwdriver? Heard the glop of color slop in the pail? Squeeze a tube of paint? Put the bristles of brush in a gob of green or black and spread it into form and life and pyrotechnic feathers?

Coffee tastes of clairvoyance and rain.

I do push-ups. My wife decorates cakes.

Once I owned a pair of beautiful gloves. They warmed my hands and inclined toward music. They were so beautiful that surrealism evolved a new form of meat.

Our stove is old but the burner bowls are new. The old ones had holes in them. The new burner bowls were hard to find. We looked all over the Internet. We finally found some at Sears. They're bright and silver and sound like the metal of the moon shouting at birds on a carousel.

The planet orbits a farm tended by Guillaume Apollinaire. I help with the chores. I have grown feathers. There are feathers all over my body. I constantly itch, but the power of flight is worth it.

The air is heavy. The rain comes and goes.

The mirror in the bathroom is large and honest. I look piquant. A bathmat hangs from a chrome bar on the shower door. It has a light blue background and a motif of arabesques and flowers rendered in white. One of the edges is frayed.

I'm comfortable in my life. More or less. But then, I don't know any other life. I would have to invent one in order to describe it to you. I would need a thermometer and a little lumber.

The city we inhabit is ruthless. My private life is a celestial ductility of fruitless subjunctives.

I need some fingernail polish for retouching the corner of the wall by the door in the bathroom where it was scratched by carpet layers maneuvering a roll of carpet into the bedroom. You can hardly see it, but it bugs me. I hoped to find the paint that I used to paint the bathroom when we cleaned out the utility closet under the stairwell. I thought I had saved a pint, but apparently not. It's a pale yellowish white, what is called "ivory sonata," and is very rare. You can only find it hidden in the sawdust of certain musical compositions pretending to be a B flat.

The most perfect abstraction is horses.

Most of the time, I'm clean shaven. I grew a beard once when I was in my thirties. It didn't feel right. My mouth felt like a hole on the face of Grigori Rasputin.

I went home and flopped on the bed and gazed at the ceiling. I watched the whine of bullets, the howling of bombs.

And those were just the spiders.

THE PARROTS ARE MONUMENTAL ON THE RUE D'ORSEL

My wallet is cluttered with identity. Cards, facets, gestalts.

Heaven's nails are pounded into the lumber of life.

Those who kill do so because the infantry expects it of them. There is division between the body and the soul. There is division between bone and meat. There is division between man and woman. Division between today and yesterday.

Yesterday I rode a horse out into the cactus. I was surrounded by an ocean of silence. The air felt thick as a wedding gown. My mind filled with reflection. Thought became a bird filled with real life.

The strain to see things clearly. Meanings harnessed to words.

Necks, butter, scratching and cinnamon.

Sigourney Weaver.

A pair of old boots painted by Vincent Van Gogh.

My life tasted funny. Like old whiskey in a bottle of Truth or Consequences.

That's where I discovered Aristotle.

And the problem of universals.

And the Dead Sea Scrolls.

And the problem of war.

And refrigerators and toasters.

What I mean is beads that pulse with description. Appeals to radicality. Quixotic prose. Secrets coiled on the floor. Eyeballs hissing romance. Words that sweeten the biology of tongues.

Death is defined by obedience, life by subversion. Life is always best served by understanding. The harness is expanded for jellyfish. The eggnog exudes intention.

The parrots are monumental on the rue d'Orsel.

To go outdoors is to fulfill oneself with private thought and still remain open to grace. The squash in the market incandesces. The pumpkins culminate in plump apotheosis. There are shouts. There are shots. There are shovels.

Even the shadows hiss with anticipation.

And Solomon Burke echoes on the walls: don't you feel like cra cra cra cra crying.

LIKE A FUR-COVERED TEACUP

If fur is correspondent to the words will the words be fur? The time and place of a writing has little to do with fur, but the parables that emerge on Thursday are full of entrails. This makes our questions yellow. Green is a calamity. It follows then that when time is chickens television equals the radius of prayer divided by aviation. Molecules are a major cause of shirts. Handstands begin as teaspoons. Reality bounces through a herd of drools furious as cheese and twice as cypress. There are discretions that shiver with engagement and times when daydreaming leads to lemonade. Kerosene mimics the mind when it burns in a lantern quibbling with the breath of night. Yet, when it comes to whiskers, nobility is papier-mâché. Antiques are more like napkins. That is to say, if a yardstick appeals to the variegations of a conversation the words will combine with larder to create apples. They will be real apples, but with eight definitions teeming with thought and bicycles. Pepper comes from incentive, not hills. A flickering purpose walks on clumsy fingers. The piano unpacks a conception of Bach. The resulting melee deserves our attention. Let us, then, slap the stars with our mouths and prepare our invisibility. There is a certain providence in grebes that remembers the coordinates of gambling. Nothing is a similarity without a resemblance. Existence must grow from stress, or else it is mere windows and only marginally soaked with nerves. What is a worm if ambivalence calls its dreams into spicy turmoil and dust echoes dust with the toys of ceremony? What is it to be? It is to be, that is all. Being and water fat with examination. Inquiry earns its incandescence from stone. Libraries hooked on oblivion. The abstractions of a pumpkin are still a pumpkin, but the auroras of astronomy pull their oars through the solitudes of a pocket comb. We send our balloons up through space and time. The thrill is Pythogorean. The cream is thick and copious. If we name at least one sensation we will be that much further home.

JOHN RUSKIN DOING A SWAN DIVE

Needs simplify life. For instance, today I need a farm. I'm in a mood to grow beans. I'm no greenhorn. I once petted a cat.

Not only that.

I once saw a woman crushing cans with her breast on YouTube.

Her breast was huge. Both breasts were huge. She used her right breast. Lifted it to her chin, aimed at the can, and shoved it down as hard as she could.

And crushed the can.

That must have hurt. That can't be good for a breast.

They say the mammary glands evolved to keep the eggs of early mammals warm. It is hard to say, because breasts do not fossilize well.

I feel quite certain they did not evolve to crush cans.

But what is emotion?

A high cliff overlooking the Pacific ocean.

John Ruskin doing a swan dive.

FEELING A FEELING

Consciousness is haunted by the prospect of eternal life. Paper swans milked in the heat of a window. Heavenly dots slammed into decoration. The sand sags by an open fire. Name your favorite emotion. Mine is snow falling on a river. I like that feeling. It makes me feel clean and graceful like a hat. What I see in the sidewalk is gum and time. The concentration of a moment falling into big fat words and creating a sentence that clashes with reality. But in a good way. Like dreaming a conversation with a guitar. There is an open dynamic in music that drips with the silk of intuition. Surely the whole thing is more than a brightness crawling out of the neck. I have a great respect for mint. But the cabbage mistakes our digestion for Ohio. This is not Ohio. This is vapor. Rain on an antenna. Symmetry carries other obligations. Even the way a serape is folded bears certain implications. Secrets spun into the yarn like water. Like tears, or warts. Similes are always so eager to be fulfilled. Metaphors are different. They just sit around and moo. Coins slosh around in my pockets like the symbolism we find in anthologies of French symbolism. Which is to say their metal is not of this world. And so I wander around in my head until I fall asleep. I herd wildebeests. I open doors to other worlds. I bring opinions to the wind. The wind doesn't care. The wind has its own opinions. I can smell them. They smell like headlights and mustard. And when Mick Jagger asked me to join the Rolling Stones I didn't tell him I couldn't sing or play a guitar. No siree. I just got up on the stage and wiggled. Everything changed when André Breton arrived. He lost some buttons and was trying to find some sand for a fable he was writing. I helped with his allegory and he helped me find that moment of the day when there's nothing to do but explode into light. If reality is as real as it thinks it is, well then, all I have to say is get on with it. But does reality think? Reality is an abstraction. Abstractions don't think. What would happen if I reached up and touched the moon? I'll tell you: absolutely nothing. It's gravity that juggles the stars. Perceptions are there to flatter consciousness into believing that England is punctuated by time and that time itself is a paradigm bursting with pickles and incendiary nouns. Crisis carves its horrors out of the air, not the clock. The clock just sits on the shelf ticking and tocking the way a clock is supposed to. The hands move, the hours follow. And at three o'clock in the afternoon the Hunchback of Notre Dame arrives whispering of bells and waterfalls. Feeling, he says, is one way to feel a feeling. Another is to hop from bell to bell in a glorious hysteria of sound. This is how the rain gets nailed to the stationary and words evoke everything there is in the world except how to be silent. And that takes guts. There is nothing in the mind but shadows, and the mind itself is nothing. We swim in the sounds below our life and when we agree to remember the cabbage it jellies into concentration.

WRITING À LA POLLOCK

Writing is a dripping dropping drooling smearing smudging daubing lobbing energy of smells and Möbius strippers, goats, ghosts, ejaculated nouns, fluttered toboggans.

A fugue drops out of my mouth and assumes a life of socks.

The signs are cartilage and bone. If I had a hammer I would build a pair of sparkly feet.

I need to pry the air open and let it bleed Christmas.

Structure is a napkin folded into an ounce of courtesy.

This is an ear with a bright future.

And a shining star dangling from a lobe of junk mail.

There is an ocean in my head sobbing with headlines. Thud, thud, thud, thud of a heavyset, middle-aged man wearing a sweaty T-shirt that says Texas State.

Rain agrees with morning in a taxi. Cloth is living testament, a perspective made holy by conception. Coffee under perpetual construction.

Because tin. Because erratic. And because it explains my sleeve.

Do anything you want, I say. Be rubber be rubbed. Sip mind. Hallucinations in the wrinkled fat glitter of calliope copper.

Feel your skin. Your anonymity. Your weariness.

Clicking of the burner on the stove.

Cat toy in the shape of a cowboy dinner.

My heel looks like a squirrel, the distant hush of a jet fading into the sky.

Whatever kind of weather this happens to be, the air is dimes. Hectic oysters jingle their prepositions and elude all index.

Metaphors crack the coordinates. History is sliced into mushrooms. Daylight crashes through my eyes and reifies steel.

The truth wears philodendrons.

My intent is birds.

Water comprehended by a few nerves. And if I'm missing a sock, I accept the logic of denim.

I feel like a clarinet, a pornography of pronouns.

I hold in my hand a worm of unpredictable syntax. It wriggles and curls. It is lyrical with struggle. It is lovable with turmoil. It produces a strong radio emission associated with washing machines.

Here is my advice: stay in bed.

The human mind is a very messy place.

MY FAVORITE EMOTION

My favorite emotion is crystallizing into a mind. It hangs inside my head twinkling like a cartoon.

I believe the goal in life is masturbation, and candy.

Falling in love is helpful. Falling in love expands your options. You can, for instance, join a rock'n roll group and walk out of a nightclub in a splendor of rhizomatous audacity, hugging the world with roots and oophytic megasporangia.

Think like a geisha, act like a potato.

Examine your face for traces of blood. There is cotton for such things, and cafeterias.

Water is shaped into flesh with the pastels of thought.

The pecan is stretched into a station wagon. A hinged board at the rear may be lowered during loading or unloading. It is here that we find the human anatomy doing what it does best, grunting and lifting and showing a readiness to undertake any adventure.

The human body is the entire structure of a human being and comprises a head, neck, trunk and various types of organ. Many systems and mechanisms interact in order to maintain homeostasis, which is a way to sleep on the couch and watch TV, or read a book, or masturbate and eat candy.

The knee is a mechanism legion with bone. You can fill it with sounds and imagine Charlotte Gainsbourg living in it, or go for a walk using both knees simultaneously.

So much depends on a wheelbarrow glazed with rainwater that it's hard to live inside a house or toolshed and not want to eat something.

A mouth is a wonderful thing. It has lips and teeth. It can reveal the yarn or tartan of paradise and still have room for Jello. It can glitter into armadas of incidental scenery and hoist a barrel of pennies with a single breath. It has a tongue, which is a kind of muscle that it extends to savor a mound of whipped cream, stimulate a partner's organ, or reach a summit of towering rhetoric constructed of nothing but syntax and wire.

So much depends upon a mouth glazed with dentistry beside the white narcissus.

Nudity becomes monotonous after a while, but a mouth is all cause and effect. The lungs push a column of air through the throat, the larynx vibrates it, and the tongue sculpts it into a book for Gustave Flaubert and his parrot.

If the mouth is a marvel of skin and personality, the book is even more so. The book is a structure in which words kiss and bite and suck in a manner analogous to the emission of light. Everything in the book is a noise like Lebanon.

It is often said that there is nothing in the intellect which is not first in the senses. And yet various occurrences are fat with allegory.

I give the body what it wants: warm clothes, an airport, a little hot water from time to time.

And when I descend from the mountain I carry the words of heaven in a wallet of blood and sleep with the bears at the edge of town.

EXPLORATION IS FOR FEATHERS

Exploration is for feathers. A mouth full of words and a damaged journey that sells for a dollar at the local emotion. Murdered syntax and a pound of sound. A blast of fingers and a color walking in bones. The muscle bulb is an open process. Description is held by a bas relief climbing into itself on paper. A lobster is thinking because its behavior stumbles on a turmoil and the sound of it hammers a sheen with agates. The head pounds into consciousness gulping propositions. My meanings spill into the foam of stupefaction. A sparkling crown of erratic life occurs when space is concentrated in language and thoughts have no substance other than the beatific tinkling of lassitude. The brocade churns like a river. And there's a street in Seattle called Aurora which is often misunderstood and discharges a strange gas full of auras and keys. The cat likes to sit in the window humming George Gershwin tunes. My existence on paper reaches for your eyes. It's always a little strange to sit in an exam room waiting for the doctor. The human anatomy is glued together with a kiss. Daylight is not allowed to enter. A burlap sack holds potatoes like a placenta of jute. Objects may appear larger in the mirror. I have three eyes, four thumbs, eight legs and a banjo. Great Britain has taken umbrage with Amazon. There's an animal in me that strains to complement England with snow. Pathos vibrates like a cocktail lounge. The snow groans under the weight of the sky exciting thoughts of tenderness and convolution. Parrots recite Shakespeare in all the popular clubs. We admire the endeavor and touch on Wisconsin in a quiet corner where there are no agitprops. We have tickets for Paris and the piercing sounds of an orange cloud are utterly silent. The sensation serves the fertility of experience and we find that our feathers have grown longer and now resemble kelp and balloons. My perceptions, too, have altered a bit and include shadows and blood. I feel the cement beneath my feet as I walk in exhibition of myself. I enter the house of language and find that I've been there all along oozing adjectives and simmering with nouns. An embryonic argument expands into a vascular novel. I flail at the perspectives on a canvas of hammerhead gold. I dangle from the ceiling eating a pupa cooked in a pluperfect sauce sprinkled with commas. I rip the rain in half and discover a pronoun reflected in a pound of legend. All my feathers rupture into a suitcase and I leave immediately for Bohemia thrilling with participles and hop on a Corot pulling a long blue dream.

MONT BLANC REDUX

Percy Bysshe Shelley and Jack Kerouac climb the western flank of
Mont Blanc.

"The space around us is charged with divine energy," remarks Percy.

"Clean needs start in destiny. We're incongruous hats pushed into
snow, you and I," answers Jack.

"Heaving crustaceans muscular as sound. Embryonic bubbles blown
into mountain upholstery," says Percy.

"Painting is unfettered by steel," says Jack. "Proximity trebles the
spectral molasses. Tuna served on broken plates."

"Apparitions knotted in gaslight moss," answers Percy.

"Push-ups bend the air into bananas," says Jack. "The lake is excused
from enthusiasm. But I will wrestle your gaze. I will give you iron."

"The pines haunt everyone's ambivalence," says Percy, knocking
snow from his hat. "The physiology of swans is upside-down."

"What I mean is beads," says Jack. "Totems! Art! Rectangles!"

"Our words," says Percy, "will earn us an agreeable spring."

"Being is bells and viscera," says Jack. "Which is why I'm a Buddhist,
a spilled glass of water."

"And the shine in the water," says Percy.

"It is the hunger in our eyes that awaken our words," says Jack.

"You could say there is a mouth that opens in the wind," says
Shelley. "An invisible power that hides where it is most apt to be seen.
We know it's there. But the door has curiously slammed."

"And we shall open it," says Jack, taking out a harmonica. "The ruby
is bright. Yet the horizon is clumsy."

"Finally it is all words," says Percy. "We shall act seminal at the gate."

"The juice is in the head," says Jack.

They climb to the summit and look down at the earth.

"A wind is hovering o'er the mountain's brow," says Percy.

"Yes," says Jack. "out of exuberant nothingness."

HOLLYWOOD SUGAR

No pain is private. How can it be? All pain seeks expression. Pain demands a theatre. Sometimes that theatre is the face. Sometimes that theatre is the mouth. Or the voice. The voice trembling like a giant handshake with God. The face dangling little fragments of bone.

TV cheapens emotion. The radio returns to get things done. I think it's only fair to describe the radio as a huge orchid of understanding. A testicle emitting consciousness.

Movies need to be seen on a screen. A colossal screen. This is where pain spins in eternal glory. This is my clothing. These are my desires swarming with expression.

The pain of truth is strangely violet. Sometimes even vermillion. A young woman helps an old woman to the door. The old woman suffers, among other chronic illnesses, sciatica. The young woman is seized by a shiny knob in the wheel of her heart. This is called blood. It's what moves her.

Thought implies flight. Thought carries pain through the brain in the form of remorse, memory, regret, guilt, sensations structured as the ache of consciousness. There is a sense of thingness to thought in the same way that there is a sense of thingness to waves. Waves have shapes and cohesion but they're not things. A wave is an energy moving through water. A thought is an energy moving through the brain.

Pain is flipped in diagrams. This is osteoarthritis, this is fibromyalgia. There is acute pain and chronic pain. There is existential pain, called angst, which punches the being with granite recognition. The sticky pyramids of abandonment. The stirred vermilion of hope. The howling of ghosts at the edge of the abyss.

The edge of the mattress in a Kansas motel.

But if you want an experience of true oblivion walk down a street in Manhattan on a business day afternoon.

Find a respectable wedge of space on a subway and stand there feeling the velocity of time steal your life away.

But hey, why dwell on the turnstiles when we can expand into simple being and walk among our bones in the serene immediacy of any given moment. That's gold.

Give me the anodyne of abstraction.

Give me the morphine of rhythm.

Coltrane. Davis. Jones.

Give me the darkness of the theatre. Lights and shapes on a screen. Actors enacting magnitudes of confusion and anguish. Marcel Proust hunched among the angels of sensation.

THE EARS OF THE CRICKET

The ears of the cricket are on its legs and a voice like opera comes out of the ooze to answer all the questions I have regarding Peruvian x-rays. Only yesterday I saw an octopus developed by hunger choose its own chemicals and experience itself as a poem. It dawdled among secrets and argyle until it was time to characterize its absence from the box office with a heavy sharp tool.

Toothpicks return us to crickets where our ears mirror the appearance of sound in a dead man's name.

If you haven't already noticed, my face is in labor. It's giving birth to a nose. I had to borrow one from someone last night in Costa Rica.

As for memory let us say it's a giraffe with its head above the clouds. Anything remembered is nibbled in a gestalt of uninhibited rumination.

There is a chromosomal syntax that remembers how to create living beings that are the color of desire. This is good to know as I live in a zip code so full of pathos that even the boat propellers are soaked in meaning. Sometimes I can feel the air decipher itself as a form of tarantula tugging at a thought. One day I hope to understand reality with the same level of intimacy as a dragonfly paying attention to itself.

I can distill a parable or two out of this day. Two p.m. is my favorite hour. Meanwhile I need to talk to the milliner about her appendix. There's an emotion in the scrotum of the bank manager that might otherwise be dismissed.

The afternoon is built with money. Because it amuses me to say so and I feel like bearing the armada of my lips to you. There is the thinness of wasps to consider and large azaleas consummate as mountains. Bigger than your laundry. But you can always catch an elevator and flare into garlic if it upsets you.

The splendid blue talents of the yucca kiss your jewelry. And I am assuming that your avocado fits my eyes. My face is unanimous as dirt.

Poetry is sometimes so blatantly autonomous it will never win a prize. The fetus sweats among its doorknobs and when the chest opens the heart falls out in a delirium of cruel tenderness.

That's when I lie on the bed and rub my legs making sweet music. Chirp, chirp, chirp.

When all is said the waterfront is nothing but mist and history and is nothing like a cricket. The candy is a nasty fire and my beautiful lassitude languishes under the boardwalk like a compound eye.

HERKY-JERKY STATIONARY

The room is glowing with longhand. Hair tends to be more like apples than guitars. But when it's fierce and tilted toward Sunday it becomes a feeling that requires appliances and alpaca. These implications are paths to Etruscan money. The rug is more like tumult. It's a cold temperature that we like to build by miming despair when nothing else works and our comedies are bungled by vagueness. And so Sunday I woke up hung-over in Dagwood. I kept bumping into the walls and furniture until Blondie kicked me out. The wild prospects of the great outdoors enriched my collisions with reality. People snatch at my charcoal and run. But what exasperates me is symmetry. Symbolism has greater audacity. Therefore I must make a pair of wings. The proverbs of our culture emphasize ablution by flight. Time is a secretion. It oozes from our clocks like moon pudding. Truth bursts out of our drawers in underwear and monogamy. And if it happens that there are clouds on the prairie we must paint the oceans with fog. Meaning, I suppose, that I like to vacuum the floor naked. But who doesn't? I know a cat with one large blood red eye and she likes to sit on the steps and socialize. As for me, I like words in strings. Behavior is malleable. So is language. It turns grey in the bargain and creativity blossoms like a haircut. Permit me to touch you. The atmosphere sneezes Portugal. I sense a trace of Paris edged with dust in my perspectives. I want to explore time. I see Baudelaire stroll through a hothouse. I feel autumn in my bones. I smell like an elevator. And from time to time I talk to a bird named Skeeter Slagboom. I've decided to go through life without a name. You can call me anything you want but don't call me late for dinner. There is dignity in food. If language were a food it would be lettuce. Or Forgotten Offerings by Olivier Messiaen. I'm not sure which. We use crackleware. Nothing in life is truly incongruous. We even have ceremonies for our expectations. The sky leans over the horizon and kisses a single blue orchid. This reminds me of water, which is everything. It guides our feet through winter slush and extends undulations of grace all the way to Baton Rouge. Think of a warm farm crowded with shapes and time will thicken in your assumptions about squid. There, I said it. Now I can spend the rest of my day lamenting the color of my stationary, which is pink, with gilt foliate borders flanked by scrolling acanthus. In fact, it's not even stationary. The borders are gilt but open to negotiation. Descriptions climb into whatever language they can find and sputter like handshakes until they ramify into shadows. There's lightning in the bubbles. And as Blondie bends to forgive me, my spirit flies toward her hair.

DANCE OF THE BAMBOO NIPPLES

This morning as I fed the cat I realized that a sense of imbalance can result in a romance with gravity and that nearly all of my opinions are forms of speculations raised into speech. For instance, when a map is milk and smells of dwelling the dynamic is sexual and full of audacity. Intentions begin yelling. The atmosphere turns silk and grammar propels it into textural immediacy, like a bright envy echoing paragraphs of shocking jelly. I put the emphasis on hills. Fingers crave symmetry. But hills, hills are like white elephants wearing ethereal fedoras. I know I sometimes do. Generally when it's raining and the orchids are bathed in an amber light. This is how I make most of my discoveries. I drop from the sunlight and burst into conversation like the sidewalks of Paris. Then I ask to join the Rolling Stones and Mick Jagger asks why, why do you continue to ask me such questions? Because, I insist, the world is full of musicians, but what band has a member that can't play so much as a triangle? If knowledge doesn't bounce, it floats. But how, I ask you, how is knowledge acquired? That is to say, if you already know something there is no reason to go looking for it, but if you don't know something, then how would you know to look for it? The human mind is haunted by its own mouth. Because when those lips get going and the tongue gets to flapping anything can open. My existence on paper explodes into light. Once I get the words out they take care of themselves. They go where they want, they say what they want, they create books of brazen chitchat. Time disperses its syllables in tics and tocs. The empire of space has wings. If I smell like an elevator it's because the driftwood is unconscious. And I awoke to find my mouth flying around the room like a moth. Other mornings I feel more like a road in a forest. A quiet thing of dust bending occasionally around the side of a mountain or ascending into Switzerland. It is there that I find the referents I was looking for. Until then my words had no meaning. Not really. They appeared to have meaning but when they began a newer journey I could drink them like wine and eat pretzels in winter the way pretzels were made to be eaten. You know? Like when a nail is pounded into a two-by-four of pine. My life hangs from necessity like a waterfall. The hunchback of Notre Dame walks among these words. And the sweet Mediterranean air flows through the tangle of his mind luminous with saints and roses. We chime through the centuries harboring narratives of grace. Philosophies are deepened by torpor. I feel most alive when idleness visits my simmering mind and bamboo nipples frolic on the lips of an accommodating innocence. There's no irony here, only a badly shaved Pythagorean pain. I feel open to anything. The afternoon lifts itself into the eyes and the world pulses in a Montmartre window. This is how it was meant to be. Existence, fingers, riddles and being. Good, simple being. The kind that struts on a hardwood floor in footwear soft as belief yet thick as the cotton of October's sad conceptions. The path of the rug is more like a shadow in the mind. A story in which nothing happens but the jingling of mints and the laughter of pronouns clicking their descriptions at a street.

THWACK PLAQUE

Goldfish are the change they tug. Urge conference, swan the green-house beneath a twinkle. Frill your photogenic tigers with papier collé. I will nerve my sparkle until it smells. Faucet a hunger until we happen to ourselves.

Henna is a sense there is a dot. It's the inch we dribble so that we sob emission at its extrusion. Bobble a bubble below the clock by bubbling bucolic. Crash process, experience it as sleeves if it's drawn by pencil. We can condense Wittgenstein's alchemy by ruffling circumference.

Norway's anguish trickles its vowels. Severity flows from the clapper and vomits necks of sound. Curve it, carve it, blaze it with alpaca. Inspire boxing. This I nail to imbue bacteria.

Distill your scribbles through propagation. The bruise I opinion plays feeling by unrolling itself into trinkets. Our bulb aches defending them. Dig art, thwack our absorption behind a plummet walk. Energy is a fantasy that my proverb weighs.

The willow is so scrupulously itself that I've turned monstrous with cabbage. Galaxy an old garment that a pump accepts and get wet by gripping its ascension. Passion in pounds grows proud by amplification. I slouch there where gratification wallows in oddity. The thumb is besieged with honesty.

Fingers ripen in pungent suspension. Abstraction happens to everything sooner or later. Luxuries crawl to their abandonment. Consciousness fills this hair with pretty eggs and turns stuffing to thought and thought to stuffing. The pumpkin, my friend, is a paradigm.

I feel a life beneath my ribs. I hit my mouth with its debris. Snow is the swollen component beneath the words. The lucidity of it anticipates growth. We stir the prose and sip a whale.

The luminous altitude shook itself into a personality. This perturbed the ocher and made everything pull into bumps of poorly sewn conference. I spit my energy at a belt and developed a dream that shattered the atmosphere into Africa. If we continue shrewdly we will find that a meaning imitates the mineral wonder of Zambesi, and so grow to a pound of stunned conclusion.

THE BOOK OF FOG

There was once a book of fog. It remained to be written. It remains to be written. The elusive fog of the book of fog. The rain was nailed down perfectly. We had loopholes. We could do anything. Anything but cage the fog. Cage it in words. Like things in embroidery. Flowers and such. Muffins and afternoons. The fog is a certain aesthetic. It's more than a meteorological phenomenon. It's more like a dump. One of those forlorn places where objects are crumpled and forgotten. I remember the day an RV blocked our driveway. We needed to go to the store for groceries. I knocked on the door. A harridan came to the door in curlers and told us she was stuck there for eternity. Her name was Tilda Fogg. I had a feeling that was going to be her name. I could see it in her eyes: fog. There was fog under the flaps of her eyes and fog in her voice. Sometimes you have to take life as it comes. Vague and roiling about in wraiths of churning ambiguity. There are implications that burst into streams of consciousness and float the mind into shadows and curious sensations, like taxis moving at a crawl in front of an airport. Or swimming. You know? That feeling you get underwater when a vermilion mermaid appears from the depths and bumps into your head? You can't rehearse life. All you can do is wander around hoping to find a script somewhere. All I've been able to find is a box full of *National Geographics*. That's why my conversations are filled with volcanos and palm trees. Grammar propels me toward circumstances tangential to summer. I interact with sediments that slide through my fingers like gravity. The silken kind of gravity that holds planets in their orbit and sticks to your mouth in burning parliaments of starry solitude. Who doesn't speak to the universal with the particulars of our costumes? Experience tastes like chicken. Reflection is a drop of sunlight. Morality is the pith of character but miscarries in places like New Orleans. Driftwood ornaments the beach. I'm worried about our planet. But what good does that do? One day I'll write a book of fog. It will answer everything. It will answer nothing. It will be filled with premonitions. It will be stolid as nails but smell like Plato. It will be a

Republic. It will be a reproductive organ. It will operate slowly, like the gears and cogs of an ancient clock. It will float like a balloon. It will report the darkness with a lisp. It will flutter through the heart of a rattlesnake glazed in excursion. The fog. The shapeless accommodating fog. And swallow reality. And move like a mountain through the weight of its distortions. And walk through my sleep. And moisten my face. And drip in the window. And blossom on a tip of grace.

HOW I SPEND MY DAY

I gossip. I push and embody. I look for redemption wherever I can find it.

I get up in the morning and drink coffee and listen to news from France and scribble my way into sweet oblivion.

Beauty is elusive but I'm bent on finding it and wrestling it into words. Is that what made Mark Twain shave his head in Florence, Italy? I do not know. That is between Mark Twain and Mart Twain's hair.

I scrounge for food and shelter. I am, improbably, a collar stud. I hate anything vague. A word slaps my lip and indicates tinfoil.

I argue with zippers and hoist meaning from rope.

I wheel and stir and tremble and endure. I convulse and turn and despair and measure.

I display feelings of experience and bump. I plant big ideas. I thunder pugnacity and bite the air. I convulse and grab and purify and slap the buttocks of my mule.

I sell books. I crack jokes. I trudge the winter streets of the soggy northwest and sigh.

I speed down the freeway. I nail abandon to the air.

I mutate. I plant adjectives in perfectly good forsythias.

I do the wash. I explode into light. I embezzle. I embarrass. I emboss.

I walk in circles dripping redwood and moss.

I like a lot of things but I don't like routine. I'm athletic. And lazy. I'm athletically lazy.

The hives explain nothing. It is the honey that articulates the secrets of the pine nut.

A wizard once told me that the winter is sublime and this made me feel long and woody.

Please. Sit down. Have a pancake. Watch your head. Think of this as a PhD in leisure.

I'm excited. Aren't you? I feel enriched by this excursion.

When I get home I'll send you a loaf of pumpernickel. The highway is long but the pleasures and pains are pearls. Nevertheless, I must often strain to make my emotions pull hedonistic predicates into glandular tissues. Later, they will grow into kisses and lost horizons.

Infinity must be sampled intelligently, as if it were a contest in Florida involving math problems and breasts. It hurts less than bikini waxing, but the orgasms are worth it.

PLINKETY-PLUNK

If nothing means nothing anything can mean anything. Shoe can mean innumerable and endless worlds. Because words are worlds and reality fulfills its filling stations.

I once saw an owl on a fence in Wyoming. It was late. The owl had come out to begin its mysteries among the shadows of this poor forsaken world. There is severity in the air, and creation and death. For it is the nature of a substance to conceive itself and coruscate with arpeggios in a minor key.

It is the forehead that imparts defiance. And dishrags with faces moving over the trees and rocks that welcome the era of thought and have much to do with easels. For the mouth is molded in the mouth and I don't know what reality is anymore. I used to think reality was gasoline and diesel. But now it is March and reality is bristling with preludes. Massed chords correct the embroidery. If I dip it in blisters the fog is harnessed to its prodigal talk and something bigger might be said about dangling.

Here comes the bus. The bus is a leviathan of rubber and glass. There are twelve people on the bus and a refrigerator named Vertebrae and a ball of nerves named Grace. Twelve people not including the driver, and Vertebrae and Grace, who are protruding from a Flügelhorn. The driver, whose name is Pablo Picasso, is the fragrance surrounding a camel's muzzle on a desert night when the sky is full of stars and one's illusions are Cubist and ornithological.

But who am I to say such things? I am a ripple with an impersonal snicker. I am a bubble hugging my own escape. I am a cross-eyed indentation on a lactation of misanthropic hair.

Here begins my story: I am swimming in words like a drugstore. Any moment now the sky will get funny and start shoving words out of my mouth. Airplane propellers will lift them into your eyes where a new story will begin. The story of clouds and claws. The story of clank, the story of clunk. The story of a mouth opening its lips to let a story

out. Words of the Amazonian basin. Words and worms and little
packets of sugar. Words and worms and an upright piano. Words
and worms and sprockets and jaws.

Plinkety-plunk. Plinkety-plunk.

ACCESSORIZE YOUR EYES

If there is an emphasis on the particular tethered to the whole idea of
fish, faith becomes a radar with a blip of radiant spit. Salt is a monster
of endurance. Sewing favors concentration, and permits the apparition
of form and stupefaction. The immediacy of salt and thread and needle
and crack awakens the topography of cement in a sidewalk. At least,
that's the rumor. The great philosophers tell us that there are versions
of cement that are more romantic. Honor has little to do with it. To
swallow life is also to occasionally gargle. This is what the gargoyles
tell us: gargle. The comprehension of space, on the other hand, only
requires a sense of space and an amphibious sensuality.

I say these things not because I'm hungry but because the use of eye
shadow is intergenerational. The arrival of dust in an igloo is another
indication that the color beige is equally herbivorous. I saw it swallow
an entire suitcase once and spin like a dress in the rain. We can begin
the hymn when the enamel dries. Meanwhile just let the colors burn in
a puddle of modest astronomy. I have often wept to see anything as
wild and cotton as a bank account. The flesh grumbles to the bones yet
approves of the squeeze of transport. There are days that the bus is
crowded. That's just the way it is. The only reason I've embarked on
this journey at all is to escape the sediment of familiarity.

Cement is respectable, but the metamorphosis of bicycles must not
be held for ransom. Conception begins with a ship and ends with a
bottle. The sonar is full of life. The tide-pool does a handstand. The
mosaic is freely understood to be a parable of pliers. And why not?
Even the deodorant has something to say about warts. Why warts exist.
Why warts never seem brand new, but ancient and small. It's a very
hard thing to crackle like a cherry at the power of grease. Language is
its own rock and roll, gallant as an intestine yet intuitive as asphalt.

I'm in no hurry, obviously. I have a mouth. I can sprinkle the air
with names. I can groan. I can prod the word 'ocher' until it moves,
shows some sign of life, and quivers with comprehension, a deepened

understanding of seals. Who hasn't enjoyed floating in someone's living room absorbing the details of a kilowatt? Opium engenders cherubs of seminal validation. I think I'm in love with a predicate. There's a mushroom in the forest drooling money on an illusion of masculinity. I'll tell you what masculinity is: it's a reaction to flutes. The world is a calligraphy of cuticles and contacts. It's touching. It's fathomless and hazy, and yet I hold a dream in my hand and feel it squiggle, squirm into something legible, like garlic, or stone.

CELLS

We live in a world of cells. Prokaryotic cells, eukaryotic cells, parikaryotic cells. Flagella, fimbria, organelles.

My body is constellated with cells. How do I accomplish this? I don't. I have nothing to do with it. Cells generate cells and I go on with my life eating and digesting food. I'm just along for the ride. When the ride ends, I end. I am, after all, no more than an identity. This I achieve by liking and disliking things.

I like the way bubbles float and drift in a room and catch the light and sparkle and pop never to exist again.

I don't like getting out of bed in the morning, but when I do, I like the way the carpet feels beneath my feet.

I love coffee. I usually have two full mugs of rich black coffee in the morning. That helps get me going. It sparks my neurons into action. My blood unravels its gold.

I'm not much on religion. I have religious feelings, which are ones of sublimity and reverence, but if there's anybody in charge of this universe, some intelligence that assumes responsibility for its creation, for all of its stars and jars and Orion's belt, I'd sure like to meet that intelligence and ask why some infants are born into poverty and disease, while others are born into royalty and wealth.

Or why do cats and dogs have such short lives and turtles and parrots live to be a hundred?

Not that I have anything against turtles and parrots. I like turtles and parrots. I'm not against turtles and parrots. I support turtles and parrots.

Turtles and parrots. Turtles and parrots. Turtles and parrots.
Just saying.

I believe that blood and water are real, but is that truly a belief, or more like an experience?

Hair comes out of my head thread by thread but I can't hear it.

My legs are Apache. My feet are airplanes. The bone in my chest is a clarinet. My head is a planet my heart is a lake. The bone surrounding my brain is round and opaque. The bones of my fingers are moderate on buttons and anathema to cake.

A tiger burns out of my mouth whenever I think of England and I lift my knife to the moon to induce expansion and all things towering and symphonic.

Meaning gives muscle to the brain. Meaning is the sun burning and Jake LaMotta banging his head against the wall in his jail cell out of frustration and remorse.

That's another kind of cell. The cell of regret. The cell of penance and guilt. The cell of the self which is the most solitary cell. This cell is an illusory cell whose bars are vermicelli. There is no self. The self is a ghost.

The squid escapes in a cloud of ink. Give me a pen and I'm a Houdini.

ZIUHITSU

I've never been into sailing. But there is a nautical term that has a great attraction. The word is ziuhitsu, which means "follow the brush." Writing, which bears many similarities to the practice of sailing, requires a shiver of light. There is no shame in changing direction, particularly when the winds are curious sensations. If we remain stubborn and refuse a change of direction, we find ourselves groggy with torpor, and if there are no clouds or moonlight, there is a sensation of floating in space. There are times when it's good to have a little calm. Some time to reflect. To make some propulsion. Each effect has a cause. The cause of color is dreams. William Shakespeare says hello. He is a frost giant groaning in the bitter Arctic air. He vacuums an elevator for roughly five minutes. Or is it ten? Did I mention that there are woods nearby? The woods abound with acorns. The age demanded an image and so I gave it acorns. Hummingbirds and wine. Oak. Oak is a beautiful wood, brilliant in its moral of pushing the poem forward, causing it to branch, emerge from the dark and run into the streets of Manhattan full of terror. Because that's what poetry does. It makes a reckless infrared tennis shoe plausible as a construction crane. Tentacles of a giant octopus swishing back and forth over the windshield and hood. I never take the sun for granted. I lapse into obscurity whenever I feel like it. I'm timid at parties. I despise anything that involves badges, or potlucks. It is useless to worry. But I do it anyway. Somebody has to do it. Meaning, like radar, determines the sound of a shovel plunged into soft dark earth, and gives us a skull to ponder. For this is the realm of ziuhitsu and margarita means daisy in Spanish. The elevator rises to the fourth floor. The fourth floor offers housewares and kitchen gadgets. It is, I agree, sad to bring delicacies into this world and then get tyrannous about it. The man in the bakery shields his face from the heat of the oven. An upholsterer daubs a box joint with beads of glue. Life in the United States always tends naturally and inexorably toward the Whitmanesque. I do not know why. It must have something to do with space. Enormous shopping malls. Walmart. Home Depot. Target. It cannot solve itself. It must lose its geography to speed. The Navajo believed the soul to be part of a divine being called the Holy Wind. The Holy Wind suffused the universe, giving life, thought, speech and the power of movement to all living things. Their sand-paintings are full of symbolically expressed motion: whirling snakes, rotating logs, streaming head feathers, whirling rainbows and feathered travel hoops: magical means of travel. Easy to see why Pollock was so enamored of Navajo sandpainting. Again: Japanese zuihitsu. Starting at one place, ending up at another. Like life. The trembling of gauze in a quiet African room. Air mingling with air. Form mingling with form. Emily Dickinson watching through her window the light spread over the dark imagined land. And finding the eyes to bring it to life.

FATS

It began the night my parents took my brother and I to see *The Vikings* at the drive-in and the trailer for *The Girl Can't Help It* came on the screen, introduced by the completely acceptable Tom Ewell, which the folks could swallow, he was one of them, but as soon as we saw Fats Domino sitting at the piano rocking out and looking joyful as all New Orleans during Mardi Gras my parents freaked. There was no way on earth I was going to see that movie. And that's when I first felt it. Rebellion. Anger. The exquisite feeling that something dangerous and exciting has occurred. That acute sense of division and the first thrill of subversion. You awaken to a power within and recognize it as something crucial to your survival. Which is also a little scary. Because you love your parents. They give you food and shelter. They give you guidance and council and comfort. But that feeling is telling you something different. That feeling is telling you that you're not still just a kid but a developing creature. A thing that is alien to your parents. A life and an attitude different from your parents. I don't think I knew what a chrysalis was at the time. But I would've appreciated the metaphor. That metamorphosis all living creatures including human beings go through. That propulsion out of the chrysalis and into the light where those goopy wings stretch out and start to dry and turn translucent in the sun. Which becomes years of growth and frustration and disappointment and occasional triumph. Sometimes sweet redemption. But mostly the shine of potential. Which becomes car wrecks and drugs and music. Which becomes philosophy and finance and medication. Walls hurdled, doors slammed. Arrest and conviction. Perfume and addiction. Collisions, frictions, mosquito coasts. Nine cars. Three marriages. Champagne popped in green rooms. And years later listening to Fats Domino you discover that moment is still there, even in old age, there it is, shining behind your eyes, hot and edgy and dangerous. Mad. Totally crazy. Like the French Quarter during Mardi Gras.

THE GHOST OF AN ADJECTIVE

The ghost of an adjective chews a noun into the Philippines. The noun catches fire. The noun fire catches fire. The fire feeds on an allegory in search of a theme. The theme catches fire. There must, therefore, be adjectives for the fire. Adjectives that will burn: hot, inextinguishable, monstrous.

Time is a monstrosity. But so are fingers. Fingers are procedures of bone and skin designed to carry rapiers to their logical conclusion, which is vigorous and steel.

Words cry continually for eyes. My cuticles gleam like root beer. There is deliverance in a guitar, and breath to fill the scent of clover. Even the rungs in the refrigerator shelving ring when I shut the refrigerator door, thus revealing a mode of structural undress.

I like the scene in which King Kong breaks loose of his chains and sends the audience fleeing into the streets. This proves that adjectives are both necessary and cruel.

The mind is a climate. This is how nothingness becomes rungs in a refrigerator.

One day in October I discovered the true meaning of string. It twirls.

Ever so slightly.

Twirls.

And twirls.

I can hear the pulse of a weeping helicopter. It sounds like a Viking in a discount store.

The dishwasher is scatological. But it works. It gets the plates and silverware clean. The telephone rings. It's the oranges. They're holding Fiji hostage. They demand a jet, a gamma ray, and an alphabet with a Geiger counter. As for me, I enjoy push-ups and the muscles that make a gentle resurgence of them.

I sometimes read *Finnegans Wake* under a contagion of chandeliers. This makes me rise and fall within a seed-bearing organ which I call a sanctum.

I've been behind bars at least once in my life. This is where one learns how to make silhouettes on the wall mimic the beginning of time.

A man dives in the Rhone searching for Caesar. He finds Caesar in the muck at the bottom and brings his head up with the aid of a crane and a highly skilled crane operator. This is how structure wanders through the poem looking for three arms and a margarita.

Did I mention the pliers? They, too, have reality. Something akin to brass doorknobs in an old Norwegian house, or the ghost of an adjective turning syntax into sun tacks.

WHAT HAPPENS WHEN WORDS LEAVE OUR HEADS

What happens when words leave our heads?

Who knows? It depends on the word. Is it a big word like anacoluthon, a small word like daub, or a short and skinny word like keyhole? Is the word floating idly in a sentence like a lily pad or communicating nocturnal aberrations while converting molecular nitrogen to ribgrass? Is it longer than it is broad or subdivided into precious stones? Is it seamed with oakum or hanging in the air like a banjo or a shaving brush? Is it a ball of vibrations enameled with assurance and glittering like a lake or is it more like a portent, a shiver of shadowy import?

I know this: when a word leaves the cradle of the mouth it assumes a feeling response. Its being depends upon being heard and understood. This is why words go around accompanied by other words. One word makes a sound. Two words make a situation.

For example, winter. The word winter is six letters and two phonemes. But it's a whole drama. Blizzards, ice, holidays, death. Brittleness and beauty, fragrances and pain.

A simple phrase like "most of the time" becomes a whole dynamic if it's turned into a song by Bob Dylan and sung by Bettye Lavette.

Words fall from my mouth in the form of rain and reflect marabou.

I carry a pitcher of ghosts and pour them on a guitarist pursuing a PhD in gastronomy. A feeling of lost animals sparkles in these implications. It always does. I could do this better in a bar in Milwaukee.

Why Milwaukee? I've never been to Milwaukee. But if I say the word Milwaukee something Milwaukee happens to my imagination of Milwaukee. Milwaukee fills with Milwaukee.

Watch me squeeze this gland until it turns into Montmartre.

I desire nothing more than a radio with shiny evergreen leaves and a song of kinetic energy contained in a high-pressure, ionized, moving combustion of gas.

Deepen your acceptance of ice. Don't insult the maid. Interact with liniment.

All I want to do now is visit Wisconsin.

SPEAKING IN BUBBLES

Knowledge doesn't bounce it floats. It must, because the brocade churns like a river, and the world is full of bananas. This is why I jingle when I walk and that I find subtleties in architecture that make me want to sit down and write about sounds and odors. There are smells in the Palace of Salt, for instance, that bark like a dog and some that cradle a whole philosophy. Proximity is only an approximation. The real smell of power is when it creaks open like an old weathered epitome. Other smells are just plain purposeless, which makes them all the more special, particularly when opium stirs the brain and the blood congeals into shapes of crystal. You ask why don't I carry my mouth into the hills and glue it to a closet door. Well, maybe I will, maybe I won't. Despair has purged my words of illusion. The shiny metal of a bad joke impels a more circular engorgement, or opinion, if you'd like to call it that. Me, I like to maneuver words and can sit here doing that all day. This is how I nailed the rain to the air yesterday as I was sitting in my chair gazing out the window and improvised a box of pink stationery. I wrote a letter to John Keats describing a giant handshake that burst into a stream of consciousness and carried me away. Swimming is incongruous when you feel more like crawling, which is exactly what I did when I arrived in Chicago. I just got up on stage and played a guitar and let all my emotions pour out of it. There is no despair that nothing can bungle like music. This is what happens when we embody the symptoms of our pain and wake up feeling hungover like Dagwood. Blondie stands there with her rolling pin looking baffled and frustrated and the dog looks up at her with watery eyes wondering whatever it is that dogs wonder when human beings speak in bubbles.

MY TRIP TO PLUTO

I'm falling through a jukebox like fingers in distillation. Like a martyr
to wax. Like a song to the beauty of seclusion. Like a puddle of sound
hinged to its own commas. Which are non-existent. Various kinds of
cloud whirl about me. Everywhere you look you see coconuts. There is
a drugstore full of brightly colored birds and drugs so generous that all
their machinery bounces through the bloodstream like insects on the
verge of feathers. All of which urges sensations of lightness and
euphoria and poetry. The kind of poetry that is written in a fever past
midnight. For no reason other than the need of words to come together
and assemble a rocket to Pluto. The rocket is easy it's the trajectory
that keeps me up nights. All that math is so beautiful, so heady that
it makes me want to roll eyeball to eyeball in a mania of lyricism. You
know? Like the smell of a lumberyard early on a summer morning?
This is what thought tastes like when it's not resembling chocolate, or
belligerence as a way of life. Don't mistake me, I have plenty of disdain
for this world so Pluto is still very much alive on the drawing board,
sparkling in monarchical ice. Buffalo are a different matter they require
gerunds, as in "the stampeding buffalo drowned the sound of crickets in
Wichita last night." But yes, I do have plans to bring buffalo to Pluto.
This happened to be one of André Breton's last wishes which he com-
municated to me in a dream. The ocean is paper, after all, and the waves
on its surface have been inscribed by the wind. I think of wind as a
form of consciousness, but who wouldn't? It absorbs the language of
bells. And carries the drone of a diesel locomotive as it lurches out of
Waxahachie. That, too, is in the cards for my voyage to Pluto. And
maybe Arizona too. Who's going to miss Arizona? Maybe Mexico,
though I very much doubt that. I also have plans for a metal hat. Not
a helmet, exactly, but a shaggy Beefeater hat with a band of platinum
abstractions. That will see me through the solar winds. I have reason to
believe in tubes. Mansions in outer space. Space itself, particularly as it
relates to the sound of the bassoon. This is where the ghosts of water-
falls wander corridors of spaceship exhilaration broad and flapping as

the wind messing around in the feathers of a heron looking for frogs in the Camargue. And over there is where the consonants harden into crowbars and emanate vowels. This is a piece of air and this is a mirror that tells you what your face is doing when you're asleep. This is a conflict I'm having with the table and this is the table. Hello table. Hello, says the table. Shut up table, I say. Get lost, says the table. You're not going to Pluto I tell the table. But don't feel bad this isn't about you Mr. Table I'm not bringing any furniture. All I want in my spaceship is prayer. Licorice, grandeur, and enough morphine to pull a fire out of sticks of language and warm my brain with thoughts of cinnamon.

TARZAN ON MARS

Tarzan peers through a telescope. Earth, in its aphelion, is approximately 40 million miles away.

A star.

He lives alone. He is old. He worries about cataracts. He worries about going blind.

Mars is cold. But there are ways to keep warm. He reads poetry. He lets out bloodcurdling yells. He pounds his drums in a fury of savage release.

He swims in a subterranean pool. Its name is Maldoror.

Names give intimacy. Names give being and individuality to things.

Tarzan rests his head on a pillow. He remembers the names of things on Planet Earth. Lakes and rivers and oceans. Immense cities. Giant waterfalls. Colossal philosophies.

He remembers Paris, and Portugal, and the Cote d'Ivoire.

He remembers eating ndolé with fermented cassava wrapped in plaintain leaves on a table of bubinga wood with friends in Cameroon. He remembers learning to play the stick zither of the Fang people of Gabon, and to dance the Bikutsi, which means "let's beat the earth," and the tongue of the chameleon, and the howl of the Fennec Fox, and wrestling a crocodile in the Mungo River.

Is the soul separate from the body? Where does the soul go when the body dies?

He falls asleep. During the night he dreams of the Dibamba River and a battle fought over stolen ivory tusks and wounds that never heal.

Morning arrives. Pterodactyls wheel in the sky.

Tarzan gets up and pounds his chest and lets out a blood curdling yell.

Today, he thinks, I will savor the feeling of water. I will ride the back of a giant reptilian beast and visit the Princess of Helium. I will wear a cape of black feathers. For I am Tarzan, master of the swift-footed Willy Bird.

What is death? What is time? What is eternity?

These are the things that fill the jungle of Tarzan's mind during his journey to the Kingdom of Taj Hajus.

The sun is a 141 million miles distant, a blob of opacity against the jagged edge of a rock.

Tarzan continues north.

What is reality? What is consciousness? What is Ding an sich?

This is serious.

Not it's not.

Not at all, says the wind and the rock. Let it all unfold as a story. Let it find questions in skeletons, and answers in ice.

BIG PLANS

I'm going to build a catalogue of flags. The feeling of a knife blade sinking into a cherry pie. Images developing in a darkroom. The sound of a car starting on a cold morning in March. I'm going to hang from a yardarm and cook a drugstore. I'm going to punish the innocent with a pinch of salt and sit down and initiate a cackle and luxuriate. I'm going to immerse myself in ophthalmology and irritate a superstition. I'm going to splash blood on the walls and drive to Louisiana humming a Bob Dylan song. I'm going to slam the door when I get there and mourn the loss of my outlook and impersonate a mirror. I'm going to follow the sun and inhabit a present tense and sing of the past. I'm going to hire a poet to construct a bubble that clatters like a broken ladder. I'm going to arrange a series of hoes and deliver them to the president and demand a refund. I'm going to sparkle like a prostitute and gargle a book cover. I'm going to wipe the computer screen with a rag full of pumpkin seeds and wander around the room in a primordial octave. I'm going to sculpt a pronoun out of electrons. I'm going to sip a charming light. I'm going to spill some secrets. I'm going to study emptiness. I'm going to moisten my lips and hold a word until its gears begin to turn. These are my plans. My plans for the future. It is all mapped out. I just need to begin. Begin doing it. Begin the beguine. The stucco and studs. The bridge and pontoon. The grand scheme of my life. Which is everywhere stirring. Which is latent as the afterlife. Which is chewed into harsh realities. Which is death. Which is what happens when words look good on your head. Which are dropped into a sentence that smells of abstraction. Which is prayer. Which is air. Which is rare. And crammed as a flag with plasma.

THE GLAMOUR OF REPRODUCTION

In winter the arcade menstruates. It is done for the feeling of it is
cowlicks. Meaning the correlation of icicles leads to a sprinkling in the
spring that a face can elaborate into wonky box office braids. Limestone
means timber. Bark on the lark like a snap on the back. It disentangles
the message of injection. Say, like a harp in the rain. Logic shouting to
merge with the oncoming traffic. Intimate moments like this with a
little incense can go a long way. The musicians have arrived. Over there
we see the northern lights. Blue visiting the ballistics of badminton.
A door swings open. It sweeps over the sand. England steps out and
wades into the Atlantic. King Arthur eats fried chicken. The sonnets of
Ted Berrigan substitute for lace. Laceration substitutes for radiation,
and sobbing. Imagine a giant wandering the darkness of night in the
nude. Now think of it as daylight and you have the hopeful slurps of
the zinnia bulging out of the prison of its existence. How bubbly and
delightful to find such a gregarious universe involved with string.
Everything is willow and woodwinds. Even so, an apron comes in
handy, as do multiple dimensions. Terra-cotta bric-a-brac, coal and
sweat, prunes and pronouns, wizards and elasticity. This sentence is
getting bigger by the minute each time a word is added a cloud forms
and changes shape and an aftertaste of bacon mingles with the sensa-
tion of being licked by a predicate. Definitions are crushed into words.
Or warts. Pimples massed as diplomatic forms of punctuation on a
dialectical face. Jackknives shiny in an Army surplus counter. Lakes,
rivers, ponds, brooks, puddles, swamps, marshes, bayous and oceans.
Cows mooing. Horses whinnying. Sometimes you never know where a
paragraph is going to go. It falls somewhere between what life and
death might be. There is a mathematics for this sort of thing. Everyone
sits in a booth working out their own private problems. I'm not going
to argue with life or death. I just want to get my plate of eggs and
orange juice. I can't answer the larger questions of existence without a
little something in my stomach. A few boiling words and a driver's

license. Then I begin to pop out of myself and see how truly intricate it all is, and adventurous and fascinating. Here come my eggs. Amalgams of yolk and albumin. The glamour of reproduction rampant on a plate.

PHILOSOPHY TOAST

Muscles are lush and germinate mind. Then at devotion a needle cures one's irritations and accumulates sleep. Buckskin Cytherea pushes a glass tack into an early arrival of content. There is sand about and poles and red bottles such as mussels. Warm oats pushed into a sheen of nacreous sagacity is simply chins. Camellias make the stadium wild. The ocean is ever crammed feeling for its sticks. I have thrilled with such hotels as my very sleeves attest. I have banged on foibles and cured apricot with herring, laced roller skates with fog. Or did I mean white blood cells? This is a sudden area of zip code absorption. Bog saddle. Blueprint of gauze for a paper lion amid crocodile birds. The whistle is not a soliloquy so much as a knot of power. The uninhibited knock that comes with monsters. Bikini diaphragm, or corner glazed with boiling tongues. Suddenly Tuesday appears French as cobblestones and this sentence has a plywood heart. The stomach has its drapery and archaeology has its moss. Lagniappe is a sandwich if a philosophy crackles. Distance is as beautiful as Monday. The snowshoes are a form of negotiation. It is the nature of things to spit because morality offers kites. But why morality? Why not just nerves? Geniality and canvas? The bikini suits me although I'm male and have no breasts, other than what nature has given me, which is popcorn to my dreams of Montana. I feel buxom as a zigzag. And sometimes I'm a river. Philosophy requires toast because it's Gothic and consciousness tugs at the acetylene poetry of silver and gold. Poetry is an event. Language is a phenomenon. Heartbeats come with tarantulas. There is a tarantula in all of us, and a skeleton and a pain that cannot be described as broth or leather but will require the grammar of realism and the physics of romance. I feel closer to my neck today than I have before and this is partly the result of singing and partly the result of thought. Sometimes standing in the doorway makes me feel like an alley in the rain. And this, too, is a form of philosophy. If I cater to feathers then the tourists will scrawl their names on the wall and buttons cause the morning to dive into pine. That's where the breezes go and the air smells sharply and dialectical. There's leather in light and light in leather. This makes the leather light and the raft depends on inflammations of water.

FABLE

Fable is the blood of gnomes. Fable plays with description as if description were a mole of myriad power. The Muse stands at the summit of a paragraph playing with a yo-yo. Fable and muse are examples of butterfly milk. The air is cut with a knife of stainless zeal. A chrysalis of thought grows into meaning and glistens in convulsive glamour as a pair of wings find muscle and structure in a language of garish subtleties. The frame is unequal to its content. Experience is radical. The imagination feeds it fish and goulash. I feel the heat of emotion, the opium of similarity, the ecstasy of difference, the fingers of spectral alphabets. The interior of being is the exterior of anterior worlds. There is a door that opens to a room of grammar and a door that opens to a room of clouds. There is a question in the rain and a question in the growl of wolves. This is how fable expands into the white light of kerosene. This is how the wick gets black. This is how words swell into asphalt and noise. This is how the crescendo of tides impels the shiver of mass, and the edge of the world excites the pursuit of wonder in the sleep of hungry vagabonds.

THE HOUSE OF ESTUARY

I can reach heaven with my tweezers and a feeling of intense abandon. I'm in a room full of sunlight. The walls are white as the inside of a mint. The entire house is an accident of bottles and boomerangs, sensational sarcasms and celestial knives. We make our own lightbulbs out of exotic sensations luminous as lobsters in the sands of Veracruz. The clarity of puddles is a clear indication that the sidewalk has a heart. The activities of bees are translated into beams and parables and a potato twinkling with the freshness of a recently uttered word. The heat obliges us to glow. There is nothing linear, nothing one-dimensional. We continually slide into a future smeared with nostalgia. Aluminum puppets gratify one another until their strings catch fire. We have need of more carp, more rope, more umber. My thirst has wheels and its pulse is quick with despair and flattery. It is one-half claw, one-half symbol. I'm scrupulous as a zipper and always enkindle a concentric implication with an acute sense of chocolate and exclamations of ecstasy. This is, after all, a house, not a cave. Look: here comes winter. I enjoy all the implications of drugs, including the side effects. I walk into amusements like a squid, my tentacles probing the walls for entertainment until the colors arrive in a warm suitcase of miracles and art. A paper blossom opens a door to a movie shot in Technicolor by a lunatic astronomer to signify dysentery. The movie was radically discarded, then later reconfigured as a blob of tidepool jelly flexing a muscle in a soft orange drop of buffalo piss. I'm often torn between growing a beard and hitting the pavement with a baseball bat. There is a woman in me sewing a whisper with a metal detector as Jackson Pollock slouches over a canvas arguing with an earthquake. The gantries are green against a blue sky. I only mention that because I bungled tonight's soup. I used soap instead of windows. The eyes have a virtue and they truly shine when we carry wood for people like Sarah Bernhardt and Buffalo Bill. We've arranged the silverware to clink so that each sound has a meaning and the letters on the back are prominent with nomenclature. Allow me to introduce my partners Crinkle and Cloudburst. Think of this as an imitation propeller shimmering with substance like a timeless cow in a squirt of shaving cream. The world is great with dirt, but it is cement that holds the sidewalk together, and a reminiscence of skin embedded in abstraction that brings such extraneous success to the fish and the butterflies straining to calm the calliope in the jungle. The subjective is often remarkably echoed on the forehead. But the bend in the river is personal as breath and tailings of mutable omens enjoy chewing the scenery into cats and reindeer. Envy evaporates with each guzzle, and the surrounding objects graze on space. The furrows in the phonograph record are deep. No one plays it anymore. Even its nipples sound scratched like cathedrals of ocher, an edifice of nothingness erected solely for religious exploration. The song is clear and navigable and sung in veneration of The Phantom, a comic strip that ran a while back when the Beatles were just getting started and The Rolling Stones were still looking for adaptors in the supply room. Nails and plugs are vowels writhing with sound, but when the consonants age into pulleys it will be possible to lift this sentence a few inches higher and get a look at Stockholm. Each new perception is expressive as birth and sanguine as motion in a monumental chair of pituitary upholstery, a monstrous bergère with legs like Nibelungs and arms like pendulums cradling a baby gravity. This is the effect of bouncing in public with an indigo cochlea. If there are tacks on the steps of the stepladder, then don't foster the illusion of grebes. There is brightness in obscurity and morals mirror the elevation of fog. There is a flavor of gender prowling around the pronouns, but this means nothing. This means that the windows have been left open for a reason and anything that flies in might also fly back out. If you must exit, then do so now. I have just squeezed another tube of paint. I long for the experience of seclusion and ride a bicycle on the moon. I want to complement this action with red. It has a length of shadow and five new strings of salt and pepper for a spiritual voyage despite the current shape of the world and the black night dancing like rain in the telescope. If you have a new finding you wish to share, send it by mail in a bag of cement. I will construct a bridge and find you. And together we will unwrap this box of altitude called a garret and watch as it spits lotus after lotus into our mutual flutter.

LET THE ACCORDION SQUEEZE ITSELF

Let the accordion squeeze itself. There is magic in it, and exemption and stools. An emotion wobbles on its stem redeeming the mint with a monumental proximity. And because the tranquility we find in boiserie is sometimes freighted with mythology, there are luxuries fulfilled in the application of hand lotion. The intentions of the chisel are apparent in the sharpness of its edge. Fingers are more intriguing. I think the Fauve dots of a plausible insecurity may be entered into the lists of an insatiable crusade for conversation. That's when I realized I was writing something.

My intent here is neither to attack or disturb but mount a Technicolor duck and ride it across the Martian plains in quest of an aroma I can fondle and explore. The duck would have to be large, mechanical, and stocked with groceries. It would have the look of authority and its eyes would be the color of nutmeg, its feet palmate and fluorescent. Flirtation is only part of the story. The other half is a museum in the sky containing statuary and gloves. It's why these words are engorged with corridors. As soon as anything else gets written, it anticipates the pleasures of elevation, babbling brooks and quiet haunts. Romanticism, pretty much, with a helping of alabaster.

It's only natural to want to crush a fork into one's mashed potatoes and to create illusions of power at the dinner table. Invention wasn't invented in a day. Meanwhile, the milk is boiling and the train is running late. If I were you, I would take a long hot shower and forget the true meaning of the word 'property.' There's no such thing as property. What we think of as property is, at best, water and mineral rights. But these are abstractions, the stuff of law books and courtrooms. The reality of water is something else. Water is busy being water. Or mud.

Or at least a farm. It gets soft in the evenings and even the earth urges conference. They say that sorcery can be an asset but funambulism is a skill. An asset comes by bareback, a skill comes by crawling under barbed wire while being fired upon by Prussian mercenaries.

Don't worry, the bullets may not seem real, but they are. You may consider the experience to be genuine. Just don't stand up suddenly to talk to anyone. In fact, if I were you, I would exit this paragraph altogether and go on to the next.

I once saw a smear of paint tremble like an equation and add something to an artist's rendition of Dutch linen. This helped me understand the beauty of anonymity. The quiet dignity in the fold of anything. Even a chin. Especially a chin.

The folds of the accordion are a special case. No accordion is going to squeeze itself. That isn't going to happen. Not unless you let it happen. Afterward, when we get out of the simulator, we may feel differently about the actuality of life, its kinesthetic pulse and general orientation. When the air leaves the accordion, it elopes directly with a miscalculation, and so becomes music. Manipulation has its place, but contemplation is the domain of the vertical, the beanstalk and the giant, the feeling of silk and the majesty of process.

THE LONG EMOTIONS OF GRAY

I have an emotion in me that irritates golf into moaning. Meaning moaning is the meaning of the moan. But more than a moan, a moon of moaning. To moan is to be a moon, a moon of moaning. It is to entertain the possibility of a moon that moans, that a rock hanging in space dimpled with craters might be capable of moaning, an emotion that puzzles golfers, that puzzles the human will, that puzzles science, but that nourishes and clothes poetry. Which is silliness. Which is literature. Literature is silliness. We know that. Even Hamlet is silly. Perhaps the silliest. I mean, the man talked with ghosts. Or at least one ghost. We don't know if Hamlet talked to more than one ghost. Next time I see the ghost of Hamlet I will ask. Can it be that in conjuring Hamlet's spirit I myself might be Hamlet's ghost? Does the play become a vehicle by which we inhabit the ghosts of the players? And give imagination a stage? Color and wire? A bivouac in our skulls? Is that what words do? Words make hallucinations possible. They're signs for things that are absent. Mirrors and trout and scented oil. Odd compounds and curiously sculpted stone. Words are the bright machinery of meaning scribbled into dream. Look at Hamlet, how each time the play is in progress he wrestles with consciousness, with thought, with the possibility of suicide, with existence itself. With violence, with love, and especially the violence of love. The King cries out for light. Because Hamlet has brought darkness into his skull. Theater and everything that goes with it. Shadows on a wall. Dilations of spirit. Dualities of black and white that blend into complexity and nuance. This is the delicious torture of words. The goulash of the brain, the grammar of muscle and bone. Refractions of light carried into ecstasies of contradiction. Life and death. Love and hate. Words and the clash of swords. The clang of the real. The ethereal which haunts us with its possibilities, its lure into oblivion. The melody of the stars. The hilarious definitions that form around the divine. The heartbeat we can hear in the softness of gray.

SMART AND BLACK AND FULL OF BIRDS

There can be no mistaking it: I write poetry for the delirium. Thought is reflective, quiet, that's not it, not what a poem is, not entirely. It's too wild, too eccentric, spinning out of control. It's flashy and ridiculous like an amusement park ride. Lights flashing people screaming. I want a hat like that. I want a hat ringed with flashing bulbs. A marquee hat. A hat that bridges dream and reality. A hat that describes life as a difficulty so entirely palpable it tastes of bells. Something mechanical, a machinery of words, a rattling of bolts and screws, consciousness unzipped and obscene. Something immodestly aquatic. A hat like that. Delinquent and wax and scarlet and warm. Pickled in calculus. Glissandos around the brim. Maybe a Cubist comb or two stuck in the band, which will be a band like the Beatles, no leather band, no silk band, no sireee, A Hard Day's Night band, a henna band, a Hannah Arendt band, a crease on top, and dipped in Keats. I want to traipse around with the music of helium on my head. Contemptuous and desperate and full of graceful articulation. I'm not kidding. I'm not being ironic. What am I saying? I'm being very ironic. I'm being so ironic I can't but help being sincere. I can be sincerely insincere but I cannot be insincerely sincere. It's not in me. And I don't have the right kind of hat. That would take a very different kind of hat. An ironic hat. A snarky hat. Fuck that hat. I'm wearing this hat. This is the hat for me. The hat of experience. The hat of exotic tinctures. A Colorado hat. A Rocky Mountain hat. A hat crowned with snow. The kind of hat Charles Baudelaire would wear. Smart and black and full of birds.

WORDS IN SEARCH OF A SHAPE

Time causes dashboards to mimic the geometry of grapes. Everything onion gets lost in emotion, which is where time invents equanimity, and the nerves defer to dirt. Dirt, as everyone knows, is calming. Go ahead. Stick your fingers into it. Do you feel time? Memory? The march of centipedes? A lamp is a lamp in and of itself, and is not like dirt, but is more like asparagus, which is a plant with small scales and needle-like branchlets. This is a feeling I have often have when discussing plants, because they're tinged with time the same way bricks will catch the afternoon light and softly submit its symmetries to the erratic comings and goings of everyday life. Conflicts, obstacles, nosegays and parcels, the mind is experienced in syllables, and at midnight the yearning for redemption arrives in the form of ferment, drums and wildlife and salmon, all of it presented in the light of a painting by Johannes Vermeer, which is to say soft and delicate and stunningly pellucid. Not like dirt, no, but wrapped in color like the glittering words of a semantic conundrum in which an unearthly clarity creates a sense of irreality. Predications keep flying out of my mouth. I can't stop feeling the symmetry of chickens, the temperatures dribbling from idealism, as if mental phenomenon puddled in blue, and Jackson Pollock's canvases flapped around the room on the wings of a savage extravagance. Poetry is endowed by dynamite to explode its own insides into diesels of locomotive force. All the words are in search of a shape, the workings of an engine laboring to form cowlicks of meaning on the skull of the known world. And continue doing so until the door is knocked and a ghost wanders in, a spirit fresh from the road, from the wheel of a lambent Cadillac, who informs us that it's the moon that pulls the tides but it's conviction that powers the morning when it's dripping with mind and rocking chairs and metaphors for death and faith is the momentum of rain and crystal. But who needs faith when the eyes are open and a beard of rain hangs from the chin and feelings incline toward libraries of Shakespeare and Blake and intellectual candy? And God and heaven are as obvious as singing. And emotions big as area codes rub against waterfalls and all the textures of burlap are completely seasoned completely ragged completely torn and tragic and burlap, honest burlap, the burlap of barns, a burlap to complement the sounds coming out of a cow.

AND WHAT

One must think radically in order to break a habit. Some habits are better left alone. One has to ask oneself: is this a habit I can live with? If it is the habit of writing, then yes. I can live with that. Does the world want me to write? The world doesn't give a shit about anything I do. And isn't that pretty much everyone's situation?

And isn't if funny that when I say 'world,' we know what is meant by world. And when I say we 'we' know what is meant by we.

Though I can already hear someone out there saying no. I don't know what you mean by 'world.' I don't know what you mean by 'we.' And fuck you.

And who can blame them? Who doesn't like fucking?

Here is a list of twenty things I like:

1. *The Sadness of the King*, by Henri Matisse.
2. Dark chocolate cordial cherries.
3. *Finnegans Wake*, by James Joyce.
4. *Meat Science Essays*, by Michael McClure.
5. Spoons.
6. Hardware stores.
7. Toby in his paper fort looking out on the world as if from a secret place.
8. Anything surprising and unpredictable (provided that it results in something good and not something bad, like a flat tire, or a fart when bowing to the Queen of England).
9. A nice warm shower after running five miles on a winter afternoon.
10. Metaphors.

11. *The Bees Made Honey in the Lion's Skull,* studio album by Earth (2008).
12. "The Wicked Messenger," the Dylan song covered by the Black Keys.
13. "Algiers," by the Afghan Whigs.
14. "Gimme Something Good," by Ryan Adams.
15. "Eine Kleine Nachtmusik" by Ammadeus Mozart.
16. Waterfalls.
17. Rumination.
18. Formulas. Just the idea of formulas. But especially the formula for cough syrup with codeine.
19. Cows.
20. Crows

And what? What else? Pink. Pink is a crucial color. Though not as crucial as black. I can't explain black. What makes black so compelling? What makes black such an interesting climate? Because the stars shine out of it? Because old men play concertinas on darkly lit Montmartre streets? Because white is so freakishly weird and scary? Because bleak yet starkly beautiful places like the Antarctic are redeemed by black rocks and penguins?

In a word, yes. And the crunch and rusted nails and rotting timber of fantasy ships. Baudelaire's albatross aloft once again, and the sun dropping handsprings of light on the ice, where it gleams, gleams terribly, hurting the eyes, until the night arrives bloated and blissful and black.

And all those stars up there shining out of that black making you dizzy with infinity. And you wonder how something comes out of nothing. And how can nothing exist if there isn't something to make nothing nothing? There can be no nothing if there isn't something. No something, no nothing. So is nothing something? The soft dominion of snow is a kind of answer. The ice glistens saying something else. The semantic glistening of ice fulfills the glimmering abyss of the infinite and the elegant pain of inscrutability that accompanies the burning wind. The ice says cold. The ice says move, or freeze. And you move. And the skin gets twisted into another day of exploration and the search for imponderable answers and you know that death is real and no one gets out alive but because of habit which is a funny engine fueled by the basal ganglia things that need getting done get done.

Mechanical or artfully it all gets done. Even as we daydream, lose ourselves in reverie, the body knows what to do, and we arrive at our destination or sit down to a plate of pancakes.

Habits are funny. They're the little narratives that structure that flimsy overlook protruding over the abyss.

Everything else is proclivity. Mindfulness, seed, and serendipity.

GOING ALL GONAD

It's odd how quickly adapted I became to wearing reading glasses after turning forty-three or so. I cannot say the same about my prostate. I cannot get used to spending a lot of time in front of a public urinal waiting for a flow of piss to get started, staring at the wall in the restroom in a self-induced trance of anticipation, getting to know each crack, each tile, each stupid joke. It's easier at home because Duchamp's *Nude Descending a Staircase* hangs above our toilet and I never tire of looking at it.

Other maladies include the occasional headache, insomnia, and anxieties that are the product of a maladaption to contemporary western civilization. By that I mean portable phones, iPods, iPads, leaf blowers, endless war, unequal wealth distribution and zombie pedestrians in smartphone trances allowing their own brains to get eaten by commerce and banality.

After breakfast is eaten and the dishes washed and put away I hear someone breaking, ripping things apart. Is it coming from upstairs, or next door? I don't know. My brain is having a hard time processing this information.

What, I wonder, would life as an oyster be like? The anatomy of oysters, which consists of a mantle, anus, adductor muscle, foot, gills, mouth and stomach, is suited for life in a brackish habitat. It is the gonad where a pearl might form. Pearls are an oyster's response to an irritation inside their shells. Epithelial cells form a sac around the irritation and begin depositing a calcium carbonate substance known as nacre. It is this nacre that forms the essence of the pearl.

Wouldn't it be wonderful, à la Alan Watts, to try to do the same with all my irritations. Adopt a new framework for my thought that perceive problems differently, perceives them as grits of fruitful inflammation that induce a nacreous poetry, that turns the jaggedness of conflict to spheres of smooth, milky resolution.

A smell smells of time and twigs because samaras work their own gyrations. Do you see it, see it twirl, the ultimate resignation of things, their graceful descent, twirling, twirling, twirling?

The sturgeon is not a joke. It is a very large fish which produces highly succulent eggs, a.k.a. caviar.

I run water over the fork and dry it and put it away. That ends that chore. The rest of the afternoon is mine. I think I will go relieve myself and watch a nude descend, descend eternally, à la the pastoral figures on Keat's Grecian urn, always in movement, yet never touching the floor.

RIPE PURPLE

Red abstraction friendly but to bathe. Jackknife to seminal to studio. Ripe purple from flourishing to chew. A so moose operation theorem. A slide has jellyfish yell.

Abstract granite that outlines outward just independence. Black crack heard on the river. Circulate is spoons should soothe more volume. It imitates congeniality the dry step ingratiates. Red between symptoms means a hiatus.

Lift and thicken or shoal. The cactus then remedied a café. Trees with rivers overflow the throat. Freight and farm not upside-down. Shaded discriminatingly to paint a key.

Jaunty the skin of the world. Structure ripe in conquest like the horizon. An enigmatic Mediterranean attitude thrilling rails. Haul a word in language which breaks alpaca into gulps. The paragraph glitters when its pathos is echoed in frogs.

Slippery sexual fidgets are enthralling. Kaolin to spatial hills built into sky. Marks had the enamel to stew. Garish catalogue their milieu was bistros. Caress a chew for orange.

Circulate a sphere only tuna. Sense in infinite hot the volume then swamp. Late vertiginously the blossoming in phantom bursts of office crustaceans. Come entertain the myriad massive athletes. Incised mosaic the palatable truffles moved into bald Euclidean devices.

Adjust Cézanne those woods into clumsy triangles. Clatter to heft during flourishing grammar. Garden begun in trumpeted resource. His improbably bounced art is a wife. Consider more diversions a canvas can sound.

Butter in oars in wars in jaws in cotton. Never stem and examine aerodromes without grapefruit. Charge the feathers comes the tube to knit. Literally like oak the palace represents succession. The blob was equipped with light and thrilling and fastened.

A hothouse is smelly since calling it nascent tickles the biology. Steam is merely flickered Bach. Pack necessity in disillusion so that our examples may die in garlands. An abstraction enlarges summer. Suppose for banana propellers your suit duplicates blood.

Smooth in giants the climate tunneled a phantom tapioca. Medicine babble much daubed by banging shellac. Hair had perspective in willow. Indulge all personification pull a living paradox from a bug. Unofficially a flatcar is rails dabbed by sexual cylinder.

Wilderness in wire like a radical potato. Eggplant from parrots because contrasting caps dictate derbies. Mint below a glow may prophesy effervescence. The same swollen being was fencing a shadow. Engine which acts to obtain mirrors.

Inflated chin a finger just dipped. Mushroom it means many sighs. House that squashed the ovation crustaceans scintillate in river snow. Velvet or wrinkle to hooked scales lingers in narration. Hills invite visibility in whatever teaches air.

Mushroom brain its landscape to be a surface. Form maple to the sublime. Radical version box he boats the brooked moose to an anthology. Umbrella bone be the anger which elucidates opinion. Fly to fall his bicycle.

Photogenic forge to clap into pronoun. A palatable accent begins arcing toward the independence triangle. Tube struts grip the romance and numbers its suns. Sense begins butter the stew traces frequented decorations. Some wires in nutmeg improbably hypnotic.

The unrivalled spark evokes an organic skin that the overflow brims and beards. Flap so bristling that dissonance gleams. Oddity surges the milieu since birds shook. Audacity glows when the ooze immigrates to publicity. The flip willow which moccasins old personalities.

A balloon sweetens the knives of autumn. The mood spoon conducts jellyfish to crystal. Daub at affection by word. Metaphysics nebula about the chowder. Architecture by raw sienna has worlds.

Power amplifies France fastened in theorem. Curiously culminated genres develop eyeballs for drawing balloons. Cause opens within pack the pretzels. It cabbages invisible algebras which intrigue Max Jacob. Discarded syntax that he elevated everyone.

Emphasis slides the bones into imponderable wildlife. Evergreen as prodigal hermitage and paint. The contraption to thaw the pool was lost in reflection. And our eyes hosted Baudelaire by fulfilling elevations. And brightness mimicked the grammar of rain.

A BRIEF HISTORY OF INDIGO

Marco Polo was the first to report on the preparation of indigo in India, "being made of an herb which they place in a great vessel, then pour in water, and leave it till the juice is given out."

Indigo occurs between 420 and 450 nanometers in wavelength on the electromagnetic spectrum, placing it between blue and violet.

In New Age philosophy, indigo is regarded as representing intuition. Electric indigo represents the sixth chakra, called Ajna, which is said to include the third eye. This chakra is related to intuition and gnosis, insight into the divine and infinite.

Ancient Egyptians used indigo-dyed cloths to wrap their mummies.

Ibn el-Baitar, a 13th century Andalusian scientist, botanist, pharmacist and physician, recommended a solution of indigo (Indigofera) to soothe all tumors and abscesses, and that a weak solution dissolved in water and taken internally lessened not only pain but even sexual desire. He quotes another author who suggests that India or Kirman indigo, when added to a rose conserve, will check both stupidity and sadness, and that a concoction of indigo, lead monoxide, pepper, rose oil and wax will calm palpitations. A lotion of indigo, plantain oil, and honey is recommended for gangrene.

Sir Isaac Newton picked indigo as the seventh shade to make up his mystical harmony of colors. He assigned indigo A on the musical scale.

David André, a merchant-dyer who settled in Nimes in the early 17th century, created a sturdy cotton twill dyed indigo which came to be known as Serge de Nimes, which was later shortened to de Nimes, and finally, denim. Levi Strauss added rivets in the 1920s.

During the restoration of Vermeer's *Girl with a Pearl Earring* in 1994–1995, it was ascertained that Vermeer had originally given the background a deep greenish tone by glazing a very transparent layer of indigo mixed with weld (a natural yellow dye-stuff obtained from flowers of the *wouw* or *woude* plant as it is called in Dutch), over the dark black underpainting. Mixed together with a binding medium such as linseed oil they form a transparent greenish tone.

Pliny mentions the use of pigeon droppings to lighten indigo to a blue.

Joan Míro's *Tempest-Indigo* consists of a green figure with a single eyeball. The eyeball hangs defiantly, a searching engine, an organ of imperial design, a living emblem of vision, amid an energetic jungle of green, a tangle of lines and webs, with a section below, a patch of white occupied by black squiggles, the background in indigo.

Carlo Crivelli (c1435–c1495), mixed indigo with lead white for the bands of pale blue and gold decoration on the throne and steps in *The Virgin and Child with Saints Francis and Sebastian.*

Matisse's *Seated Nude* includes a square of indigo to the left of the woman's head, a bright yellow L accenting its lines, and the blue next to it of an open window, the presence of a soft velvet night, the air in the room full of vibrancy and warmth.

"Mood Indigo," a jazz composition with music by Duke Ellington, was the first time Ellington had written intentionally for radio broadcast. He turned the trumpet, trombone, and clarinet "upside down," assigning high notes to the trombone and low notes to the clarinet. The arrangement produced some interesting overtones on the electronic microphones.

The Indigo Girls are an American folk rock duo consisting of Amy Ray and Emily Saliers.

Turbulent Indigo, an album by Joni Mitchell, references a great deal of pain, madness and death, and won a Grammy in 1994.

UNANTICIPATED CONSEQUENCES

The pleasure that discarded space is insoluble. There was a horse on this pavement until the crowbar danced. The wood by the brushes tilted the hunter's attention. Consciousness, dumped under a canoe, discharged a tin ball. Gargle a stigma, comb that Etruscan.

Our bones hugged the stars. There is an architecture to writing which is gaudy and unnatural. Explicit symptoms of prophesy and ink. An attractive essay brushed by the cook. The iron looked pretty moistened.

Coffee glistening on a tray of light. We employ green to greet the lemons. The roar was desire in the library. There are insults for yawning and a purple guitar. The work rails are pungent.

Batch that a palatable hold might impart. The proposal left a residual parody. We emerged to invoke its circumference. Monstrosity in sunlight. Death in Madrid.

We were done with the exhibition eyeball. A hose as long as judgment is tangible and deviating. A muscle gardenia a clay just lumped. Properties linger that dwell anyone. The door is now a rounded puff.

An air the public only squashed to prove the existence of tickling. Talking is deliverance. More summer. Less indication. A crackling fire and a sweet crow behind the leg.

His wife was trumpeted into plywood. The drum's surface simmered in dots. The physiology of the root molasses out into spirit. Respectable hypothetical luminous hits. Butterflies and letters upholster the same giant.

Veins and intentions open your reverie to blasts of Hinduism. Autumn images swarm around the drawing, impairment as a paint story. Magisterially focused swallows nesting in echoes. The salon begins its simple implication. Which a piano confirms in staunch sonatas.

The intent is not to admonish a string but make a proverb of motion. A remedial old hinge is gray. Exploration develops the bashful. Wheels in elemental alchemy embed the sculpture. Roses blossom in an antique jar.

Truffles cry feather. And a Fauve orchard enamels your rain. Angle the sphere more invisibly to the copperplate. The paint balloon expands into gauze during the novel. A candle below my latitude tunnels light through a dripping mud.

Anguish is like a lyrical strike. It flares in syllables a resilience that can only smell of pancakes. The heart has a hiatus from lifting its personality into yourself. The light has a mind that strains to chatter. Loop language begins the pineapple.

Clatter entertains the stove. A fast wallet presented in meat sizzles in the skillet. Map these bubbles. The boat dances on its own supposition. Crawling is tailored to the moonlight.

Fulfill beauty in everything. Heave with life. Be a reckless wing between airport bugs. House gravity and include its photogenic bang. Equal the mosaic of my hat and discover your bones.

ABSTRACT MACHINE

Drift for apples when enhancing the hirsute. Bronze but outward. The path is too almond to sketch wildcats. The trestle crossing wreckage. The mosquitoes finding mustard and gasoline.

The pronoun explodes by the papier collé elevation. Depth which nutmegs a scratch. Piles such aerodrome as ear ever heard or success ever suckled.

The odor moistened and the bend was eluded. A landscape your haircut must pinch is therefore asymmetrical. General. Chartreuse. Promiscuous.

Picasso done those violins to conceits of carve. A pumped thumb would stream a money to sexual affection if the outline could be deciphered as a cord, or flagpole.

The intriguing resistance had an unprecedented deliverance. Beginning in coordinates. Worlds in knives. Apollinaire among the astronomers. Fangs.

An anarchic palette of kaolin elevates the deformation of escrow. Fiber and cloth and destiny. Up is a lyrical modification. A palette between massive teeming ideas. Of buffalo. Of L'Estaque. Of warm hobnobbing plasma.

Talking is galactic being a chin is thrilling. The heart agrees to tidepool its subtleties. Equip Cubism with heartwood. Plead offices of myriad thesis. A new emotion simmering in the airport from bumps or elbows. Garments. Phantoms. Parrots.

Eat a moment. Cartwheels painted with adjectives. Opium swans represented in glass. Intestines. Aluminum cooks distance below those alleys that prickle with illegibility. Bristling knives gurgle the chain to azaleas. Fierce siege. Reflection.

Up halibut. An eloquent expression pinned to a stunned driver does its fingers in pink. Bang! Bang!

Red bends to pungency. The milieu is implicated in maroon. Stirring with civet. A ghost spitting goldfish. A private oak poking the sky to stars.

Spectral apples reflect the realism of straw. The phantom drags a canvas. Invisible mines throughout the compass bite the leaning trees like you fall into a genetic incentive to experience rubber.

The structural gut was a severity to the biology of roots wherein an old pretzel burns by anthologizing shattered denial. Galloping pages of western spark. Cool secrets. Squeezed from audacity. Like grease.

Fickle irritations begin the chemistry of passion. The pyramids are ripe. Tea darned with yellow wool. Raspberries forked between whispers.

Ooze feeling as burning words. Journey. The sternum dollars cluttered among the stars are the flotsam of a previous thought. Blots embark in armadillos. Gunned engines. Brushes. Stimulating pains. Elegies.

A banana that stoves its art is admired in lines. An aesthetic in floating was glimpsed through a force of soda. Stilts. A moral indicative under a dark intonation.

Profligate to another is a garden with indentations menstruating bugs. Circles. Evolutions of heaven heaving with maturity. I would rather have a winter in my solution than a solace in my salon. Violins are instinct with propinquity. Pianos are more logarithmic. Like jackknives.

Dabs. Daubs. Dadoes. Wisdom's paraphernalia between nouns. The propane darting a blue flame.

Cured heart. Skulk. Laughing brush. Anger.

Yellow conjures revelation by cube in the Louvre. Knots in space draw cement by opening Technicolor gargoyles too hard to puff into yolk. Crustaceans indicate hunger by clicking consonants. Chiaroscuro is absurdly absent. A nascent leg kicks Cézanne into the world.

Mahogany France. Steam. Abstract machine. Feeling. Insects color a rattan to quicker crackling than a palpable fish treads space with its fingers. Brocade, propelled outward, has time for ambiguity. Each blaze on the water redeems a clear cynosure with a compass and a straw.

The migration proceeds with a calliope.

INFINITY'S ORCHID

Infinity's orchid is abandoned in the cartilage of denotation. The testimony of string yields a different metaphor. It evergreens the animal chair. Injures the irony of indentation. Denim too racked to mood.

Dig for fangs in combination. Clapboard the tea with apparitions. Blood is lobster red and strikes this vein with sheen. Jaw joy is ocher. The lyric strength of stone explains the storage of age in a wrinkle of falling skin.

There is a tuna ship between two radical realities. The cemetery evokes a thumb. A mode of hat on the rue d'Orsel. Meanings with a crabby density manufacture consciousness in a roughneck. Elvis Presley singing Hound Dog on Ed Sullivan.

Perspective is but a spoon we'll call secular. The noise of its imagery steadies the consciousness of a centipede in a ceremony of cellophane. Personality chews a palette of springs. Drag these smears to the smell of its opening. Tilt the granite toward the outside.

Buckle your gargle not because the ocean is spinning but because nature's symmetry jokes at algebra. Mass has wax. Awed is washed for loops. Such bone as might propose a paradigm, a wide-eyed glitter provided with red. Oil and iron spooned in a garage.

All likes a fork in lightning. The desk is treading these words in suppositions of cotton. The arrival of an image makes everyone glad. The birth of a thought grinds the biology of a town. Kerosene mingles about a fulfillment.

An explanation fostered on gaudiness figures a fat prickling crinkle in the sound of a bistro. We are within the prophesy and its growling eggnog pediments. There is a feather in the story that has been thumbed by ganglions and moistened by your interest. It may alter the dwelling. It may stink of eyes.

The biography is hostile toward its own premise. Squirt it for diversion. Power whispers on the path. Awakens the willingness to branch into pronouns. The literal drift of piccolos through a dream of calculus.

There is more palette on a palate than pallets in a palace. These echoes have been tumbled in gauze and their effects tug at a sagging reality of twigs and artichokes. A drug distilled from the ecstasies of painters. Corot on a mountain, Braque in a field of broccoli.

Despair imposes cognition when it is squeezed. It is grease to a key of gravity. An eyeball dragging a caboose to the end of a sentence. Sympathy is deaf to the cries of platitude. This is an engine that conjugates charm, and this is a liquid thrilling with spoons.

Lucidity's hospital is nutmeg's Apollinaire. Willow begins a duty by bending in the wind. Milieu is a convocation of crabs crawling backwards. Glasses, or parables, whose meaning lingers in the pews of a dead excuse. Heave at Hinduism when your vertebrae seems to float.

The ceiling must dry in a proverb. Honors tease the cake of maneuvered daylight. Swords are crossed. Songs are sung. The aurora tumbles through its clouds, perforating the fossil of a tragic adjective.

Sheer attacks of improbable hawthorn have ignited the idea of cabs. Stork on a palomino. Another morning of fiduciary ambush compelling and insoluble. Hammer the snow for another heartwood dollar. Infinity is blue when it is lifted by a Fauve religion.

Black when a laughter exceeds its wheels. The seashore rolls through its description undoing itself on the sand. The chrome brocade of a lyric violence tastes of oarlocks and temptation. A clay nude volunteers her nipples. Baudelaire stews in a blob of subversive velvet.

A red intestine singing of rivers bicycles around an oval portrait. Limestone is implicit. Unification is rain. An elbow and a farm might be catalogued as monuments. Everything else is either an excursion, or experiencing dirt.

BUFFALO WRINKLES

A suitcase packed with time pops open revealing Iceland. I get dressed in a personality expelling from a volcanic vent. I walk to the edge of the world enveloped in a beautiful blue fire.

What we think of as buffalo wrinkles are memories opened to look like postulation. Each nerve weighs eighteen pounds and signals the mind that a handful of words may incarnate the sedulous smell of creosote or attempt to define cement as a requirement for the rhythm of feet.

In any event, the beyond shatters into reality and so determines the details of a blue rag that there is a treasure in your eyes called seeing.

That recognition is another form of grasping.

That attraction is often erratic and that a memory is an implication of leaves.

That time is an abstraction and geometry balks at water.

Imagine a house full of subpoenas. The clarinet bends a sound into stone. Even the soap is jingled.

I have chiseled a T-shirt out of a fork. There the stars are at rest in their sphere.

I need to pump some gasoline into this limousine. This pair of gloves. This pot of glue. This tongue of derailment. This gob of paint.

Shadows crackle on my forehead. Can you see them? They shine like crystals of ice that dissolve when one breathes on them.

Space sweats fire behind these words.

Here is a book of Splenetic Performances for Baudelaire. It's a hammerhead doing a handstand on a fired bullet.

And here is a color that is candid and granular like a vibrating poem.

The universe meanwhile rolls downhill during a brief but stupendous period of expansion. I would recommend getting a lawn chair and taking a photograph of the beginning of time. You can hang it on the wall and call it a day.

THE STEPLADDER CONFESSES ITS CLATTER

What if a word explodes into surf and, bashful as a bride, rides an ox to Alabama where the hatchets are buried and humanity is stunned by the oysters absorbed in a dream of water? What if density has a wildcat and lifts itself into supposition? What if the mouth in our tea begins to narrate the door? Or succeeds at mosaic? Or breeds cognition? Or detonates in the olives?

A pump is spillable. Eczema is opposite. So is Alaska.

Bouillon overstates its particularity. Radical conceptions of hunger recruit bags of gravity as if a weight declared itself horses and evolved into lightning. Corot at his easel in Como.

Lines of poetry create a galaxy of goats that deform the fence and withdraw into squares of androgynous headlight. Look what walking has done to the sidewalk. Each flower is a hiatus of hands. To cauterize opinion is to anthologize the cackling of witches. Let bacteria shine out of a book. Boil the plays of Shakespeare into jelly. Let a mountain twist itself into swans.

A mind can drift through a cloud and think itself a scent of French yelling at unpredictable temperatures. Virtuosity comes in cubes that freeze below the threshold of consciousness. Mass mirrors the density of words. Fingers grow into metaphor and hold the mind like a slice of pumpernickel. A door opens in my head and a phenomenon of spoons and camaraderie culminates in evocations of blood. I can feel a fat cloud of cats and dogs rain on a map of England. I can feel abstractions of sunlight tugging my sleeve. I can feel the confusion of gardens.

The idea of frost has not been sufficiently explored. The golden glue of the estuary demonstrates the idea of union. It all sticks together after the tide pulls back revealing an ear full of imagery and a tongue of mud languishing in wreckage.

I am not another fungus come to announce the wisdom of decay. I am simply a house of language offering shelter to the nebulas of reverie ballooning into furniture. Actual chairs. Actual tables. Actual actuaries. Actual dimes and initiations.

Meaning coheres when the daydreams collude in exhibitions of cork, and the stepladder confesses its clatter.

BAKED IN INDIGO

Time to put something on the canvas. Just some tuna birds, many of them leaning. The bazaar pumps a universe into view. I am feeling abstract. This causes resonance to arrive in the shape of a bubbly mind.

A trapeze swings in this hair I have on my head. It flavors push-ups with holes. A nailing inward can pull raspberries toward brightness. The palpable lyric of a creamy song murmurs exaltation. Euclid grows a new feeling in the interaction.

A penumbra agrees to envy eating. The farm is sticky, and spoons the bumps. The maple elevator pauses in concentration exhibiting imponderable peculiarities. There is joy in squeezing an accordion. A summer which calculus corners in Portugal.

Tin with wood for the oath drug. A spectral hive which keys the pulse. Energy's philodendron hinting at rattles, and African spices. The new job requires metamorphism. Sorcery and letters. The tea describes heat with a tender science.

Oboe to burn with a ghost. Deliverance is almost confessed until the components are chained. There are wet paintings between that history. Binoculars stimulated by your mind jerked through a granite atmosphere. The shoulder is incidental to the spine, as are the wings, and perceptions are balls.

The infinite greeting of any ambiguity might be clearer in tilted bones. It steams in elemental Max Jacob. Transformations have machines for these vowels. Oppose the memorials. Peg the mountain in words to a beating heart.

Zinc begins the eyes. Know your events. A hugged honesty embarks on skulls. A cloud was that pushed despair. Its edge and structure exceeding the swallows inside its finger.

If the studio cracks at your lines, the swans will call in hunger. There is invention, or cooking, imposed on declension. Virtuosity would pull it for harmony, but the blood is clumsy. A crow in syntax that heaves lace in hibachi handsprings. Grebes which comply in sunlight.

The vowel is emphatic in its engine of soup. Envy is expansive in the way it contracts, a paradox visiting itself, solving its sheer rescue with language. By that I mean nails. A knot of chiaroscuro muscle curled in red. The parable earns a simulacrum then.

The details push themselves between these words. Hunger dwells on the canvas to feature its open throats. A book bulb washes the maneuver. This gluttonous table and its incongruities misinterpret their surface as struts. An orchard pushed out of summer and puffed up the escalator concludes the gantry, a Braque buckled to the boat.

Form can sanguine to sandstone. Experience the opium aggressively merely to caulk its indication. A plot of exhibition will soothe that flow. This alters fog when the others are lost. Space itself is ugly the piano serves to excite.

Time chains itself behind a brush. Its components pulse charcoal, or cars. The spoon of paint lags after construction. There is, meanwhile, a stove to assemble by spirit. Oysters the cartwheels put between the eyes.

The chronicle gets thrilling in its view of heat. It feathers, or presses, those inside. Cézanne carries introversion to a maximal wallet of ocher and brown. The bleeding is fenced, then initiated by swimming. Frame and delectation are therefore a harness to posterity.

Sugar is quixotic, a trapeze for Bach. A skin of bashful Byzantine anticipates sound. The spoon is long and riveting. Now beams the syntax. It cries for suppleness and roads.

The garnish on beauty is embryonic. Engine for a machine vertiginously spinning this collar stud. Sheer being exceeds the silt. Buffalo Bill and a hungry compilation sipping structure from a basket of drawers. The glockenspiel is shaken by an oath of cardboard.

Heft imposes a severity on the flavor of today's gravity. Later, January will pull an icicle out of a stillborn desire, the way it always has, always does. Butter is just another box for yellow. Thought turns green, and crackles, blossoming into visibility. The mirrors meet our eyes in a feather of rain.

DARK MATTER

Astrophysicists speak of the dark matter of space. They don't know what it is. I find this appealing. The idea of an inscrutable dark matter holding the universe together is luminous and rich, pregnant with postulation.

The masses of galaxies and their ghostly clusters can be calculated by measuring the velocity at which stars orbit the centers of the galaxies to which they belong. The answer to this infers a mass that is five to ten times the mass of what is visible. The unseen matter is a shine in the ore of poetry. This is where matter doesn't matter so much as simmer on the low boil of a permeation bubbling words.

It may also be that there is an unknown particle with an infinite number of manifestations, as in the innumerable tunes that may be composed on a single string of Pythagoras's lyre. The theory suggests how maximum complexity could have arisen from maximum simplicity.

Think of a group of people rising together in an elevator. How many are there? Five? Four? How old are they? Are they all women, all men, or a happy combination of men and women? Do they have jobs? Do they enjoy their jobs? Do they read books, spend time on Facebook, wonder why, in a universe with very few answers there is something rather than nothing? To assume what other people might be thinking is to get lost very quickly. The important thing is to notice their shoes.

It is better to notice their shoes rather than their shirts or haircuts because shirts and haircuts would merit looking more directly at them, these your fellow travelers on the elevator, and nobody likes that. Nobody likes it when you look directly at them, especially when you don't know them from Adam.

Or Eve.

Eve did not wear shoes. Adam did not wear shoes. They did not wear shoes because they did not require shoes. They lived in a state of innocence. Until that nasty incident with the apple. That's when everybody started wearing shoes.

A bald need to protect the soles of one's feet brings us by a commodious vicus of recirculation to the shoe store. Here we find deck shoes, desert shoes, running shoes, dress shoes, hiking boots, riding boots, cowboy boots, skimmers, pumps, ski boots, steel-toed safety boots, oxfords, sandals, slippers, ice skates, snowshoes, monk straps, Cuban heels, kitten heels, stiletto heels, high tops, plain-toes, cap-toes, closed lacing, open lacing, slip-ons, loafers, and brogues.

As you can see, the role of the poet is very uncertain in a mercantile society. The poet does not make shoes, the poet may not even wear shoes. I have seen poets recite their work in public barefoot. It is a complex issue. Bare feet distract from the poetry. I mean, the human toe is so weird. All of them. Big toe, little toe, middle toe: weird.

The reality of other people's feet is that they are not my feet. This is a very dark matter, refractory and fast. I don't know how to address it, and I'm not wearing shoes.

LIFTOFF AT THE COURT OF VERSAILLES

The balloon was a 37,500 cubic feet sphere of sky-blue taffeta held together by 18,000 buttons, coated with a varnish of alum and decorated with flourishes of gold and the signs of the zodiac. The crew consisted of a sheep, a rooster, and a duck. They were placed in a small wicker basket attached to the balloon by cords of hemp. Each time one of them was placed in the basket, they promptly jumped back out, barely missing an open pit in which a fire crackled. Some grass, seeds, and worms were deposited in the basket which ultimately persuaded the crew to remain put.

King Louis XVI and his wife Marie Antoinette pinched their noses to block the stench of smoke, a mephitic blend of burning wool, fetid hay, and old shoes. It was assumed that the smellier the smoke, the more buoyant the craft.

It was a warm September day. Hundreds of people gathered about the great lawn of Versailles.

The fire crackled, the duck quacked, the rooster pecked at a worm. The sheep let out a long vibrant bah as the balloon rose higher and began to drift over the palace.

Heads tilted back. Voices murmured.

Sacre bleu! exclaimed Marie Antoinette.

The flight lasted approximately eight minutes, covered two miles, and obtained an altitude of about 1,500 feet.

The basket hung still as the balloon floated weirdly and majestically over the topiary of Versailles and thence into the rougher countryside, diminishing in size as it began a slow descent and landed at the carrefour Maréchal in the bois de Vaucresson. The sphere drooped like a wounded celestial body as the wicker basket glided over tremors of green grass and came to a stop.

It was to be expected that the duck, rooster and sheep would be transformed for better or worse after attaining such height, but they appeared quite normal when the first people gazed into the wicker basket. The duck quacked, the rooster crowed, the sheep baaad. The animals were fine.

What were the thoughts that the crowd took home with them that day? The mind has a light that delights to dance on its own suppositions. For this is the day that flight became possible, and free will shined louder in the vineyards, whose bounty, it was said, exceeded all records that year.

THE PAINTER

There is something you should know about painting: it's a declaration of knobs. Yaks. Conviction. The sag of a cemetery willow. The uncanny dialects of a woman's arm. The insinuation of streets when they're wet and the cars go by with people in them dreaming, talking, yelling, crying, laughing.

How do you paint that? There is always that question when I sit down to paint. I draw a snake. I paint the snake. The snake coils into a variegated iridescence and flicks a scarlet tongue.

Then I get into density. The volumes of things. Houses, forklifts, cows. Animals with horns. And sometimes something small, a fingernail, a pin in a map, a pickle.

Or a screw. I admire the machinery of the screw. Such a simple thing. I can feel the truth of its existence in the torque of its threads.

Art is a matter of experience not principles. The clarity of any given moment. There's so much reality in a moment. But then, as we are all wont to ask, what the fuck is reality?

Reality is the activity of consciousness. It comes into being through interrelationship. Parables and paraffin and abalone and hills. The tea of incident, the brightness of valor. Bubbles rising in a ginger ale on a flight to Oaxaca. Sexual somersaults, injuries of the spur. Alligator gravity flying saucer soup a ghost hoeing a garden in Guadalajara.

I feel seized by a stunning translucence. My mind is a mass of fireworks. The stars journey over the prairie, ripping the sky open until eternity shines through.

My brush moves a flower into a woman's hand and her eyes light the world on fire.

I include a cherry. A bright red cherry. So juicy it sings. So real that it expects my bite.

I love the thingness of things. Das ding an sich. The thing-in-itself. A knife that is a real knife. A wheel that is a real wheel. An eye that is a true eye. The luster of pain in a swoon of pleasure.

A saguaro sun drawing lemon from a gourd of carnelian and jade.

Alchemist holding a blue liquid in a careful measure.

Scarlet trumpet vine. Maidenhair fern. Night scented jasmine in a forest glade.

MARMALADE

A book answers space with the milk of a page, the beauty of paper in a monologue of glue. But what is it, truly, that swims behind these words, that breathes, that moves, that has being and character? Ask a painting by Cézanne. Ask the teaspoon reposing in an emptied can of cat food filled with water in the kitchen sink. Ask the kitchen sink. Ask the kitchen.

There is the artist in her studio, busy in a riot of color. The hammer hugs its form. The paintbrushes soak in a jar. We fulfill the will of the tool by using it for what it was designed. Letters are designed to languish in catastrophe. The mind is wild and laden with sage. The sky is open, the hills are bare. A spherical mass of black rolls across a smooth wooden floor. Pins fall. This is what is known as bowling.

The fingers go into the holes of a globe, the arm swings the globe forward, and lets it go. The globe rolls thunderously down planks of smoothly fitted wood. This is done with a sense of purpose. Consequently, it is not poetry, but something else. It becomes poetry when it ceases to be a quest for personal glory and becomes a splendor of bulk and ambulation.

This is my appeal to infinity.

A cemetery pencil awakens the imperatives of smoke. The dead don't know this, because they are dead. When people are dead they become memories in the brains of the living, who carry them forward into their lives as they age, and tend gardens, and plunge their hands into dirt, the soft warm dirt, the dirt of the planet earth, where the trees agitate according to the caprice of the wind, and the hedge is a genre of huckleberry.

There is a bonfire on the beach. I don't see the point of it, which makes it perfect. From this prospect, the jar is a journey of glass, and contains pickles.

Or marmalade.

Here is Prospero tracing a symbol in the sand. A spirit appears and he commands the spirit to go shopping for marmalade. The spirit returns with a jar of marmalade. It was on sale. Prospero is happy and proud.

The senses are contemporaneous with objects. This is how things happen. This is how phenomena are revealed in perspective. No longer to see the objects in the room because I have closed my eyes is to see the curtain of my eyelids. In the same way if I put a jar of marmalade in the refrigerator then no longer see the chunks and orange translucency of the marmalade is precisely to see the marmalade. That is to say, imagine the marmalade. In which case I see through the marmalade, and the world disappears into an infinite jar of possible relations. And that jar is a word, and the word is marmalade.

ROOT BEER

I'm feeling Byzantine, intricate and convoluted. Nobody wants to see reality do push-ups. Yet the secret reality of things is clearly nothing more than a thin film of nothingness, like the glow of stage lights on a new euphonium, and the vacuum cleaner ate the closet. There are clothes everywhere, shirts, pants, coats, and three old cardigans, which embarrasses philosophy.

What is it that so stirs my being? The smooth contour of a whale's rib, the effervescence of elves. There is also the whole reality of the window, a thing external to the sphere of volition, a relational ontology of intelligible patterns as are germane to the productions of space, time, and causality, as paramount to the shiver of beach grass or gentle vibration of washing machines, a totality of involvements endowed with a distinctive phenomenological signature, a native quality which is given and observable to the senses, which is glass, which is transparent, and made by melting sand and other materials, and the totality of these effects creates a possibility of vision, and the house next door, which has other people in it, people like me, except louder, and more enthusiastic about sports.

I like to go to bed early. There's a family of sparrows living in my beard and when night comes little cuts on my hand begin bleeding worlds.

I'm tempted to say words, but that would be a mutiny, because the intent here is to seduce you into believing the bed is a metaphor and the sparrows are real sparrows, although I do not actually have a beard, I have a pair of Cubist gloves and a formulary chock-a-block with aromatic gerunds and pharmaceuticals that make you sincere and Jurassic.

My grammar takes me for a long ride into the unknown. I wear the horizon like a toga. My hectic ink is a muscle that I use to lift a pen and blast into spleen.

My preferred medium is correspondence, but tonight I am speaking to you from a podium of hypothetical spruce, a writhing mass of grease and pulleys that percolates shadows and incandesces like a carbon filament in a storage room. It indicates only itself, which is compact and well-proportioned, and not unlike the evolution of a feeling that culminates in cream. The Wesenshau of Husserl, for example, which twinkles when you fill it with water.

The act is everything. Root beer squirts from a shaken bottle, not one that has been sitting on the shelf for a long time, unsung and unwieldy, placed as it is behind a sign celebrating a mid-January sale. That is, it acquires a reality by the sole fact that the manufacturer confers on it an outside, and an inside. The interior is too delicate to bring into discussion at this point. Let's just say the root beer reveals itself as a bald expenditure, and that its color corresponds to the black diamonds of Perigord, the elusive and delicious truffle of southwestern France, which only specially trained dogs are able to smell and indicate with pointed snouts and wagging tails. The truffle, like root beer, is the fruit of subterranean affinities, and leads to a new organization of complexes.

And that's why I'm feeling Byzantine.

Root beer.

LIFE ON OTHER PLANETS

People frequently ask me what life is like on other planets. I answer that it depends on the individual planet. And, to be honest, I've never been to another planet. I don't know why people make that assumption about me. Maybe it's the trinkets on my sleeve, or the monkey that follows me everywhere. His name is Lorenzo and he once played Calpurnia in a production of Julius Caesar. As for the box under my arm, it contains a pound of legal documents. People are so sensitive these days. You never know when you're going to offend someone.

I don't know what to say about gravity. It's a grave situation. It keeps me in place. Things like that. If you get engaged to a staircase it's best to take it step by step. My intentions are solid maple. Fireworks need no introduction but the asphalt is always a little demure and as soon as the stars appear one can begin to annotate one's personal injuries. This is why so many painters love to travel and create new relationships with color. There is nothing so inexplicable as a personal injury or soybean. There's a moment during the day when a door opens in the tide-pool and the stadiums recede into the distance. It's at times like that that the refrigerator makes total sense.

But what about Cincinnati you ask. I don't know. I've never been there either. But of course I can always imagine a Cincinnati. I see a place full of wheelchairs and whistles, beaks and bones, crowbars and puddles. Throw in a few pugilists and sideboards and you've got Cincinnati. If you turn around and look at it from a side angle you can see that it's longer than your average belt and behaves like a boat when it's put in water. Which is to say it lingers. And although that proves nothing, I hold in my arms a basket of intriguing laundry. Can you guess whose it is? I can't either. Life is full of surprises. Sometimes it's not what you know but what you don't know that gives life its charm and meaning.

A few see the world as an impressive array of decorations, while others see it as a dimple in time. One does not necessarily rule out the other. As for me, I like to come at things slowly, gracefully, tossing aside crusade after crusade as I go. Sooner or later, you're going to have to sit down and listen to Bach. It's like holding the stars in your hand and smelling Pangaea. I like to feel the sky rub against my wings. If the images associated with the personality of aluminum fall into a bowl of pronouns the result can be totally anonymous unless it's protected by a house. The jungle does somersaults not because any flowers are implicated but because the rhythm requires a pomegranate. The symposium aside, we had more fun in the lobby when waffles were served the following morning. Do you see what I'm getting at? That's right: France uses a different asphalt than the United States. It's more like trigonometry than fiction.

And yes, life truly is different on other planets.

BUFFALO BILL IN THE HOLY LAND

Writing poetry is warm and parenthetical. It allows me to hold the reins to some very powerful horses.

I think religion is an unpredictable dog.

I crave the strength of the moccasin. Snakes in needles of pine. Dead leaves wrinkled and dry like the parchment of death.

It is inconceivable that men in wigs discuss ceiling fans.

If life is a game of chess, time may be imagined as a jail cell, or cow.

An empty head in an empty bed operates the machinery of heaven.

I love the lonely dirt roads of North Dakota. Places were the wind encourages width and wheat and hooks to hang clothes on a line.

Syllables get the bees going. Buffalo. Slices of orange. Wood creaking on hot afternoons. Swallows and stairs and exciting blue stones. Mud on a bottle of burgundy. An old Chinese man in San Francisco on the corner of Kearney and Clay bowing a two-stringed erhu. Each of his sounds slide in and out of time.

The world is asleep. People walk by in a gas full of sampans and river thieves.

I look for redemption wherever I can find it. Life is insoluble. Animals seem to have a better grasp of it. But that's just me. Buffalo Bill. And my Wild West Show. Everything else is sticky like blood and hairy as a tarantula when remorse bites and your suitcase won't close.

Here is my diagnosis: my horse is old. But the day is young and beautiful.

I dig a hole and plant a name. Its syllables are visceral. Why? Why do we name things?

My horse doesn't know either. But that's his shadow on the ground, gliding over the sage.

BUFFALO BILL AND THE GIANT EYEBALL

Buffalo Bill rides out onto the prairie. It's a lovely day. The air is a parable of rose. It's early spring. Buds are beginning to burst. Leaves are tremors of green. I'm old, he thinks. I ache. I know more names at the cemetery than I do in town. Getting old is like what? I don't know. Some emotions are too vague to describe with words. You have to use sand, or chiaroscuro.

Words reach out of my mind for paradise. And come back with rocks.

I tell myself: be expansive. Fly this day into prophecy. Persevere.

He is followed by wolves. If he shoots one, the others will get him. He doesn't relish dying like that. But what the hell. Shit happens.

His heart beats faster. His horse snorts, smelling death. The wolves give chase.

He spurs his horse. They take off at a gallop. He turns round and fires a shot. A wolf yelps and hits the ground. The wolves retreat and he continues his ride. He sees a giant balloon overhead painted to look like an eyeball. Surveyors, most likely. He sees the glint of a telescope in what appears to be a basket hanging like a nerve from the eyeball, bloated and unnatural.

The hooves of his horse click like consonants on the stone of a butte. The wings of dragonflies shine in the light, veined and transparent. He squeezes an orange and watches the juice ooze out. A cloud passes overheard. A snake crawls out from a rock. A coyote runs off into the brush. He remembers seeing a skull filled with sand and flecks of gold. And the skull spoke to him and said we must endure the cold. And he could feel the weight of its voice. It felt like a knife blade. Shiny and hard. Like the division between soul and meat.

He ponders the eyeball. The eyeball ponders him. The image defines his day. Until it becomes a speck. And his back aches. And he takes a piss by an elm. And gets back on. And the day becomes less mortal, like blood. The day becomes a wrist of water on an arm of mud.

DINNER AT THE HOTEL UNIVERSE

Buffalo Bill rides into town on an ostrich. It begins to rain. If you saw the day in half, the metaphors imprisoned in various religions will be released. The world will turn into a Heptateuch.

Buffalo Bill checks into the Hotel Universe. Later he has dinner. The napkins are folded into clavicles and mandibles. Buffalo Bill doesn't know why we exist. But he gives it thought.

Whenever a sequence of words are strung together we have what is called a sentence. A sentence is a place to store ideas, grow chrysanthemums, or build hotels.

Rivers start as threads to become tea or coffee. All the rivers are nerves. The mouths of rivers are just that: mouths. But these mouths do not make words. Words come from elsewhere.

Words are the embers of a long subterranean fire.

And then there's God. God is a word. Anyone can say it. Nobody can prove that it has reality. But because it is a word, and all words refer to something, doesn't that "something" qualify as a species of reality? Karats indicate the purity of a piece of gold. But how does one measure the purity of an idea?

People like to say God because it is a powerful word. Just saying it makes you feel powerful. And small. Simultaneously powerful and powerless.

Buffalo Bill sticks a piece of chicken in his mouth and gazes idly out the window. There's a flash of lightning. God appears as a stuffed wildcat in an antique store.

Pain is sometimes a diversion. But most of the time it's just pain, signaling the nerves with meanings of its own.

Buffalo Bill struggles every day against the embarrassment of killing buffalo. He makes a note: stop killing buffalo.

Someone plays the piano and a woman's voice flutters in the air like a cecropia moth. The voice flickers, powdery and polychromatic, and lands on a table. The cutlery vibrates.

Words will sometimes go on a journey and take the spirit and intellect with them. This is how the Hotel Universe was created. Words were gathered into a destiny that mandated a building of rooms and hallways. A man asleep in a bed, a woman's voice flickering on the ceiling and the occasional flash of lightning silhouetting the outline of a wildcat on the wall.

THE PACKAGE

I'm shaving. There is a knock on the door. I go to the door and peep through the peephole. Half of my face is covered with shaving cream. No one is there. It must be the mailman. He does that. He will leave a package at the door if it's too large for our mailbox. He does this as a courtesy. I open the door and bring the package in and put it on the coffee table. It's a heavy package and smells of coffee and camels and long painful distances. It looks old and battered. The paper is deep brown and the package is held together by twine. The return address says simply Arthur Rimbaud, Hôtel de l'Univers, Aden. The lettering is smudged, so that it is barely visible. I get a pair of scissors and break the twine and open the package. The paper crackles. Inside are bags of coffee and an ounce of hashish wrapped in a silk handkerchief. There is a tin of oysters and a galaxy of bewildering metaphors. The groan of a woman sleeping in desert heat and a jar of trembling nebulas. I lift out a gooey mess of passion and the motion of a hyena slinking stealthily through a village at night with a piece of meat in his mouth. There are books on engineering and mining and carpentry and masonry. A pound of tangled spring and a basket of peremptory sunlight. Various knots in old crumbling hemp and an embryonic simile straining to become a real child. There is a punchbag and a pair of pajamas. The pajamas are striped and look like the ones prisoners wore in movies made in the thirties. There is a note of folded paper at the bottom. It says: *Mon cher ami, Je suis de retour d'un voyage au Harar: six cents kilometres, que j'ai faits en 11 jours de cheval. Je repars, dans trois ou quatre jours, pour Zeilah et Harar où je vais définitivement me fixer. Je vais pour le compte des négoicants d'Aden. Je veux que vous avez ces choses pour répondre à votre question. Bien à vous, Arthur Rimbaud.* My question ? What question ? I do not remember writing to Monsieur Rimbaud. But I do have questions. I have many questions. But how are they to be answered by a solitude hemmed with sleep and a map of Zanzibar ? What does the dried blossom of a cocoa flower mean, or the noise of a door creaking open a few minutes past midnight ? Question mounts on question until there is nothing but the silence of the room, the smell of coffee, and the smack smack smack of a cat chewing his food.

HEARTBEATS AND SCARS

I'm getting old. I'm getting wrinkled. The wrinkles are often quite interesting. It's like having a story emerge on parchment, the parchment being, of course, the skin of my face.

Here's what my face says: you can't escape time. You can give it a shot. Get on a plane. Fly to Paris. Live in a dream. Put your trust in velocity. It'll work. For a while.

Being is what gets you. Being has a bottomless appetite for experience, and process, and time.

Time, unlike light, is quietly invisible. It works in private. It is longest in solitude, fastest in crowds, particularly when there are acrobats and rock stars involved. Time is a strange phenomenon. It enters the mind differently than temperature and light. It feels geometric. It slides across the ground in shadows, and the sun itself is a huge sphere of gold.

Why are hours round? They're no longer round for people with digital watches, digital clocks on their laptops and radios. Time has ceased being round. It has become luminous numbers. But I still think of hours as round, like wheels or pies, and the minutes as their more spritely counterparts, their movement being visible, whereas the hour is not. Hours move too slowly to be visible. But when one o'clock becomes two o'clock, you know that there has occurred a meaningful division in time. The vivacity of time is reinforced by seconds. It is there that you hear the actual ticking. And if you have the benefit of a stopwatch you can see the seconds popping into time like the tattoos sounded on a bugle to summon soldiers to their quarters at night.

There is no real way to describe time. Description is an incidence of correspondence and time doesn't connect with anything real, anything tangible. Clocks are not time, but the houses of time. Is time any slipperier underwater than it is at high altitudes?

Why do people find the new year so moving? Why is it celebrated with champagne and fireworks? Why isn't every hour celebrated with champagne and fireworks?

A year, of course, is much longer than an hour. When you get older, time assumes the imaginary scope of a prairie. It seems like gazing a long way into your life. The events don't feel old, just far away. Fifty years ago today The Searcher's version of "Needles and Pins" came out. Barry Goldwater announced that he would seek the Republican nomination for President of the United States. Lyndon Johnson announced a war on poverty. *Hello Dolly* opened at New York's Saint James Theater. *Meet the Beatles* came out, starting the British invasion in America.

I loved the British invasion. It meant liberation to adolescents who were different, who were poor, who were girlish. Weirdness was celebrated, girlishness was androgynous and cool, people scorned materialism and conformity, live for today was the dominant motto.

It didn't last. Things are once again materialistic and conformist and totalitarian. But that's time. The strange workings of time. The book on sedition usurps itself. Day descends into dark. The memories of one's life are mapped in scents and keepsakes, journals and drawers, heartbeats and scars.

THE GLOCKENSPIEL

The glockenspiel is a percussion instrument mounted in a frame. It consists of a series of steel or alloy bars of graduated length and pitch arranged in two rows chromatically. Sharps and flats stowed away in the chromatic attic.

I like the word 'glockenspiel,' which is German, and means "bell play." I like it when a word can do this. I like it when a word can rise like a loaf in the oven of the head and produce a fragrance of morning warmth. Words are a stirring of the odor of sound. Sound as a form of afflatus, or phoneme. Sound as sound. Sound sound. Sound on a sound in a sound by a sound.

Distortions of sound form bulbs. Burst on the page in fire and color. Chrysanthemums of fire blooming on a summer night.

It's very similar to gardening. If you plant a squash you get a sycamore.

My language is your language. I don't own the language. Any language. No one owns a language. I find this very exciting. It's how I navigate. I walk beside a fire. I pursue a chimera of echoes. My diversions are simple and topographic. The surrounding earth is sublime. I hear echoes beneath the language that extrude ganglions of ghostly caravan. I delight my eyeballs with the odor of definition. The odor of definition varies from word to word. Some words smell like clouds. Some words smell like lightning flashing in a cloud. Sulfurous. And hot.

Little Richard polishes his piano with an insoluble C sharp. The words that I am using to describe this curve into calculus and modulate the vividness of water. And this is how you begin with a glockenspiel and end up with a piano. Language is slippery. You're trafficking in shadows. My thoughts on this shift from day to day. I'm certain that language is a garden for the hybridization of words and the development of metaphors. But then I think no, that's too complicated, too static. Language is more volatile than that. It's more like a gas, or hallucination.

Sometimes the words scatter like crustaceans and sometimes the words demand the elasticity of rubber. My ears are laboratories for the study of waves.

I like the way words travel through an argument, convulsing like torrents on a map of fjords and aqueducts.

Consider a constancy and you will discover a spin.

The paper towels go so quickly. Where do they go? The words go in search of paper towels. The words are not my words. The words are words searching for paper towels.

Because there is a quiddity of things. An old poet getting on a plane. Could be me. Could be you. The question to ask is: do words separate us from the essentials of reality, or do they join us to a reality that wouldn't exist without them? And what is the language of clouds? What is the language of stars? What is the language of light and mud and the naked air? Air is the language of air. Mud speaks mud. Stars speak stars. It is the play of bells. Bluster. Potato. Glockenspiel.

HERDS OF DIAMOND CENTIPEDE

These questions, "what do I want," "what is it possible to want," and "what am I" compared reveal my relation with the universe. Right now what I want is a rocking chair, a bag of earth, and the language of rocks delivered into my bloodstream intravenously. Because if I speak like a rock with the needs and desires of a rock I will arrive at the geometry of faucets in which answers evince kilowatts of personality and a knot is a knot is a knot. That is to say, a convolution of rope, which smells of the waterfront. If I follow the logic of rope, I will change tenses when it suits me and signify texture with my bones and cackling scraps of consciousness littered here and there like words. Like the glamorous shine of a terra-cotta caboose.

It follows, then, that blood and bone offer imponderable moments of meaning. In this state, the best of ideas which can be come to me on the backs of lurid creatures blasted into lavish definition by the candy of enigma. I have often thrilled to the splendor of hardware. I can be sincere as an armadillo or ironic as a cat. I can include a conundrum of bone. I can wish for sanctity and redemption. I can hope for bowling. Asparagus. A freshly mown lawn. And yet I do not like asparagus and I own no lawn. What I am this moment is determined by intrigue and the contour and texture of time, which is 9:09 a.m., and time for breakfast.

I make scrambled eggs and toast slathered with cherry raspberry rhubarb jam and watch the news. Thirty-one hikers were feared dead near the peak of a volcano in a mountainous region west of Tokyo, Japan. The eruption was a complete surprise. There had been weeks of minor earthquakes but nothing that seismologists had interpreted as a warning of a major event. The release of toxic gases made it impossible to bring the corpses down. Ash covered everything. The volcano continued to spew billows of smoke. Military helicopters, negotiating the ash and smoke, were able to rescue a few more survivors on the volcano's slopes. More hikers awaited rescue in shelters.

George Clooney and Amal Alamuddin exchanged vows in an intimate ceremony at the Aman Canal Grande luxury resort in Venice,

Italy. They were married by the mayor of Rome, Walter Veltroni. Following the ceremony, a dinner reception offered lemon risotto with lobster, lemon ricotta agnolotti with arugula pesto, and Chianina beef with porcini mushrooms.

New Zealand scientists examined a giant squid weighing 770 pounds with tentacles like fire hoses and eyes like dinner plates.

A Chinese restaurant owner in New York City was arrested after allegedly lacing dishes with opium in an effort to keep customers coming back.

U.S. forces launched air strikes on territory controlled by Islamic State (Isis) in northern and eastern Syria. This included a gas plant outside Deir al-Zor and another in Homs that provided several provinces with electricity and powers oil field generators.

Another airstrike on mills and grain storage facilities in Manbij were mistaken for Islamic State holdings and killed civilians, which were mainly workers.

The spike in heroin use that has surged across the nation sowing panic in affluent suburban areas has been labeled a public health epidemic.

A new shape of brain cell was discovered in the hippocampus of a mouse brain.

What is reality? The question simulates wax.

But really, what is it? What is reality? A slice of toast still warm enough to allow a pat of butter to melt and become absorbed into the soft substance of the toasted bread.

The sharp granule which has strayed from Toby's litter box and is under my heel in the bathroom.

Edges, snow, studios, coasts.

Reality is that hurricane of inscrutable pink in the candle next to the coffee cup with the faces of the Beatles as they appeared in 1965.

Charles Baudelaire listening to Wagner.

As for goals, I have no goals. I want to visit Paris at least one more time. I want a haircut that resembles fog.

I'm an aging organism. An organism full of other organisms. Organelles, mitochondria, bacteria. My being is a constellation of microbes and cells and colloidal particles such as spaghetti.

Emotion is sweat. The lather of high intensity evolving into a travel accessory. Free will when it mulls a moment in a rocking chair. A conundrum ranked as a grassy thought. The feeling of fingers in electricity. Coal and the hardware of song. Spit and adjectives. Claws and wings. Eternity turning viscous with gestation, the birth of another star. And when the buttons are green the emotion is partly mercury. Who turned the faucet? Tattoos argue gloom. Their narratives obscure the parchment of skin with a scripture of the streets, dragons and roses, snakes and palm trees. As for me, I prefer abstractions. The charm of antiquity, the contempt of dragons.

Herds of diamond centipede moving toward a carnival of aphids.

THINGS EXCITE ME

Things excite me. Old albums. Thunderstorms. My desk.

My desk is a world of wood and memory. It excites my thinking. My atoms, my life.

I smell a loaf of freshly baked pumpernickel. It puts a glow in my head. A glorious bloodstream nourishes my muscles, organs, lungs.

A tug named Wahkiakum answers the waves with hawsers.

Memory, once awakened, may be experienced as jelly, or interior monologue.

I remember taking a bus to my job at Boeing in the summer of 1967, the number 132 crossing the South Park Bridge, the Duwamish gleaming below, and hearing for the first time the Beatle's "A Day in the Life" coming from somebody's transistor radio. It astonished me with its complexity and beauty. For days after I thought about all those holes in Blackburn, Lancashire.

I remember my walk down a long ramp into the factory darkness, machines pounding, whirring, buzzing. Drills, saws, lathes, presses, carbide grinders, the smell of grease. There was a huge vat of acrid chemicals for cleaning freshly molded metal parts. I imagined that if you fell into it they'd be pulling out a skeleton.

I worked with a guy who looked like Keith Richards who began his day with Dexedrine. His alarm would ring, he'd take some Dexedrine, go back to sleep, then awaken an hour or so later with a nice amphetamine buzz. Not a bad idea. One day, minutes after a reprimand from the supervisor, we looked at one another and each of us simultaneously registering the same sense of pervasive nihilism attached to doing this meaningless, boring work he said "for some reason, I just don't seem to care," and we broke into an endless fit of laughter.

I lasted until late summer then up and took off for California and Jim Morrison's Crystal Ship.

Everything is desire. Everything is chemistry. Everything is fight or flight. Everything is letters. Everything is inhabited.

There is moisture on the windows.

I admire your ability to imagine this.

Here is a hat for you: it has a large white plume and whistles.

I love the idea of a suitcase as much as the actuality of the suitcase itself. I love the idea of packing it with shadows. The sound of a stone in the middle of a stone. The hushed obscurities of a highway, a bikini left in the rain.

I hold an agate. The face of the rock is silent as the Buddha.

The glide of hypnosis is alterable. I don't know what to call this emotion. It creates electricity on a freshly folded Kansas bed. An old man making a Monte Cristo on sourdough.

BRIEF TO THE NOÖSPHERE

The hive is on hiatus but the bees gargle pencils. It's one of those kinds of motels. There are spirits in the curtain. Odors in the bedsprings.

The debris of my emotional life is wet. When I walk in the rain, it seems as if the night wears a blindfold.

I like to dive into books. My eyebrows grasp explanations and grow themselves into weather and empire.

Motion is goopy with blue. Even the leaves are prophesies.

Knowledge is what you know, said Gertrude Stein. I know that the boiling point of water is 212 degrees Fahrenheit.

I know that sunlight has no weight but that an equivalent mass for its energy can be roughly determined by the average radiation flux incident on the earth's surface multiplied by one half of the area of the earth. The formula $E=mc^2$ will thus yield an answer of 2.8 kilograms, albeit measured as seconds, not weight.

I know what time Café Vita opens at the bottom of the hill.

I know how much it will hurt if I punch the wall.

I know that a Noösphere is a sphere of human thought. I saw one in Vienna once as it streamed out of a mouth in a sentence of murmured marmalade.

I know the collective conscience of Grindavik, Iceland is the same as a pumpkin.

Glue is a purpose unto itself. It is its own sticky teleology. This is not a mere metaphysics but a refuge for the eyes. The clang of metal, the abdication of kings.

The siege cannot continue under these conditions. There is a weird coherence to the napkins, and the propellers are ravenous for experience.

Jingle your intuition. Sneeze on a rock.

There is a hit song that experiments with history. It ends badly, with truth and nudity.

I remember Rawhide on TV.

Hinduism is optional.

I just want to say, I relate completely to bread dough.

I can't tell you how the leavening of evil is purged by singing, but the chaudfroid can speak for itself.

ANODYNE

Control is an illusion. "The heart asks pleasure first," said Emily, "and then, excuse from pain; and then, those little anodynes that deaden suffering."

Let me tell you about those little anodynes. They're fantastic. But you can't always get a prescription for them, and you can't find them on a shelf at the drugstore.

It's not that they're rare. The anodynes I have in mind are morphine, Valium, Xanax, heroin, ibuprofen, St. John's Wort, skullcap and wild cherry bark.

Some are effective, some are not. Heroin works. Skullcap does not.

The best anodynes are the ones that make you put on a coat and argue the willpower of the environment. The breath coming out of my mouth becomes an anodyne, and my willpower has relations with external reality. Therefore the eyes of an inner vision are an anodyne.

Upstairs, it sounds like our neighbor is giving a walrus a scrub bath. The pipes groan and hiss like the stellar winds of a great madness. But this is not pain. This is annoyance.

The sloshing of the dishwasher is pleasing.

There are times when pain has value, but not sciatica. That's just dumb, meaningless, chronic pain. It contains its own private message. What is that message? Pain persists.

A heightened awareness of a pain can alter our response to the pain and transmute the pain itself from a leaden weight to a golden paradox. That there is pleasure in pain and pain in pleasure is more than simple mathematics. It's a transcendent glory.

But I agree with Emily. Deadening pain is the best solution.

It is the feeling of detachment, when "the Nerves sit ceremonious, like Tombs."

Morphine was first isolated in 1804 by Friedrich Sertürner and commercialized by Merck in 1827. The hypodermic needle was invented in 1857.

"First – chill – then Stupor – then the letting go."

"Life hurts a lot more than death," said Jim Morrison. "At the point of death, the pain is over. Yeah, I guess it is a friend."

HOW TO READ A RIVER

Think of a river. Any river. The Mississippi. The Missouri. The Snake. The Zambezi. The Yukon. The Paraíba do Sul. The Tigris.

We are all rivers. We vary as rivers vary. Vary in current, vary in color. Vary in depth, vary in width. Vary in shoal, vary in bank.

Some have the dazzle of diamonds. Others flutter over rocks in hilarities of white. Some feel warm. Some bite with cold. Some thrash, some more tranquilly go.

Flowing is primarily a horizontal business. It's important to absorb things, indulge yourself occasionally, have a few opinions about things.

Despair is only natural. It accelerates our ideas of transcendence.

Ask me about percolation. Percolation is hot water poured over a cone-load of freshly ground coffee. Denim trousers drying on a barrel. The first few drops of rain to hit the dirt.

An insect of a peculiar color walks to the edge of a roof and takes wing and disappears out over the water until a fish jumps up and takes it in his mouth.

Have you ever seen the sky in the jelly of a fish's eyes?

The eye sees only what the mind is prepared to comprehend, said Henri Bergson.

Does the universe have edges?

It does have a hole.

And a flow.

And an undulation.

I believe in reflections. I believe there is a face down below looking up at you. And a face above looking down at you.

Everything shimmers underwater. The eyes blur. The world blurs. Glide. Swirl. Rise and breathe the air. The muddy Mississippi air.

The human mind is charming. Open a book and study the life of ancient Egypt. Tell your muse to get busy. Tell your muse to become a waterfall. Tell your muse to become Memphis.

My story is simple. I break the water with one arm while pushing the water down with the other arm and kicking my feet and carving a stick of wood when it's over. If I feel like falling up I will fall up. Or not. It all depends on one's perspective. For some people down is up and for others what is up is down. Up and down are relative.

You can experience almost any kind of food by putting it in your mouth and chewing it but you can't describe how it turns to muscle or enriches the blood unless you sample a strawberry on the Mississippi.

There are immense subtleties in the fold of a napkin and the rills and dimples on the surface of a river have important things to say about the bottom. I can grasp the meaning of a fistful of words if I put them together a certain way. But as soon as I rearrange them they mean something else entirely different.

Water on the blacktop creates a sheen, but water in motion creates a skin.

PRESIDENT TAFT PRESSES A TELEGRAPH KEY

Let us consider President Taft. He sits, a large man with a walrus mustache, pondering a gold telegraph key. He cracks his knuckles. He leans forward. He presses the key. A surge of electricity travels through thousands of miles of wire to the west, across mountains and prairies and rivers and mills, factories and forests and bridges and trains, to put the Alaska-Yukon-Pacific Exposition into motion.

Mounted on a slope of picturesque Seattle commons, punctuated with towering firs and palatial exhibits, a huge gong strikes five times, an enormous American flag unfurls from a high scaffold, and Japanese and American fleets in Elliott Bay boom their tributes. Volumes of smoke drift over the water as the reports from the cannons resound in monumental concussions thrilling the crowd of people gathered for the opening of the fair into eruptions of unbridled joy.

The famous Bicket family performs at the foot of the Pay Streak and later there is a shoe contest. Everyone removes their shoes and puts them in a barrel. The barrel is placed in the center of a large open field. At the sound of a whistle everyone rushes out to the barrel to find their shoes. The winner must have his or her shoes laced throughout, and must stand at attention.

Calista Leach, the first American woman to visit Alaska, heads straight to the Alaska exhibit. Eight Inuit men join hands and begin circling to the left, chanting and leaping into the air, notwithstanding their heavy Oxfords.

Gas balloons carry toy flags over the crowd.

The Navy band plays Sousa marches.

There is a tug of war and a relay race and an exhibition drill by a company of blue jackets.

Beautiful snow white carrara marble statuary ornaments the entrance of the Oriental Building where there are displays of coral, cut silver, and Roman pearls.

Strains of music pour from the D.S. Johnston Company's Krelle Autogrand upright player piano housed in the spacious Manufacturer's Building.

Bud Mars makes his first ascension in a big dirigible balloon and circles the grounds while Princess Lala dances the barn dance with writhing reptiles in the Turkish Village.

Curtains are drawn on The Baby Incubator Exhibit, housed in a two-story neoclassical pavilion with Ionic columns and ornamental pilasters, between the Temple of Palmistry and the Gold Camps of Alaska.

Shouts and laughter come from the Fairy Gorge Tickler.

The Theater of Sensations opens its doors.

TENDENCIES TO EXIST

Physicists speak of "tendencies to exist." Matter at the subatomic level does not exist with certainty at specific locations or definite times and in identifiable form, but rather show "tendencies to exist," "tendencies to occur." The tendencies are expressed as mathematical quantities which take the form of waves. These are abstract mathematical waves, not the kind of waves that slop over the edge of a boat and get you wet. They're the kind of waves that give reality a certain feeling and flavor and happily elusive character. You get wet, but you get wet in a different manner of wetness. The water is wet. Blood is wet. Coffee is wet.

Reality is dry, like a nail.

Mallarmé arrives by bus.

The smell of an accordion serves to branch into semantic candy.

A life moves toward Grand Forks as Bob Dylan sings "Queen Jane Approximately" on the car radio.

Metaphor is a stuff that fattens on meaning by folding two separate realities into an architecture genial as a face.

Peter and Gordon. Who remembers them? "A World Without Love." "I Go to Pieces." "Lady Godiva."

The ocean has hills and busy pronouns have curls and mirrors. This means that you can argue with the shadows behind the taxi.

A mindful awareness of bone hops along in a semantic jewelry shining in the Andean sun.

Every cause has a wiggle. Rub what shield you have. The sky above is not what you think it is. It anticipates our visit. The mind will linger in it. The particles will make it polynomial.

Angels and clouds are benedictions. Forces of density will fiddle into an embassy of air to the glow of glows, which is the glow of morning.

The glow of snow.

The glow of singular pleasures held together by shoes.

The glow of the tendons in the clench of the fist.

The blood of the fingers the blood of the wrist.

The glow of nylon tents in the glow of a moonlit mist.

Beating and breathing and hallucination. Glue and outlines. Elongation. Tendencies to be cooperative. Tendencies to be in Paris. Velvet and lingerie. Immediate as wheels. Or however this feels.

THE COLOR

The artist glides through an art supply store looking for a color within. She can feel the color, but she can't name it. She can almost see it, but it's not that kind of color. It's not like, say, blue or red, a primary color that animates flags or exotic ceremonies. It's not green, definitely not green. Green is the color of nature, trees, shrubs, ferns, grass. This color is preternatural. It may not exist in nature at all. But it needs to. She needs to find this color and bring it into existence. Preferably in oil, though acrylic will do, perhaps even gouache.

The clerk is a middle-aged man with a mustache and thick brown hair who may have once been a pilot for an airlines but must now clerk in an art supply store. She doesn't know why she thinks that about him but she does. Can I help you, he asks. No, but thank you, she says. Ok, he answers, just let me know if you have any questions. He leaves her to her silence, her inner search, that ever-recurring cycle of questions that haunt most of us during intervals of quiet in our daily affairs. How many people at any given moment of the day that you see walking down the street or sitting in a car are experiencing their own private interrogation, their own private detective work, who am I, is there an end to the universe, what will happen to me when I die?

The color, she is sure, is a form of yearning. She can feel that. So it might be something purple. Or violet. Hyacinth or heliotrope. Mulberry or plum. But no. She doesn't feel a correspondence there. No true rapport, nothing that has that sound of soft summer rain late at night when the car doors have stopped slamming and voices are gone and there is nothing in the night but raccoons and wandering cats. That's the feeling but not the color. That comes close to the feeling. But it's not the whole feeling. It's only a part of the feeling. It may be there is no color for that feeling. It's not like the dots in the Sunday paper cartoons giving Dagwood and Blondie a life. That's partly what colors do, they animate things, people and seasons and birthdays and jokes.

Clowns.

Fruit. Embryos pulsing with life.

Bluish tints of membrane veined with blood.

She tries to imagine the color as a phantom, an ocean wave, the white robe of an aikido instructor, a gardenia bobbing in a light breeze. None of it will do. It's simply not that kind of color. The kind of color that gives things an identity.

And then she sees it, there on the bottom shelf. So obvious. How could she have missed it? She picks it up and brings it to the counter and the clerk comes to the register as she fishes out her wallet and credit card to pay for it. This astonishing color. This omelet of flame, this translation of pain, this perverse light shouted into cold oblivion. This madder red, this gob of blood.

BLACK HEAT

I get crazy over sewing. If I see a needle I grab it and crawl toward an image. I ooze from a line of poetry and the gray thread mingles nicely with the intestines.

Fasten a spoon to your lip, the emulsification of eggs in Miracle Whip.

The churchyard is sweet as a drug. Graves talk of shovels. We plunge into ourselves which awakens the grease of rumination. Picasso rubs a plasma TV.

Mohair happens. It just does. There is nothing else to add.

My ghost clenches a shirt. I rise and bring you a napkin.

Here. I need to hit this emotion with a roaring highway. The swans are dark water. The snow falls on the hood of our car and we are imbued with the grace of hypothesis.

The medicine is working. I wander reality in my Christmas opium.

I bewilder my earthquake. The radio emanates experiments in smell. The piano flares with red. The steak sizzles in the pan. The knife is sharp and the day is incendiary.

I stare at the stars and lift a sentence out of my brain. Its colors are strawberry and pink. I can feel the sugar of a running woman, a wound heal and grow into luxuries of thought. My plumes are diversions. There are oceans in our veins. Our ears are weird and explicit. We farm a convocation of eyes. If a paragraph floats, the engine is spectral as a horse galloping in a corner of leaves.

There are waves in our fingernails.

We stand on deck and watch the grebes spin out from the cliffs. We glide along a deformed syntax of rock and the black heat of the Arctic realms. The signs crave attention. The wound of existence brings us instinct. We cram it with gasoline and rub the day into velvet.

BRIGHT BLUE SLAPS OF SLOPPY CONVECTION

I find truth in my fingers and fidget until the letters I'm writing appear to make better sense as a wet hat, or a fiery brocade of hothouse glass. I make stupid decisions. It isn't a matter of thinking so much as bumping into things in the dark. The dark is a metaphor for a lost prescription and must be sprinkled with adjectives. Squeeze the moment. Some things can't be changed. Once sand always sand. I sip coffee from a mug with the Beatles on it and have some feeling of being of use to the universe, albeit in an emphatically useless kind of way. I am in a state of drifting, which is achieved by swinging on a trapeze of the imagination. Meaning has swings. That which does not swing is a root in eternity postulating light. Everything else is shaking or expecting rain.

It is wonderful that water has swimming in it. Swimming which is round, the way swimming was meant to be, aesthetic as a basketball. It is difficult to adapt to paint after summoning genies in words. The insistence is only natural in a pasture of buffalo. The spiritual unfolding of a moment is imposed by the stars and a singing goddess with fierce green eyes eating French fries. A simulation of fog assembled for just such a moment as this is tumbling around in a limousine and I have a parrot on my head. I can't remember why. My intentions get lost in the jewelry hanging from my throat, and the faulty GPS in this Subaru of words.

I think I was made to agree with skin. And I do. I agree with skin. I can wipe my lips with a napkin, and arrive at a sensation of cloth. This makes me brilliant and fun and worthy of a napkin.

We are on a hunt for meaning, you and I. My meaning may not be your meaning but together whatever chains and pulleys we work to make this happen will mean something one day. The chains will mean chains, the pulleys mean pulleys. The intermediate air will have to arrive at its own meaning, which will be a meaning separate from the meaning currently gestating in this communal dream of whipped cream and pork. It will be impelled by shoes, and involve prepositions and cork.

I am in a state of feathers and hear a waterfall. It is unpremeditated day, consonants scorched by reality. There is no burning but ice and cans of paint in reveries of fog and fire. The artist at the edge of existence rips the knowledge of asphalt in half and floats into a state of light that is neither electricity nor Wednesday but a sweet pure muscle that feels the weight and tug of testimony. The sky, full of bright blue slaps of sloppy convection, is pumped into life like an inflatable insect and weighs four hundred pounds. Autumn cavorts in the street. It is immediately stabbed by a strong wind and plummets into a local emotion. The sky makes everything look easy but it's not. Most of life flies through itself like an airplane.

The ugly feelings are the fertile ones and in grammar the nerves attract words that lead to the bones of the poem. The air is a lyric on the tip of a horn. Poetry must be an insurrection until the curl of frostbite is arranged by the window into a joke. The city stirs into life and Jackson Pollock stands before a kitchen sink scouring a pan with all his might. He has to. It's a pan. Pans must be scrubbed. Paint splattered. Paint dripped and ladled and drooled until a universe is born.

GOING ON ACCOUNT

It's true. I'm a pirate now, sailing my own private Caribbean, sails flapping, halyards straining, desperation feasting on the pearls of obdurate hope. I am scudding the seas to redeem the dream of romance. The moon shines like a glass of milk breaking on the floor. How do I shape reality? I twist it into a flower of iron. I am bursting with confusion. Rain walks on my head. I hear the fabulous echoes of a thousand sirens singing a thousand songs. My beliefs are long and wide like the flight of swallows. Well then, let's have a toast! There is a whisper of blue on my suitcase and a memory caught in my nerves whose suppleness of perspective has become spatial as a drop of rain and unravels the ghosts of murdered desires. My fingers burn. I work the yardarms. I cram each sentence with an ocean and a catastrophe. I ignite the gaze of midnight speculation. I wonder if I can write as great as Kerouac. How far does the sky go? It spits images against the eyes. The dead walk the waves with apples and balloons. Technicolor angels brush the clouds. Coral snakes and alligators swarm in my sperm. I live the studio life of the Bateau Lavoir when Picasso painted his harlequins and sad blue women. I study the architecture of hunger. I listen to intuitions. I have a map of heaven and a map of hell and they are the same map. I've seen great wonders. I've seen colossal beasts emerge from the depths and skeletons dance on the waves. I've seen Paris and London and the Beatles on Ed Sullivan. I wear a hat built of carefully chosen twigs. It moves me to build a worm. The feeling is rendered in syllables. The feeling twitches into life and squirms. What is despair? It is Europe weeping in the gloomy rain. It is a subjunctive mood broken into fjords. It is being alone in Mexico City. The life we lead is invisible. Reach into yourself and pull out a blazing evocation. The horizon lures us into travel along the rim of a bowl. Wounds are healed by the sound of the harmonica. Word by word I feel a poem aching in the bone of the arm making its marks on paper. I feel the rupture of a wave with a thousand wild arms. The mind plays with the dark. Jokes about the cemetery have the smell and chill of the ocean at night. I feel the creak of shifting planks, the hungry egos of poets. The brain is a pudding. Audacity is its own reward. Iron is widely literal, and that is a good sweet sound when it is uttered by a harmonica whirring round itself in a delirium of music. I like my coffee black. I like the woman who sells combs at the public market in Havana. I like Noguchi's Great Rock of Inner Seeking. The water is yawning above this structure of sculptured thought. What amazement in trying to scrape the cartilage of need from the bones of disdain. I sense the presence of fish. It is the sound of drums. I'm cold as a wet boulder. I move against the current. I smell the breath of old wood conversing with its element the sea. I feel the agitation of an invisible placenta in the ancient womb of night. The worse pains are the ones that sit on your heart like egrets of regret. The greatest treasures have nothing to do with gold, or jewelry, or coins. They are the things we find in corners. In dreams. Goats on an emerald hill soft as the break of day.

WHAT REALLY MATTERS

I'm haunted by morning because your neck is beautiful and a word crawls out of my mouth and crackles with Strindberg. Your heat feels so good infinity bursts out of a coin of pure sterling and spends itself on a definition of chrome.

My mind is empty and parallel to a hug. We age together like hawks.

The garden is a component of dirt. Handstands venerate the earth. Let us chat and imitate clarinets. We are little streams to one another beside the post office. Our thoughts flow through a canvas of rain.

A head is for healing the erudition of rubber. Cotton redeems the audacity of flags. Words are tangential to cabbage, which is a literal confusion of whispering intestines.

The tattoo squirts peacocks whenever I open a midnight towel.

I see pink horses gallop around a porcelain washbowl in which soapy water glitters with words. My injuries are amusing. My beliefs are shiny.

Poetry is a device for understanding water.

Go, grab a dream and sleep. There are parables to discover.

What really matters is being unconscious. That's where the fun starts. The surfaces drop through themselves like little fingers of rain over and over again.

My pen is talking to me. It says anguish is singing in a cemetery.

It says the river keeps going.

It says the blisters smell of mythology, and boats.

BLOSSOMS OF ERMINE MOSQUITO

I wear the mask of a wizard. I like to groan when I'm sick. I am pushing this sentence into your mind. I'm driving it like a tractor. I'm plowing the air. I'm seeding the air with words. The words grow into metaphors. Meaty metaphors. Meataphores. I am king of an invisible empire. A thought drags itself across this sheet of paper and becomes a fish. I have to write a pool of water for it. Write write write write write until writing is water and the fish has a place to live. I think of the brain as a fishbowl. I think of my body as a shape that is capable of motion and that the motions that a body make have something to do with the shape of the body. Take legs, for instance. Or arms. Who doesn't love to swim? Or walk? Or run? If I see a palette and a doorknob poking out of the sand I dwell in sympathy and perception and this is a sign that is good for me and compels me to think the universe has some meaning and order but that often that order is random and chaotic and there is nothing merrier than a sack of nails. Or the feeling of heat on a porch after the sun has been shining on it all day. This is why violet is the least literal of colors and there is a tug contending with space and time and there is a vowel that smells like an area code and a consonant that smells like rubber. I can hear an image crashing among a body of words and hear it approach what is it why it's an extraterrestrial eyeball supporting itself on a thousand legs. Imagine that. Imagine a man speaking into a microphone and saying things that nobody understands. Imagine an animal constructed of sugar standing at a brightly lit bus stop. This is why gravy sometimes resembles a fabric and a bowl of conversation is heavy as a terrarium. We embellish the cabbage we have with the cabbage that we don't have. And the world is no wiser for this, but the fish are happy, and there is now a primrose pushing against the wind where formerly there was nothing but a sheet of paper and oceans of space and palaces of mist and fog. This is why I often dream of owning a canoe, and a streetcar named Fiduciary climbs the hill with a clang and a rumor writing itself into blossoms of ermine mosquito.

TRACTATUS TARANTELLA

My voice comes out of me as snakes. It finds shadows in words. There are shadows and there are men. There are women and there are names. The world divides into facts. My tongue divides into Joyce Carol Oates.

Ask not what your embrace can do for the sky ask the sky what your embrace can do for talking. Space is what happens when gravity opens a door in your head.

The fence wobbles with its own essential fact.

The fact is experienced as an epiphany. The method is codeine. The fact must be rendered frankly or else it is personal and smells of consciousness.

The fact must be appreciated as objective and unembroidered and jolly.

The fact crawls with the fecundity of plankton.

Walls occur equally to a stepladder. The cemetery winch has its peculiarities. The fact of space is rooted in its phantoms. Here we have a contradiction. Contradiction must be welcomed, for it is a form of exhilaration.

Let us examine Bach. If I plug a cord of Bach into a wall, I see that it becomes cellos and trumpets and there is an infinite number of names with different meanings. And this is because of the organ, whose sound is so huge that it buttons eternity with gold.

The sentence works if the parrots are water. I wish I could cloud the literal with metaphor, but the helicopter is fueled by abstraction, and the mountain wrestles an infantry of water in my face.

I laugh at the idea of outdoors. I wax hormonal. I plunge into pronouns.

Go ahead. Take a picture. It is possible to form a picture of the world once the facts have been painted green and there is a motion that finds its expression in a tarantella.

In the atomic fact, says Wittgenstein, objects hang one in another, like the links of a chain.

In the wet fact of the afternoon the streets shine with the sheen of the rain.

Death falls from a strawberry and the spirit protects the beauty of similarity. The women form a circle and dance themselves into delirium. And this is called syntax, for which there is no other fact than the gargle of its own construction.

GOOFY

I feel goofy. I really do. Goofy as a goat. Goofy as a thumb. Goofy like a
shrug made of rawhide. Goofy like a shave. Goofy like a scarf. Goofy as
dots in a comic strip. Goofy as frangipani. Goofy as phosphate in a
urine sample. Goofy as a bloodmobile on Puddinghill Road. Redwood
dripping with cosmos. Fables and intoxication. Fever dream preserved
in ice. Antique liquids creating color in a traffic light. Some things tend
not to be goofy but are sometimes goofy. Sympathy can be goofy but it
can also be cruel. Sympathy is cruel unless accompanied by empathy
and the empathy is as goofy as it is brushed and luminous. It some-
times feels good to be a mollusk, and nautical to feel the world gone
wrong. English is a form of clay. It's malleable, savage in its acquisitions
and permeable in topaz. There are philosophies useful to carry around
with you, definitions of mulch and mulberry, acetylene catfish magnetic
as dissolution and delicate as the expressions of shoes. Emotions akin
to surgery flooded with epitome. Voices lengthen into daylight and in-
quire: is a faucet possible? Yes, if water can boil, anything else is a mere
tattoo on the limbs of the waterfall. Call it an alligator if you want. It's
always a little like eggs inside a noun. Name anything and it will draw
itself into your mouth for utterance. It'll make you goofy. It'll ejaculate
English. You'll spin around archaeology like an experience spilling into
words. Any texture will make you happy. Part of this means burlap and
part of this means something else entirely. There's significance in the
taste of cinnamon. DNA in rope. Tactics in cactus. Let things happen.
Why is the dawn so goofy? Why is everything suddenly a locomotive?
Reality is too obscure for a grocery receipt. The logic of crosswalks
defeats the cackle of asteroids. But it will not defeat the details of every-
day life. Belts, lulls, yo-yos. You name it. I can imagine other dimen-
sions. Arguments multi-layered as onions. Violence comes natural. It's
the fat light of hilarity that gets you in the end. There is such a thing as
seepage and it's the nerves that reveal its squirrels. Cellophane wrapped
around an apricot. Harmonies glimmering like negligees in the rainy
evening of a gooey fug. The smack of savor waltzing in kilowatts of

salted herring. Fuzz hemorrhaged as hands. Scripture busy with conjuration. Embouchure trembling with the language of insinuation. Telescopes whose organs pump foxglove into whirling intervals of meat and meaning. The meaning of meat is in the blue of its energy, its correlative barley, its totems of buxom verticality ravenous for the eyes of insects. The perfect temperature of syllables committing themselves to the fullness of being in an oyster and the gradual formation of a pearl of beatitude or barrel roll or bearing. Metamorphosis draws indigo into Edinburgh where it becomes a volume of the history of sexuality and simmers with ancient mirrors. Feel the halos surround the pulpit lungs. If a flag flaps an emotion in blue an emotion in mercury will bang into consciousness and curl into vertebrae. Dog scale. Ego spoon. Negative squad of glacier diaries. The smell of the willow. All that description on the beach waiting to elicit glass, a bowl full of prunes, a bonfire in a dream of sound.

ENFOLDINGS

Napkins have become theater. They're folded so intricately, uniquely, into such a variety of animals and objects and patterns and shapes. A man talking into a microphone, a meat loaf, a soliloquy of cloth, a brain crawling toward a thought. It is astonishing what worlds can be created by folding a napkin. Jimi Hendrix strumming an electric guitar, a lost cat hiding under a hedge of laurel, Elvis Presley singing "That's Alright Mama" on the Louisiana Hayride Show in 1954. One enters a restaurant and is led to a table and invited to sit down. You sit down. Everyone sits down. You all stare at the napkins. The swans, Ferraris and Impalas, Elizabeth Taylor shouting at Richard Burton in *Who's Afraid of Virginia Woolf*. I'm pretty good at folding towels. I'm not so hot at folding shirts. But fold a napkin into a suspension bridge or a scene from *Wizard of Oz*, that I cannot do. The sun forges a new day. The sun folds the day into a lute. The sun folds the day into a glass of root beer. The sun itself is folded. A ball of light folded into a nuclear furnace darting its flames into space. Space itself is folded. There are folds of gravity and folds of time. How does one fold the phenomenon of distance? Of a propagating wave of light? How does one do that? Where does one begin? With the right corner, the left corner, all four corners simultaneously? How does one flip it, crease it, tuck it? One begins with a periodic lattice in a higher dimension. Fold the lattice by taking one end and sliding it under the other end. Make your folds exciting and smooth. Make them subtle as the heart of a bubble. Make them as convoluted and many as the folds of the brain. As a golden mean convulsing in a glass of milk. Make your folds deliver tendencies of shape. Shorelines incidental to the memory of a dance. Storm waves, sea caves, columns of rock. Make your folds long and wide and cinematic. Make them glide and hover over a table of horsehair fern and browsing brontosaurus. Make your folds balance a metaphor on a vacuum. If you can fold a sweater, you can fold a hem-stitch cotton napkin into a telescope and hold the universe in a lens of incidental linen while you bring a mouthful of tender halibut to your lips and the room expands and the weight of a thousand shadows ripples through the rings of Jupiter.

CHARGE

My charge is being a horse. My hunger is nucleation. My drapery is a simple shout toward punctuation. My providence is a photogenic king deepened in ecstasy aboard a Greyhound destined for Tuscaloosa. I am the rascal that stipples in raw peppered light while falling forward toward a haunted thud of grammatical flies. I am a hill in a calendar for the year 1852.

Buffalo Bill discusses his comb with a mons pubis. The landscape is infinite in a flower. I fasten a pumpernickel across a flap of swollen scenery. Max Jacob manipulates clay around the cook. A book is born from his puffs of steam.

I am a monster so riotous in nouns that a blister haunts a delay in glass. I garden a Möbius star beside a surgical color and produce a whisper of sails by strumming a gas station flint.

I am a dimension tied together with string floating a lovely propane in a pool of musical wax.

I'm a phonograph playing a 45 so fractious that it seeps a glaze of rock mountain jelly. We watch the drums. My yearning pins a blaze to the wilderness. We lift endeavor along the middle groove and lean into barcaroles.

Riddles happen when glue happens. We scratch the skin to mark our talk.

Incense is what so gleefully incentivizes a hit song during dispatch that it crumples the fire in a grandfather clock. Sirens stretch exhibiting suction and ooze.

There is a pressure that grows around gravity and is called a vortex.

The concept of brightness eludes itself. My arm occurs and obscures a lobster I hold in orchidaceous emotion. There is a greenhouse where my rock emerges and pushes an array of potatoes up through the dirt of a thousand intentions and cuts the sky into pieces of time. I agree to the use of turpentine but pound the milk for a better performance. I don't like to navigate unless I have wings, or at least a bone I can pull into music and sigh.

LET US QUERY THE BOILING SUN

Let us query the boiling sun. There is snow on the linoleum. How did it get there? And that stirring in the air just before it rains, that easy murmur in the trees and flowers, what is that? Pain is nature's way of holding our attention. We already know that. But will the day get warmer? Will the pumpkins grow into oracles? No sensation escapes the pound of my fist. I cover the waterfront, as it were. However anarchic the words may be, they harden into guns. Life is notoriously difficult to put into words. The celerity of the cell is amphibious as a penny in love with a barrel. Think, for instance, of the wiggle of snakes, staircase infidelities, crabs in bags. The Tiffany lampshade reflected in the glass of the Matisse print. A burning photogenic horizon clapped to the wall in afternoon elation. The day drifts, as always, into desuetude. My papaya slowly sours. My forebears perpetually glower. My guitar gently weeps. I went to get the clothes out of the washing machine and put them into the dryer. The corridor was so crowded it was like swimming through people. I did a butterfly stroke through a conversation about London tailors. Hotels are like that. You are far better off to stay at home. Or prance around naked on the desert of pagan Nevada during that Burning Man festival. I mean, if you really want to get down to it, everything is alive and imbued with consciousness. The sky speaks to the mountain in thunder. It bellows. It groans. It rains. Before you know it you've got a soliloquy on your hands. The sky is crying look at all those tears roll down the street. Nature's propositions thicken with each new crisis. Which is why I don't understand sports. What difference does it makes how many points are gained by carrying a ball across a chalked line or pushing it through a hoop or kicking it into a net past the outstretched arms of a man hurling himself into space in order to prevent that very thing from occurring? I am in quest of meaning. I have to get up and blow my nose. The mind dilates under the influence of poetry. Did you know that? Of course you did. Why else would you be here? But let me ask you this, and I want a sincere answer, have you ever thought about becoming a star in Hollywood? Each afternoon for the past several weeks I have passed a small group of Mexican men constructing a driveway with bricks, each brick meticulously measured and put into place. This is the way to push consonants into nerves. How else capture the lurid meaning of a pair of shoes? There is joy in opening a parachute. Even when you're still on the ground. I can always sense when there's a good metaphor in the vicinity. They happen by intuition and elude the deviations of authority. The rain stumbles across the ground in a blustery wind and the paragraph engorges with heat, as if it were plugged into spring, and fragrances ran through the wires, galvanizing our ears with the smell of an emerald idea.

BARRACUDA

If I begin a novel can I begin it like this? I will consider tattoos.
Nothing evolves without Shakespeare.

I sit on the deck of a sport fishing boat off the coast of Bermuda
thinking of Prospero and Caliban and such stuff as dreams are made
of. The engine roars into life, the propeller churns, and nebulas of
purple dye swirl in a Phoenician pool.

Words are neurons. Syllables thrash about in a bed of mud.

I am a giant inflatable Santa Claus on the lawn of a dilapidated
house. I sew words together with a thread of mist. I make gestures to
no one in particular.

I am a chow chow wandering the figures of a crèche. I wag my tail.
One of the wise men topples over.

I am an emotion painted in Montmartre. Threads of indigo shine
beyond the canvas of night.

I feel the private steel of a crescent moon.

Morning arrives like a parenthesis of pine.

I shower. I like the feeling of water running down my skin.

The fingers of dawn smear the highway with gold. I drive a '65 Ply-
mouth Barracuda listening to Elvis sing of burning love. I see Buffalo
Bill ride a palomino to the crest of a butte.

I feel like a form in quest of a silhouette. My heart crackles with the
wood of revolt. The town recedes in the rear view mirror. I hear a siren.
I step on the gas. A hopped up 360 with dished pistons gets me safely
across the border.

Some of us worry about morality. I write letters to dead poets.
Sometimes they write back.

PHANTOM SENSATIONS

Bounce the structure until it imparts vitality. This is so reflection sticks to medicine. Flow science into this smear. Glow close to your anguish. It will engorge you with correspondence. Widen yourself with subversion. Pin a tear to the tidepool elbows. A railroad happens in the mind. Heart gloves protect the fingers and what fingers perform which is accommodating and drills. Paddle a modified emotion. Escape your grammar. Disturb a fire. This will all make sense when you toss mahogany into the light. I sense spit. Emptiness behind eyeballs. This will develop over the generations into an area code for phantom sensations. This will evolve into a thesis. There will be mustard available if the glaze begins to sputter with palominos. Connection is the most important thing. Connect yourself to a pain and see it if it becomes a resource or history. This will confirm you. Despite the sparks the emotion painted beneath the religion has a certain aesthetic that authorizes outdoor volleyball. This is a gallon of soothed gasoline and this is a rock prophesying a monumental rescue. Let us oblige the anonymous world with our explanations of elsewhere. Coffee will build us into men and women. Employ spoons scrupulously. Syllables are straw. Elevators flap open inviting ascendance. Hum the bacteria before the insects get to it. If you turn chiaroscuro make your fingernails glow. Freely nutmeg the infusion. Gallop slam beside crackle. Rub the springy secrets. Our outdoors is Cubist. Hymn a bean ball. Bend your eyes to the sweet color of oil. Share your sphere. Sew the snow. Extrude indigo. Urge an arm dot. A singing circumference assembled in string. Pile sunlight on a cod. Exult the space around a noun dumping salt. Spur your interior to groan for our lobster. It agrees with virtue and flickers with gold. Construct a slender animal. Cartilage will declare us wrestling it out if the canoe leans more in the water. Our grace smacks of naked hypothesis. I think my duty urges this. I suck the candy of despair. A surge of lightning garnishes the horizon. Gray is absorbed by purple. A fountain gets up and walks away after it becomes skin. A magician juggles eyeballs. Belief searches oblivion for signs of redemption because the greenhouse was damaged by metaphysics. Nevertheless your breath is beautiful when it is engorged with abstraction. I open my cage to greet you. Tell me if my diagnosis fires. Advance yourself in a wild demand. Plunge your heat into sculpture. I will tell you when the tin turns churn.

THE SHINE OF ETERNITY IN A POSTCARD RACK

Language is shaped by abstraction. Which isn't saying much. But it's true. The luminous roots of a ripe truth blossom into similes. A mouth is like a spout and a tornado endorses the airport spoons. The structures endure. Envy hurls its descriptions of wealth at a single wool glove and unemployment is ghostly. Anyone will tell you that. A dazzling evocation is longer than a murky sensation and the day convulses with parody. I'm not joking. The travel agent dialed the wrong number and got Kierkegaard rather than Socrates. This is how we ended up in Corsica rather than the Canary Islands. The sculpture in the corner startled us with its exhalation. A small stone condensed the ocean into a hard inscrutable wrinkle. This is how perceptions happen. They begin as a stimulus in the nerves and travel to a place in the brain where paper lanterns float in the river Oi and images crash among the ganglion attracting mosquitos and flies. As soon as you begin writing poetry you find yourself in a foreign country. It may be the country of your origin, but it will soon enter your eyes and skull as a foreign country. That's pretty much the whole point. The reason for the endeavor. We walk among the cactus saying I like this, but I don't like that, and the world doesn't really give a shit. Space pulls a truck into the distance and lets us engage in our virginity. Our presumed virginity. Ha. What a laugh. A little paint goes a long way. Look at Picasso. How he oozed the torment of stone. Here is what I want these words to say. I want these words to flow through a sentence echoing intention as if they were a garden hose discussing water with a parenthesis of dirt. I want these words to slide into your eyes and tell you the pavement spits when the cars go by. I will fold these syllables into a swordfish if I have to. I will remain still and spin. I want to be your travel agent. I want you to go somewhere calm and beautiful. I will bring you soap and socialism. I will give you a ticket to an airplane. Here I am flailing the air. Here I am attempting to perform these wonders. I don't know why, but it is always the birds that explain the secrets of the sky. The clouds just wander through. Imagine what they could do if they were freed into words. They could become abstractions. The absence behind the words. The shine of eternity in a postcard rack.

NO COMPLAINT

I saddled my horse and rode off the page. I sensed something larger outside the margins of the paper. Outside the millions of laptop screens. The day convulses with parody. Everyone seems hypnotized. But maybe that's just the cocoon of silence that protects us from one another. The river honors its unraveling by mirroring the trees along its banks. It arrived in New Orleans the next day fresh as the proverbial daisy. Why a daisy? Who knows. I try to avoid overthinking things whenever I can. The field is open. Someone is painting the meadow. The canvas slobbers with balloons and drums. Name something in life that isn't completely open to interpretation. Which is why we are creatures of chronology. That is, ultimately, the easiest way to create a sense of coherence. And which is why we are always absorbed in navigation. I wrestle with this all the time. When did the pronoun 'I' acquire psychic reality? My ear is soft and itchy. It contributes its share. My sorrows are parliamentary and wax. Sunlight travels through the fingers. Bones hold everything together. I see the wind far out on the horizon and wonder excites the urge to swim. I spend so much of time just sitting around maneuvering phlegm. Clearing my throat. Blowing my nose. Biology is messy. All the poets sitting on the shelves at your local bookstore will tell you that. There is a feeling in me that is large and musical and demands to be shared with someone. I roll a ball to the cat and he just sits there. He looks down at the ball and looks back up as if nothing happened. As if to say, what's this about? I'll tell you who I admire is Montaigne. He went to his library and forged so many inquiries of this world they're still waiting for me to get to them. I pull the book form the shelf and hold it to my ear. The language burns and crackles. The next thing I know I'm in the water and the more I absorb the more expansive I become. This is not my normal latitude. But I'm not complaining.

CONFESSIONS OF A CLOSET HOARDER

I'm a closet hoarder. That doesn't mean I hoard things in the closet (though in fact I do), I mean it more in the metaphorical sense as a peccadillo invisible to the random gaze of John Q. Public. I refer, specifically, to the hoarding that goes on in my wallet. It is a large wallet of finished leather which I purchased some years ago at a public market. The generosity of its size is compounded by the intricacy of its compartments. Even in its infancy, when it held but a few plastic cards, I had trouble wrestling it out of my back pocket. Lately, it has become unusually fat and unwieldy. I save everything: receipts from the ATM, grocery receipts, new shoes and shoe repair receipts, doctor appointments, dental appointments, movie ticket stubs, business cards, poetry manifestos, deflated balloons, disarmament treaties, cooking recipes, flower petals, American primitive paintings and a Triple A card even though we no longer own a car. In order to function in the public and produce the right card at the right time, I have to shift and rearrange the vast assortments of card and identity housed within its chambers. It is a labor conducting transactions with this behemoth of a billfold. Why, one is bound to ask. Why do I not purge its contents of detritus? In a word: fear. The fear of missing a receipt to prove to the bank that a quantity of missing money is their fault, not mine. This has never happened, but there is always a first time. There is the fear of accident, the fear of arrest, the fear of liability. The fear of pandemonium in general. Loss of identity, loss of direction, loss of esteem when it is discovered I do not have the proper tickets, the proper sanction, the proper license, the proper documentation. Many years ago I visited a nude beach. I undressed at the car and walked with my companions onto a California beach as naked as the day we were born. It felt odd, of course. The sensations of wind and heat and sand and exposure were all novel and awkward and strange. But by far, the strangest sensation, the one that proved most difficult to assimilate, was the lack of a wallet. There was nothing about my person to declare officially and indubitably who I was. Nothing happened. We enjoyed our day, returned to the car, dressed, and returned to normal society. But the feeling persists. The feeling of security I feel when I wrestle this leather prodigy out of my back pocket and slide a credit card or library card or organ donation card from its bowels, and endorse my needs with a stratum of permits, privileges, and approval. For as long as I can remember, I have never been without it. It is an appendage as pertinent to my welfare as a kidney. It is a comforting lump pressed against my buttcheek, and in it is the story of my life.

MARK TWAIN'S TYPEWRITER

There is an image among these words. I put it there earlier this morning. I wrote it down. I used words to describe it. I used words to identify it. But now I can't remember what it was. Was it a sun? A moon? Mark Twain's typewriter in Virginia City? Where did the image go? Am I sure I even wrote it down? I may have dreamed writing down a paragraph with an image in it. A strong, powerful, intense image. Or was it a more tenuous and ephemeral image? A web? A ripple of moonlight? A stain on the rug? I know it's there. I know it's here. Lurking. It must be an animal. That's it. I wrote down an animal. But what animal? Did I refer to Mark Twain's typewriter as an animal? Did I call it a hyena? I would not say that about Mark Twain's typewriter. Whose keys must have been dusty. Mark Twain refers to the constant, ubiquitous dust of Virginia City. How they even had to put the assaying scales in a glass case to prevent the dust from compromising the accuracy of the weight. I'll bet that's what I meant to write down. That's the image. It was dust. It wasn't the typewriter. It wasn't an animal. It was dust. The dust of Virginia City. Quiet as eternity on the keys of Mark Twain's typewriter.

JUKEBOX GENESIS

Why is it so hard to start something? A conversation, a sauce, a correspondence. There is a teleology to swallow. One becomes Quixotic. One must renounce the place where one has become settled and sure and risk the hazards of destiny and fortune. There is nothing sadder than a dream in formaldehyde. The fossils embedded in limestone haunt the imagination with ancient beginnings which have since developed into ears and vertebrae. Vowels emerge from the clash of syllables and shoulder the primal life of the piccolo. All commencements diversify into adjectives and cantaloupes. We accommodate the veins of a swirling philosophy. Once something starts, there is no telling where it will go. This is particularly true of paragraphs. This paragraph, for instance. It wants to be a belt buckle. But I refuse to let that happen. I will stand in the way of this paragraph. I began this paragraph, and I will end this paragraph. It is mine to guide. It is mine to cultivate. Nevertheless, when it ends, as all things do, I don't see a paragraph. I see a fountain of words answer to the ghostly embryo of a belt buckle. I see a ghostly embryo step into the nerves of being and jump into a jukebox and narrate the genesis of a kiss. And I strain to get out of this paragraph. This paragraph in which a needle has come down into my back and scrapes a song out of it.

TANTAMOUNT TO MAUVE

Morality is a feeling, a fast green ocean in a decimal. Scent means sent if our granite darkens a raspberry soda and our opera gets shaken into bones.

This is tantamount to noise, but is experienced as chowder.

The mind appears to be nerves and blood. But this is the materialist view. Some believe the mind is a language dilating with elation. I believe the mind is a majesty of quick bright glitter.

There is honesty that is deformed and aluminum. This kind of honesty is good for stirring soup on the prairie and serving it to hungry men.

Wrinkles are pink and cluttered and scientific.

I wander around in my head and fall asleep.

And wake up as a philosopher. This makes me feel equal to the moment, which varies from minute to minute, like impulse and gravel.

Somewhere below this sentence there is an event cowering in its own wisdom. If this can be imagined, then what is a table? What is a chair? What is the United States?

Truth pops like a balloon. The shreds come down as words. The words become libraries. Analgesics gleaned from spider venom.

Why not just fall off of the edge of the world and bounce through space like an RV with a harridan inside?

I feel the warm weight of my body preparing to make a sound. This will be a radio made of cauliflower in which the actors do somersaults and the universe is worn like a tie clasp.

Friction scatters my reflections. It chitchats into hands and scratches. The climate of a spark twinkles through a reproductive organ. This is it. This is the organ as it twangs. This was embellished by language before it happened. And then it coughed into life and a color appeared that enriched our ears with tornados of syntax.

Reality bounces into a wall. Music bubbles out of it puny and wet like an eyeball.

I continue my research on the harmonica. The hunchback of Notre Dame walks among these words. It's that moment of the day when hallucinations turn henna and retreat into art. I fold the air into a chimera, and step back to find joy in the sound of the weather, which is dreamy and soft today and tantamount to mauve.

Why mauve? Why not teal? Why not cobalt?

Mauve is the color of the mind when it parallels the curve of the watermelon, and goes gentle as a thought into dissipation, an example of thinking in the deification of trout.

READY TO SURFACE IN ALL RESPECTS

Our realtor is worried about selling our apartment. He believes it is a submarine. We cannot convince him otherwise. I agree that our apartment is a little small and more than a little cluttered. We have a lot of books. The sensation of standing or sitting in our apartment is not unlike being in a submarine. It is also partially underground, so that the view from our living room window is that of a few small plants and a snail or two. But it is not a submarine. "How many fathoms deep are we today?" he asks. I tell him that we are at sea level, on top of a hill. "I can feel the pressure," he says, "the inconsolable darkness of the abyss." He sits down on the couch, a look of awe and stupefaction in his face, and points to what he says is a flashlight fish. "This is wonderful," he tells me, "but I cannot sell this property until it surfaces." "Ha ha. Good one!" I say. "What do you mean?" he asks. "I mean, we're not in a submarine. Our place is small, and we have a humidity problem, but calling our apartment a submarine is a little exaggerated, wouldn't you say?" "Then how," he affirms, "do you explain that?" "What?" I ask. "That hotwater geyser spewing a black billowing mass of minerals and liquid carbon dioxide and what appears to be a Pacific Blackdragon with a long chin whisker dangling above a giant isopod. I won't lie. This property will be a hard sell. People are fussy about mold, but when they see a hydrothermal vent enveloped in giant tube worms they may balk. I see you've got a new dishwasher and smoke alarm, and that will help, but there is so much more to do before we can get this place properly staged. And for that to happen, we will need to surface." "But we are," I insist, "we're on the surface. That's the door to the hallway. And look, over there, that's the kitchen window. You can see the porch. The mailman was just here. Didn't you see his legs? The man has the hairiest legs I've ever seen. How could you miss them?" "I did not see the legs of a mailman," he said, "I saw the tentacles of a giant squid undulating in lyrical inquiry as it went gliding past the window." He bent his arm around to his back and groaned. "It's my back," he says, "these underwater pressures affect my spine. I must leave soon. I just want you to look through the notebook here at some of the properties you might be interested in as soon as we return to land and can spend some time visiting a few addresses and neighborhoods." We look through the glossy pages of the notebook at beautiful kitchens and beautifully appointed bedrooms with views of the city or a nearby park. It occurs to us to hire a realtor who can better represent our apartment as an apartment and not a submarine but we have a made a promise to this man. We will have to stage it as he insists. We will need some radar masts, communication antennas and periscopes. We will need to have someone clean out the ballast and trim tanks. He recommends a little oil for the rudder and a maid brigade for the mess deck. I don't know what to say. He hands me a list of numbers for contractors, electricians and welders. He gets up slowly from the couch and we shake hands and walk to the door and stand there. I gaze into his eyes as he waits for me to give the signal to surface. There are pressures in his eyes, fathoms I cannot plummet. I shout "stand by to surface," and he smiles.

ROMPER

If a dynamic impertinence impels the greenery, than the sensation of flipping will pleat the damask. Rain's illusionism circulates it. Your pamphlet makes nothing but sense. A stepladder walks the transformation to the end of the wharf and plummets into grammar. The strain of everything emerging brims with chiaroscuro and so confirms the enormity of Rembrandt.

A metaphor fulminates along the next line, this line, and enters the book in the form of a leg, my leg. I have four legs since blazing into conquest. My elevator embarks at dawn. Inventions tease the paint. A paraffin yardstick drips with sexual innuendo. I push it to the back where it educates a knob.

I have the duty to convulse with breakfast. This concerns simulacrams of space. The bikini burns quicker under the hive of antiquity than the oil of hereafter. The proverb has mentally adjusted itself to wax into gravity and assume the camaraderie of prose. The harmonica is an incarnation of rumor.

I am eager to equip our experience with bone. Black manipulates our summer fugue. I scrub the candlelight to believe in yellow. A wave is because fiddles are moonlight. The fat around the sweat of the world stirs with life as it slithers through space stealing glimpses of heaven.

We basket a Corot and split through the lobby. I rattle a spur and the grebes make echoes. I have greased this odor into dream. Religions smear my sand into a life of farming. I rock the garbage to jewel my concentration.

We stab the broken wind and grapple with rain. The mosaic butters its energy in an armchair designed to catch meditation. The brain beneath the drill sews ruffles into banging vermilion. A radical empiricism occurs with the percolation of morning at the forehead station. The train beneath my steering embodies a story of turbulence and spit.

The monotonous lamp is blackened by burning. I patch my ancestry and carry the spin past the resilience of history. There is an upheaval at the car wash. The nails snatch a door and grip a new frame. The flower is incidental to its seed.

Poke purpose and it will splash the orchard. I fall through a paradigm cooking rice on a blue fire. Your tongue is a blade. You cut the air and a sentence falls out. This is how we talk.

The wind grieves for the paint flaking from the barns of Montana. I happen to clapboard a house I imbue. A mountain circles its telling of rock and I believe it. The bitumen is new. I agree to haunt the abstraction until it projects an airport.

The gulls are funny. They stab the sky to watch the sublime. I stiffen from what I feel is real and brood in cogitation near the trash bins. There is a description of boxing that has been sewn to a wedge of library storm. Some debris has been added to make the clouds look cut and bleeding.

I have dangled scrupulously above this paper causing words to come into being and be here and describe something, anything, a feeling or grosbeak. This spring I shake with papier collé. I stand on the locomotive and rub. Here I must excuse the trembling. We are all enigmas of insult and yearning sailing out of subtleties of gabardine and mind.

PARABLE OF THE PARABOLA

I held the steam and scrubbed it. How do you do that? asked Willy. How do you scrub steam? It is so, you know, diaphanous. I said to Willy, because Willy was a good man and listened with both ears, we adapt to the heart's convulsions. I send my grammar to a public decipherment. It comes back as a dream. I am hirsute, Willy, and there are parts of my gut that have been forged in goldfish. What do you mean by that? asked Willy. It means that change is a tough and ornery lobster and once it gets you in its claws Maine will never be the same. I bowed my head and pulled a flood of words out of my arm. Afterwards, Willy stood naked in a paragraph looking clean as a sunrise on stilts. I can hear the dead, Willy, the dead straining to get back into this life. If I write a few words down it seems to help them. They boil and box according to their destiny and inclination and the music of the spheres. You want a good parable in life, Willy, a guideline by which to measure your conduct. What's a parable? asked Willy. A parable is a large dish to catch the hollering and caterwaul of the stars. I think that's a parabolic dish, said Willy. Ok, Willy, let's call it a parabolic dish. A dish of splendor hoisted into the sky of our discontent. I want to hear the birth of the universe. I want to see the legs of Divine Creation spread and the head of Being to emerge into the Nothingness of space. Can you do that? asked Willy. Why sure you can. All you need is a little patience, a good shiny belt buckle, some sparks and spars and wrinkles and doors and you've got yourself a human diesel in dominatrix boots. You've got the equivalent of a fugue clanking around in the metals of love. You've got something tender and pliant and potentially pink. All it really is, all any of it is at any given time, is consciousness, that flywheel of the head creating sequence and existentialism. I don't think I want any of that, said Willy. Who does? The whole idea is to get rid of it. Or concentrate real hard on not noticing it. That I can do, said Willy. Ah but it's tricky, Willy, trickier than you think. Because as soon as you begin to concentrate on not noticing it, the whole shebang gets bigger, magnifies, and before you know it there you are, dripping with moonbeams. The stars come and throw their light over the world and the dead finally do, do get back in.

MY AFRICAN EAR

One first has to think it, and then one arranges the words in that queer order we call a vulva. My African ear adjusts to your procedure. It packs its sleep in gauze. Walls an algebra to hats. My slouch agrees over a big idea. A fish my phenomenon catches. If you don't believe me these cubes will fang the edge. Drive the wood until it mingles. This is because gadroon. My finger sparkles like privacy. For example, this walks slowly with your olives. And why not? I know a role in such perception. So I say fur and adapt to wings. Puzzles I like epiphany with sputter. I play at elves. Hooked infinity that Nigeria miracles by pulling cork. I am much amazed but structure ribbons prettily into smells of consciousness. Definition in little pieces of pink light clutch all the roots in emission. The railroad shoots by stunning into power. I sweep my hunger into an emotion of salt. Nerves are words that swim in mirrors. Bouncing which a twist of lemon whispers some flip and is bombed through a fish. The studio has scribbles since medicine is pretty among ourselves. My trouble with ooze knocks on soap. I slip through my powder during gold. I blow my life through propulsion. The odor of elephants is worded until architecture absorbs the waitress. Egypt is lingered in sand. Sleep sparkles in space. Moving happens when the mass we wanted has tools which steam in twinkling Harar. The soar of necessity is luminous with eggs. Fields fill a forehead to pull us into grace. Warm hum of a fan. And this I like. I feel it thick and slapped and ice is sexual as rain on bamboo. One morning by ship stirs the senses to images where it hills into heft. The hull is sheer ears. The waves wear violins under the air. There is faith in occurrence since we smell bells in our pockets. I am burst into truffles and left. I crawl to Mali and bump the dirt. The thermometer grows my delivery. And when I'm a beard I extrude bronze like a swan brimming with feathers, bits of truth assembled to look like hues. The warm song of metaphor permits holes around the elbows and suitcases more forge than fire. One moment cloth the next moment flaps. I'm going now expands that rock before my tongue. Time and twigs to make nothing of nothing is sewn into spit, so semantic that a dent squirts eyeballs. It is powerful and knobs. Words in circles when the art chromes pipes to blazing sounds of sweatshirt sisters. Loom is wrinkle to the sky alright. Pain with a pattern to hold my coins.

THE ADVENTURES OF DRUKPA KUNLEY

How does one reconcile reason with divinity? Drukpa Kunley's erection stupefies a demon, while I pull a buffalo out of a retina. I'm equipped with sympathy and shirts. Personality caulks the leakage of wool, and forms a court plaster for the inelastic and Pennsylvania Dutch. I see life as a long emblem similar in quality to wind, though with messages written on it for one's progeny. Imagine Drukpa Kunley at a Home Depot. Crimson dilates the birth of desire and Christmas lights festoon Drukpa Kunley's dick, flashing on and off in an ecstasy of zeal, as if a drop of sound could be shaped into a word, and that word was 'hydrogen.' Or 'pelican.' Or 'cambium.' Or 'Ishallassoboundbewil-sothoutoosezit.' Success is a lure that never succeeds. Swans are signs and semen is warm and prehistoric. Language is simultaneously interior and exterior, as is consistent with faith and reason. You are in a cathedral of tools. Wheelbarrows auger bits edgers chainsaws caulking guns trowels cutters wire strippers pliers drop lights hammers. The shovels swarm with emotion. The vespers of eyebrows brews the cause of a livid tacamahac. Why does consciousness choose to annul itself under the form of desire? I see what I see, not what I want to see. Why does this keep happening? This entropy, this innovation, this Ptolemaic stepping stone to Dionysia? Once the world has been renounced, the desire to possess it is accentuated, which is the very meaning of the world. The adjectives awaken to pain. Cheddar mollifies the slap of eternity. The problem is always uncertain and can turn on the tension of a moment. There are certain pharmaceuticals for this, and they look like beans. The strange beans of fable, in which the sound of the rain is charmed and delicate and charged with life. The truth of the noun filters life through the ovum of withdrawl. I write because it's perverse. And trickles with brass and scholium and comedy and puppets. My hand is a frenzy of filaments. I tremble to affirm this fever. There are hundreds and hundreds of cows and cowboys slouched on their horses, sleeping in the rain. Today's social paradigm kills the Quixotic urge, but your modern cowboy stays true to his rope and saddle, lassoing the stray doggie when the herd scatters and the wind howls. This is demonstrated by the swaying of feathers on the back of a snake. Life is complex, contradictory, and laced with fugitive sensations. Dagwood sits down beside Drukpa Kunley and utters a truth so large he turns paler than yak milk. The tension between faith and reason is resolved by absurdity. It surprises me how much I'd like to get in a car right now and speed away into the night listening to old Rolling Stones songs. Mineral rights are ticklish. It helps to think of everything as a form of grammar, an iron emotion obtruding from the tongue of a Pythagorean sombrero. Shadows amuse the irregular shapes of purgatory. Consciousness comes into existence when it is conscious of being conscious, and Drukpa Kunley goes for a walk in the morning, his heart like an open drawer stuffed with the drug of language.

KIERKEGAARD AT HOME DEPOT

I lie in my hospital bed dreaming of Laputa. The longer you live, the more your personal life becomes a conjunction, a sprocket of spectacular wizardry. Experience is always blind. Reflection gives it eyes. Grommets and morphine.

Or a little leisure, at least. A little idleness now and then goes a long way toward understanding silica, its chemistry and zigzags, its charm and tetrahedral coordination.

I don't understand the scorn toward the semi-colon, or the literary. Leaves bob and toss lightly in the rain, rejecting minimalism, espousing Proust.

Why does anyone write poetry? The intentions of the accordion are implicated in its folds. Imagine, for instance, Søren Kierkegaard at a Home Depot. He fondles a pair of self-adjusting slip joint pliers with a red handle and thinks that religious belief ought to be based on a strenuous exertion of will, but that the existence of God cannot be proved.

A voice over the loudspeaker announces a sale on halogen pendants and polished brass ceiling lights. What is it, he wonders, to be God's chosen? Is it to have denied in one's youth all the wishes of youth in order to have them fulfilled with great labor in old age?

If we did not have consciousness of the eternal and if all that exists were but a fermenting turmoil convulsed by obscure passions, what else would life be but despair?

The best way to install a ceiling fan is to hire an electrician. But if it's poetry you want, then you've got to find what you love.

Consciousness comes into existence when it is conscious of something, and conscious of being conscious of something. Make an incision, then remove the lyric: look at it wriggle, full of anxious life, unconscious life, a placenta swarming with words and avidity. Can anything more closely resemble the lineaments of gestation than a sphagnum frog?

Language is simultaneously interior and exterior, like these lawn chairs. The tension between faith and reason is redeemed by absurdity. Grill accessories, patio umbrellas, resin sheds.

There are apparatuses, and then there are apparatuses. The world is alive with transcendence. Swans are signs of semantic absorption. Our interactions with the invisible forces of our lives can be partly achieved by fulfilling that wish to be drunk by one's own body, to become the pulp of a nourishing nullification and carouse into existence like a carnival. The history of a life, no matter what it may be, is a history of frustration. You can use that to your benefit. The coefficient of adversity engorges the physical with divine extension.

Drukpa Kunley's erection so stupefied a demon that he was able to slay it with a single blow.

The wheel recalls its circularity by rolling. The novel is avid to expand its scope and so becomes a fez. I am not here, thinks Kierkegaard, so much to exalt tools, as to use them. But how does one reconcile reason to the divine? How does a big-box retailer create a consistent merchandising voice?

The pagan was gripped by anxiety when great fortune came his way, for he had a certain distrust of the gods. But in Christianity! One craves and strains after earthly goods, and then, to free oneself of that anxiety, thanks God! That is just how such Christendom becomes more worldly even than paganism.

The first stage to wealth is to become a sociopath.

But that's not how Christianity was meant work. It was not guaranteed by the manufacturer, and its relation to the temporal individual does not fit neatly into conceptual frameworks, and the outlet box and its support must be able to able to fully support the weight of the moving fan. The eternal is paradoxical because you cannot insert God in time.

The rejection of the actual and the projection of the possible is crucial. But don't reject everything without first sampling a little of what life has to offer in the way of webbing and paste. Being free means determining what one wants, not getting what one wants. These are the structural aspects of any given situation.

Making the electrical connections will be a little different. It is possible to solder aluminum but it is not easy. You can make crimp connections, but the contact resistance will be different than for a soldered piece of copper.

The divine is always present, we just don't see it. Don't let that discourage you.

Being is everywhere and offers a multitude of flavors, from cherries jubilee to the nutty coconut of perpetual possibility. We must question the meaning of being in order to be conscious of being conscious, which is like imprinting a sunset on a leather belt. You will have the impression but not the colors. You will have the general idea but not the breath and smell of it. I can identify almost any emotion by its weight. Though if it suddenly grows dark outside when I open a drawer of old letters, I cannot tell you why "salon" is such a pretty word. You might try selling wedding dresses on the side, or study granite. I am trying to fulfill my promise to the fjord. I have an iron emotion that obtrudes from my tongue. It's been a hard and difficult winter and now I'm in the market for some patio furniture. I like to go for walks in the morning. This is when the divine is most apt to be trembling with vinegar. I carry an umbrella as if it were a universe of thread and little thin ribs. The weight of it proves the existence of rain. The sound of rain is charmed and delicate and charged with life. I'm not calling any more lawyers in North Dakota about mineral rights. I'm done with that. All I want now is to nail my worries down to a plank of indifference, and head toward that mountain in the breath of the morning.

EIGHT POUNDS OF FEELING

Umbrellas are wonderful. Umbrellas are umbilical to being. The rain makes a certain sound on umbrellas, a patter and a splatter of spectacular matter. The umbrella flaps in the wind, bat-like, a membrane with ribs, and a pole, confusing it metaphorically with a bat and a pole and a house in the form of a membrane. Rain slides to its edges then drops to the world.

The rain is intense, then quiet, then intense again. Spouts burble. Syllables drip.

The rain insists on being rain. There are no metaphors for the rain. The rain is rain.

This is silly. This is going nowhere.

Everyone colludes in watercolors. The sky is walking around like an Unchained Melody. Phil Spector enters a music studio and fires a gun.

I often think of going to Iowa. Spencer Selby lives in Iowa. Hi Spencer!

On April 14th, 2012, a tornado entered the kitchen of Celestia Cobb, ate all the mayonnaise in the refrigerator, then deposited house and goods and Celestia Cobb in the middle of the Bermuda Golf Academy.

The surface of the earth reflects the moods of heaven. The crust is brown and beige and green and molten gold inside where Haphaestus works, making weapons for the gods.

I miss the Beatles.

It is the Season of Hell.

Today I am constructing a paragraph. Each sentence will be ten feet high and walk around in a robe of salt.

I am either sedate or ridiculous I'm not sure which. This type of thinking reveals that the bus is driven by Little Richard. His eyes are aflame with Tutti Frutti.

There is always the threat of nuclear war. David Letterman laughs and brings on his next guest. Death sits down. His head is a skull. And eggplants and singing and warts.

If you saw a seesaw would a seesaw see you?

Think of it as eight pounds of feeling.

Something tart, like a present tense. The sky leaning over the horizon dropping light and water.

GEODE

Gravity is grave. We know that. It is why there are tombstones of granite and marble at the cemeteries. It is why names and dates and epitaphs have been engraved on them. Gravity is grave. It holds time and space and tarpaulins in place. But what of fog? What of that nebulous mist that obscures the evergreens and wanders the earth like a refugee from the sky, where it more properly belongs? Or foghorns? The sound of the foghorn is grave. And more than grave. It has gravity but it has something else, something ineffable, something like the tremor in John Lee Hooker's voice when he sings about covering the waterfront. His voice is soft and unhurried but with something hard and endurable in it as well. There is a rock somewhere with the truth of the sky in it, the glitter of otherworldly charms that falsify the ugliness of the literal. But it is buried in the earth where it reposes in eternal silence. It is buried in the words of poets. Its universe is encased in granite, like the astronomy of pain encased in the heart of a spurned lover. You can find a geode and break it open with a hammer and find the scintillation of crystal on the interior walls. Or you can take an old vinyl 45 of John Lee Hooker and play it and hear the ultimate sadness of the world, which is also its joy, and mooring and load. You can hear Hooker's voice bring the sea to your door. A big old ship. And the creak and barnacles of the dock. The reality of all that. If you smashed Hooker's voice open you would find the scintillation of crystal. You would find an old beauty. You would find proof of heaven. You would find the brood of gravity.

LIKE EXILES IN A TESTICLE MUSEUM

The fat light of Easter throws pathos and faith into the tawdry, ugly world of senseless reproduction and amazes the eyes and urges the conference of birds. The air assumes the consolations of sawdust and lace. We make documentaries about infants, thunderstorms, and color. We dig deep holes in the earth searching for water and oil and metal. We throw balls. We roll balls. We bounce and kick and bat and juggle balls. Balls excite our interest because we live on a ball. We travel through space on a ball. A large ball of light shines on our lives and habitations. It is the charm and physiology of the ball that shapes our destinies and rejoices in our hearts and heads. But it is the scent of wood and sad delicacy of curtains that completes the conjugation of touch. You cannot touch this ball or any ball without the subtleties of incarnation and folds of dangling skin to translate sensation into ivory and ivy and string. It is why I always twinkle with compliments and keep my suitcase packed with thermometers. If you see me walking down the street looking tilted and angular it's because I have a railroad inside me screaming to get out and my grill is engorged with crepuscular dandruff. There are spirits who handle our true credentials and serve chamomile during intercourse. Perhaps you've already noticed these things and would prefer to tango with a heavier construction, Georg Wilhelm Friedrich Hegel maybe or a rocking chair made of popsicle sticks. That's ok. Do what you want. I have arranged for the rest of these words to continue making anarchic slaloms of seesaw beer. There is a maple tree that urges a quiet ascension to plausibility, a place where we can hang like exiles in a testicle museum and exempt ourselves from the hazards of logic and tinfoil.

RECENT FINDINGS

I like being perverse. It's a minor form of archaeology.

I miss tickets. Now the theaters give you a slip of paper like a grocery receipt. Tickets have substance. They're stiff. You can put them in your coat pocket and if you need to grab them they're easy to find.

I like what Hamlet says to Polonius: Good my lord, will you see the players well bestowed? Do you hear, let them be well used, for they are the abstract and brief chronicles of the time.

You betcha. Emotions turn our lives into plays.

I once saw a girl reading a book in a box office and thought, now there's a curious thing. The book is probably better than the movie.

Yesterday I saw a man eating an apple in the hole of the sculpture at Kerry Park. It's called "Changing Form" and is by Doris Chase. It overlooks Elliot Bay and the Seattle skyline. People like to stand inside its fifteen-foot high steel form and take pictures of themselves. On this occasion, the man was simply enjoying an apple. He appeared to have at least half of it eaten. He gazed at me. I gazed at him. He took a bite of his apple, and I continued to pound the sidewalk on my afternoon run.

And this afternoon again out on a run I heard the Butterworth crematorium vent blasting the sunny air with someone's exit from this world. It reminded me of my first real eight hour a day job at the White Center Funeral Home after graduating from high school, and on cold damp Seattle days standing in front of the big metal door of the crematorium after it had been in use, reading Homer's *The Iliad*.

Materialism has triumphed over the spiritual. Everybody knows that. Just look around. There are places where goods may be bought in bulk, but no places where it is possible to just sit and think and dream of souks and bazaars, places where fragrances evoke an ancient sensuality and cobras uncoil from baskets woven of reeds by the Ganges. Where sadus bathe in the cold water of the mountains and spices are put in jars.

There is a jar on a hill in Tennessee, and it's going to stay there until someone comes to move it. Here in Washington State jars do not take dominion. They get put in the garage, and are filled with screws.

If prose is rubber, poetry is wax. This formula permits ukulele coal to power the audience.

Some days I can't get Antony and Cleopatra out of my head, and some days I can't get them into my head.

There are dramas, and there are dramas. There is the drama of application and the drama of invention. The drama of turning, the drama of leaning. The dramas of sand, the dramas of rain.

The quiet drama of the ineffable will inform you how the weight of a box of cat food tends to get heavier as you walk it home. How the bronze arm of Chief Seattle Seattle lifts in reverence and is a thingness like pain.

SHAKEN SHAPE OF MIDNIGHT

Shaken shape of midnight. A hive broadcasts the room. It's hard that our rattles are a piece of soap. The bruise is breathing in veins of rose to blue. I butter my resilience. Ointment is my prompt. Chemicals won't blossom flipped in a mattress. Hallucinations huddle into what riveted depth. Trouble is an emotion so big it occurs orthogonal. Clay is a way to begin to shiver. An exhibition convinces drawing an ocean is abandoned by beads. Opinion incarnates a dump from candles. Clatter wears the eyes except sleep if a giant moody vapor becomes a flower and vagueness becomes an architecture. The motion authorizes rising green and the carving goes in air to lip into fights hanging by including bugs. My clothes are in a yell to hit a sternum. The rationalizations are like quarks in the intestine of a desire. I feel the need to knock on a mosquito with trees. The paradigm rattles a world the hunger turned bubbly with oaths. My appearance plunged in a bistro at simple needs. Definition has a magnetic old Cubist chair dreaming eyes of the morning. A crowd of words huddle at my window of rain. The appeasement of squeezing glides through thought. Wrap the pickle. I hear the sound of my life holding a kitchen sink. Locomotive groans under the weight of alchemy. Corot strains shrewdly to transcend the sky in crisis. I'm sanguine as pepper. I feel the silence of this abstract ice is correspondent to a tall pink tower if the paragraph throbs like a cherry in apprehension of itself. Implication is considered to become a waterfall. I continue to make the sound of sympathy on a harmonica. A hunchbacked goldfish is harnessed to these words. Silk is a word incarnate in the arabesques of a single blue orchid. The grebe falls suddenly and plunges into the water. The savor of mayonnaise is hypothetical with eggs. My cynicism crackles among my fingers. The silk of listening necessitates thought. Focus on a hit song and eternity will attract thinking. Pounce on a consonant if a vowel occurs. I give my hat to the wet oddity pressing my pencil into description. This is called an iguana. Temptation tilts a fence. We live life differently in glory. Beyond the acceptance of compost is your opening the mouth into the invocation. Act softly if feeling gets naked. Things convey pummeling by form, and drills and cradles are a paradox. This is called brocade. Call it dissonance. Affirm this flare into yanking what this ancient garden produces in the sky. The distance provides enough theorem for the nerves to make pronouns. There is a sensation from the evocation of meaning that we recognize spreading in hypothesis. There are thumbs among the pages of metaphysics. We flourish in the prodigality of talk. We flutter in closets. We enrich our glasses with ugly towels. The phantoms crumble under the absorption and vault beside the driveway. Protein clenches our mohair. We walk in a cloud of butterflies. The sentence circles itself in cream. Birds are everything. I moo in phenomenon. I feel the ghost of a dream throwing a rivet up to the eyes in a wilderness of feeling. I heft it onto paper and ponder space, ripping feeling to shreds of Cézanne. Language is affectionately being alive to the splutter of stars.

NO EXCUSE

Writing is real life on paper. It doesn't require a reason to exist. It is aloud and contiguous. It is rhythmic and crucial and happens like a heart. The sky gargles clouds. The kitchen drawer provides a discourse in cutlery. Breakfast evolves in conception until it becomes utterly irrational and epic, a form of oratorio imbued with celestial vibrations.

And bacon and eggs.

I like to communicate with images. But I don't care for paint. It's messy. And frankly, I'm appalled at how often I have to go to the bathroom these days.

I gaze at Duchamp's *Nude Descending a Staircase,* take out my dick, and piss. This is what I call writing. Principally, a huge question mark. I have no excuse. Thoughts come and go with the ephemeral journeys of clouds. Someone has to write it down. No one steps in the same language twice. If you don't chew watermelon then dream of fish. Nipples, ointment, and bourbon. Whatever gets you through the night.

My emotions are monstrous and chrome. I jingle when I walk and push an ancient steam called embellishment. There is a sneer in my coffee and a kangaroo in my ambulance. It is not for nothing that I carry a shadow across the sand. Language is hostile to the particular and nevertheless seeks its rescue. Said Adorno. Who was really smart. And lived in Vienna, Frankfurt, and Berlin. And even Los Angeles for a time, where he made the acquaintance of Charlie Chaplin.

I have a sky in my head. I'm not kidding. We all have skies in our heads. Let's try to bump some details together and figure it all out. It's all that matters. Figuring this stuff out. This mystery called gasoline.

Infinity tastes of malt. And you, my friend, are the visceral sand of my spectral wheels.

Whatever that means.

It means this: wings and eyes. The flutter of leaves. The smell of rain. A full open space experienced with the entirety of our being.

I sigh to think of Greece. The rise of the oligarchy and privatization of everything. I don't know how to combat it. All I have is a pen, a computer, and a subscription to *Harper's*.

Facebook don't cut it, that's for frigging sure.

So really, what is the purpose of all this writing? There are now so many poets out there the stars are nervous. They don't shine like they used to. They shine like a creative writing class.

Now if my friend Nico were here he would shake his head and laugh because it doesn't really matter.

It's how things feel to the fingers that matters. Hot work moistens the sawdust. Arabesques caress the accident of the dunes in the susurrus of beach grass. I think of James Schuyler and immediately feel better. About everything. Even the sad banality of marriage proposals.

We search for stimulation wherever we can find it. Hunger unlocks the mystery of toast. Chains accomplish the sonority of form. There is singing on the road in the burning autumn and pharmacology to help us with our mistakes. The kind of mistakes that are bound to occur in life. Such as becoming a poet instead of a refrigerator repairman.

It's a good day to be visible and that's just what I intend to do. The milieu of the lip is water and skin. Poetry drives the blood. I am the captain of an imaginary zeppelin. My black leather gloves commemorate the sonnet. The slightest noise upsets me. Puts me off course. All art is reminiscent of masks. Which is why I have an appointment with an effervescent moose.

With an elaborate set of antlers and a boisterous obscurity.

Later, I will make a phantom pepper and sprinkle it on paper.

Because I'm a mammal and the bathtub is bronze.

Flicker a tiger and the swan boils.

That's what writing does to you. It grows under your sweat in bed at night until it becomes an architecture of thought and carries shadows of a higher reality. Shadows that must be shared with the world. Or at least set down on paper or pounded onto a computer screen. There is alchemy in the invocation of fire. Philosophy and eggnog at the rummage sale. Holes burlesque the illusion of substance. As for me, I like the simplicity of plugs. You stick them into the wall and a lamp lights up or a CD player sets the Beatles to singing "Norwegian Wood" again.

What else is a writer to do in a non-literary age? Gilgamesh wrestles the universe alone. It's sad. But interrelation, one soon discovers, is an eloquent sensation, like the history of the forehead, or the rim of a coffee mug, which has been a bit cracked, and feels good to the lips, interesting and irregular, a text on the pleasures of touch.

What more do I need? Oh sure, I'd like to live in a palace of glucose and gin, but I can accept the general weirdness of drapery and learn to live with buffalo. The landscape of the mind is rendered in postcards. The creak of the postcard rack at the drugstore is an important reminder of this fact. There is a reason the biggest assholes generally have a lot of money. My best friend is a cat. He keeps to himself a lot of the time and can be a little obnoxious at night when I'm trying to sleep, but he knows how to enjoy his food, and he has no money at all.

SWANS ON A SQUEEZED ACCORDION

Soap feels good because little bells jingle on the horses and needs are fitted to the individual. Volumes walk around in skin believing time is metal. The hours flame with tiny incisions and the sky breaks into little pieces. When our lives have finally begun to be libraries a smear of music will whisper at the edge of the cemetery. If you open that drawer you can expect to get wet. I'm not granite and vertebrae. I'm kerosene in the diagnosis of a rock. Constancy brims with aluminum and the sweat on your veins insinuates the pathos of Whitman. This is garish but here is a knot of tilted light to quiet the nerves. Bite this shape. A spoon will expand it into astronomy. The events at the bistro sit on the horse of language. Some of these metaphors may not be violent, but will tin the ocean with a stern heart. I can no longer be sure of anything, unless it squirts. All that sculpture does is provide a pound of antiquity where all the ghosts of our weekends are touching one another. A stone announces the rails of our belief. You must nail them to a camera or moor them in a religion. Nothing is literal. Except floating, which is consistently wet. Oysters are palaces of rain. Hectic curlicues of mucus. This could be the sternum of a highway and ooze life. Moss and mosquitoes knit the world into perspective. It is always a joy to study a table at the side of the road. And now that the train is arriving we can finish our opinions and slice the air into conversation. Nothing comes from nothing, except the marble block in which a sculpture walks out to squeeze the eyes into stars.

THE BIRCH DOCTRINE

The birch doctrine in summer summons emeralds. Algebra is friendly to the lucidity of evergreen and exempts many further allegories from incessant vinegar. A metaphorical bistro has been emphatic. Mohair by the aerodrome, a bikini by the mushrooms. Virtue, in a later pyramid with a bone black expansion, wheels forward on an oath of oak and popcorn.

Fiction is square as well as ripe and flavored with nature. Ocher is the path to mustard and its emotion gives a hunger to the inflation of carp. A jungle in cake, a napkin pinned to a hungry wind. A diagnosis fondles a mirror pulled out of a disease of bone and drum. The Rio Tinto zinc mines which aggressively drag around on stilts are further symptoms of pith.

Libraries are better suited to the greed for grammar. The kind of grammar predicated on angora, dirt, and portulaca. Fireworks pulled from a ball of gurgled hallucinations. The ascension is detailed in oblivion. Perception alters the pickles.

A funny morality exhumed from a hive of wasps teaches us ideas of jackknifed coagulation. Morning scribbles its abstractions on a pumpkin. A wild time dangles from a violin. And a bald trombonist pulls a fold of protoplasm out of a wallet to pay for an impersonal consonant. One must always draw the clutter of life as if it were both vulgar and parenthetical.

The vowel I discovered on the top of my head was heavy and red, like a scratched mineral. Apollinaire unrolled the lotus of his mind and varnished it with wisdom. Medicine left us all feeling new and grand. Knots of verbal fiber inched its way toward a deeper meaning in a stew of prose and luscious hysteria. Greed murdered a goldfish.

The galaxy, in its elegance, felt visceral, as if a pineapple had rolled out of the door and into the hallway, tripping one of the neighbors I dislike. There is a door in the pigment opening to a wonderful seclusion percolated through a cone of isinglass and morphine. Each muscle is personified by an engine of spinning chairs. The humor of it is total flagstone, hectic with heat and paper.

The crab, contrasting with the hammer, has been reluctant to settle down and do crab-like things. Blood, meanwhile, comes in daubs, haunted and serious. The sternum collar stud has married the chair to its gloss. Our drawers are filled with summer, little potpourris of sloth and shittimwood. Below the aurora is a neck in the river that holds the secret of itself in cottonwood and willow.

My intent climbs to my mouth and jumps out in words over which I appear to have no control. Even the butter of morning bends into fish. A buffalo exclaims headlights are the eyes of a grizzled cacophony peremptorily rubber. I believe in nothing but my own two axioms: description is shaky, and bitumen is solemn. Mass and density are two sides of the same halitosis.

Crawling is enriched by hands. Grow strong from hammers. Touch the trapeze upon the pulling of it toward you. Then swing. Swing in squirts, like a rubbed tube of precipitous tinsel.

Smack that oar against the water and splash the clouds with camaraderie. Nothing exists that has not been mouthed by the smell of effusion. Coordinates scribbled on a café napkin, or a trumpet wrapped in silk. Those sweet experiences we sometimes hear in the fragrance of sheer endeavor. Algebra, with its surge of symbols, creates a feeling of consciousness, faucets arranged by kinetic mosquitoes in a dream of beauty.

Astronomy makes itself available, then later photogenic meat. Everything has a certain weight to pull. Stars, or zippers, things you would not expect interfaced with thousands of inconceivable sensation, walks on the beach, an anchor descending into the water, a romance littered with jokes. The baking of sexual dollars in the Federal Reserve inflates a phantom wealth impregnated by a syringe of gooey improbability. The brushed fangs of an unbridled autumn converging with the tender meat of a day old harmonica.

There are some irritations that turn peculiarly aesthetic. Others are just plain irritating. A stove, annotated with strips of chrome, awakens the palpability of watts in its coils of gloss and glory, then recedes into shadow when the light is turned off. I have no further thoughts on this. My words revolt, grinding the world to a swollen indeterminacy, irritating critics, but otherwise providing a platform for the reverie of crickets. The metaphysics of a jerky chiaroscuro warming the shadows of a vagrant cantata plunges the rest of the story in straw.

A LETTER FROM ARTHUR RIMBAUD

Yesterday I received a letter from Arthur Rimbaud. He tells me he learned how to swim in the Mississippi. He canoed. He said there is no other sensation like it. Being in a boat. Drifting. It is wonderful. Even the trees speak to me. They say "You are not the world. We are the world."

He likes watching Nirvana on YouTube and maneuvering his canoe around rocks. The voyage has only just begun, he says, sounding oddly like Karen Carpenter.

The landscape has deepened his appreciation of beige. There is catfish in baskets, echoes in duckweed. When knowledge collides with ignorance, the result is television.

The door exhibits butter.

What door?

He does not say.

My smooth new opposition to the world, he says, is no substitute for elephants. I am not Hannibal. I is other. Gravity assumes the irregularity of sandstone. Pollock promulgates the pathos of paint.

What are the causes of attraction?

Ablution. Absolution. Henry Miller eating osso bucco with Brenda Venus.

What is osso bucco? What is enuresis? What is illuminism?

I am impatient, thin, and upside down. The metaphor realizes itself by secretion. Green holds the adjectives of ghosts. Leather necessitates idealism.

Don't you find this true?

Nor do the wealthy comprehend death. They do not comprehend it because a magic camera has displaced it from their incumbent gut.

The organ trembles with Bach, disquieting as a Martian sunset.

Why am I here?

I cannot tell him. He did not include his address.

He avers that his point of view is sometimes bitter, but that this is due to the camels, the rigors of a punishing and merciless landscape, and the creak of the winches dredging feelings from his heart.

He is sending me a package of red silk. The dye, he says, is excellent.

The power of light does push-ups in gold. I have a spider bite on my biceps. I remember how my bones felt when Blaise Cendrar drove his Alpha Romeo across the Amazon. How drops of space drifted through my sleep.

My intentions are never equal to the diversions of language.

I want to kiss your eyes.

I want to juggle a pirate, a porthole, and Jan Vermeer's pearls.

I like to gaze at water.

DREAM OF DISTANT SUNS

First think of a knife and next to it a joke doing edges. This will only take a minute. Then tangential to a nimble France believe in a workshop for making snowshoes. And now I ask: how much does a mind weigh? Ten pounds of blue squeezed into cotton. Only later will it become a bruise.

The personality is catalogued more appropriately as a pumpkin, or species of conversation. The liberation of old apparitions dances a novel into cuticles and bulbs. Depth is alive in its heft. Opinions balloon in Montmartre. Duty is not the same as an elevator.

Here is the hem the elation erects. A canoe of monumental eloquence out to enthrall a scruple of feathers draws itself through the sentence creating vowels and waves. Dimension truffles are not the same as astronomy or eggs. There is a light which spoons the heart and causes gloves to mount impairment. Timelessness is always needed at the smell of abalone.

This is written while coffee, as pumpernickel, pleases feeling. It is dusty to gasoline the violin. Clumsy from almonds, I can tumble toward the synchronization of cardboard. Only heft is charming, and those are railroads. You will have to look here to see an elephant dipped in symptoms of jurisprudence. Grammar treads itself to shift a nerve or two into buckles.

Circumference is fast to honor its surface. The moon paraphrases a tide pool wherein the vowels are thrilling and slow. The mud sparkles into structure and ears. The bank denies its inertia. Grain from a surge of intent brings ocher to the heart as a shape inspirits the clouds.

The occurrence of mahogany means the table is a cat. Figure itself is square and exhumed and arms that fill the embroidery with an army of shades. A mink arrives in infinite ganglions. The sleep in delectation blazes a wilderness of stethoscopes and tigers. There is a winch which gives nature a lap and a ritual that swells into paradox, harmonies carved from chaos and a circle disturbed by parallels.

Bracken chafes the pilings. Flotsam bobs on a greenish water. There is a monster within that distorts the world to vapor and parenthetical odors leaning into it with pulse and neon. A hoe marks the ground. A kill becomes sand.

Semen is the same as legs. The sensation works its way up another punished universe where pleading is fast and sighing is mohair. Space stirs within a block of dimes. A pineapple umbrella entertains the asphalt. Decipherment exceeds its clothing.

Charcoal is a resource in feeling. A daub of paint becomes conspicuous when space holds the lake but not its propellers. The revelation is enhanced by fencing, or radiation. Etruscan spars give the air the subtleties of an indispensable racket that plays its way into ink and harmonicas. The paragraph turns green over its peculiarities, declaring a door that burns with elucidation.

The saga, tailored in its beginnings, turns naked in elation. Paint this road into your mind with a scrupulous predicament. Assemble a gaudy caboose. Swans break the hospital. Description sways with a spirit of process.

Interiors are personified by a stinging clutter, a certain clarity in fabric that fondles the eyes, dragging their scrutiny to a creaminess invented by Braque. They scribble themselves toward the upheaval of clouds. Name at least one sensation that doesn't ignite a guitar. The house houses itself by blueprint and snow, not a mawkish suppository of perfunctory stucco.

Being examines its blisters, exceeding itself by imitating an algebra of roots and boiling modulations of punctual blue. It is natural to push a wrinkle into grammar. But do not expect the bones to get up and dance. The air is indulged on a string of words. Echoes perturb the adjectives imposed on the structure of a fast consciousness heaving with autumn and infrared hats.

What is required is an aesthetic that reclaims trigonometry, performs like Buffalo Bill, adheres to unpredictable planets, and washes infinity in ghostly thermometers. Flirt it stern, then tickle it around. Hobnob in the ceiling. Gold and jellyfish smell of pulse. Be parliamentary by denying the next plague.

But be wise by accepting willow. The sawdust is much admired by our staff in the lumberyard. Consonants clean the explosion of thought in a cap of increase. Not since circles were circles did a rectangle seems so modular. An odd emotion modeled on cedar illumines the incense, and a brain bent by oak maps itself as a bent idea.

Ideas bent into moonlight smell of evocation. A song of red, a poem by Stephane Mallarmé, a sorcerer soothing a wild ocean. The glaze of a kneecap can shine like a fugue unbinding a terrible moose. Carry a jug in syntax peremptorily cornered by sound. Flap that sky into Picasso, headlights innovating the highway in their dream of distant suns.

HERE IT ISN'T

Here it isn't: the poem I can never write. I cannot write it because it cannot be written. It isn't made of words. Or thoughts or dreams or gravity or gravy. Or denotations or detonations or combinations or nebulas of stars. Gravity in gravy or space with a consonance of spice. It has no metaphors or phantoms. No semaphores or rivers. It is a poem of nothing. It has nothing in it. The poem itself is nothing. It does not exist. It means nothing, promises nothing, leads to nothing, professes nothing.

Think of Wyoming. The clouds, the air, the wind, the rocks, the plants, the birds, the horses, the roads. Now remove everything from your mind. Remove Wyoming from your mind. Sweep it all out. Sweep it clean from your mind. Everything. Bridles. Stirrups. Ropes. Corrals. Lassoes. Cliffs. Buttes. Canyons. The poem is not Wyoming. It is not even Death Valley.

The poem does not exist. If it had an existence, it would no longer be the poem that it would be if it was a poem made of words. A poem with an existence. A poem that meant something. A poem with feelings and fingers and eagerness and possibly an accordion. This is not that poem. If it was that poem, it could not be that poem, because it would have an existence, it would have these words making it exist, squeezing the accordion, pressing little pearl buttons, creating melodies and ideals. Spectral energies. Pegs. Eyes. Crows and giants. And so this is not that poem. Not the poem that cannot be written. The poem that I want to write by not writing it.

The poem of non-existence cannot exist. If it existed, its existence would rid it of non-existence, and by not existing, it would cease to exist. The act of writing such a poem would destroy that poem.

Consequently, this is not that poem, can never be that poem, however much it tries to not exist, the act of not existing causes it to exist. It undoes itself in the process of doing itself. Doing nothing. Being a poem. Not a proverb. Not a wad of leaves. Not a trunk. Not a branch.

Not a web. Not a root. Not a grain. Not a knot. Not a knot in the grain. Not a knot in the bark. Not a gnosis. Not a gnomon. Not a gnu. Not that. No knots. No gnosis. No gnomon. No gnocchi. No gnat. Not even that. No nimbus. No Noh. Nothing. But not quite nothing. Never quite nothing. Always something. Something heavy. Or light. A shape. A form. A dereliction of air.

ONTOLOGY 101 PART ONE

Using the human nervous system as a representational medium, are there parts of the universe that are innately unknowable to us?

Artists struggle to extend our perceptions through the library and out into the world where the wild things hurry and hurdle and hurl in turmoil and proposal.

Explain the ocean. Trumpet your perceptions in sonnet and paint. In squares and circles and heaving tongues of steel. Vibrating chords. Scurrying fictions.

There is a marbling in the mind, intermixtures of transcendence and bewilderment. Hold a rock in your hand. What does it say? Whatever it says will convulse in the mouth. Ooze life and garret, pavilion and dock.

Braque and his rocks.

Increase is decreased by the increase of decrease. Whereas decrease is increased by the decrease of increase. And increase is outdoors whereas decrease is apparent in concentration.

The world is remembered in copper and clapper. And the way the waves move and the tides come and go and a seagull is reflected on the sheen of the shore.

In your left pocket.

The universe we do not see is tangential to our blood. A radio squawking, hugged in vibration.

I love this chair and its framework. The neck is a structure. The head is an explosion. The voice emerges from the throat and its sounds are shaped by the lips and tongue. The bones bend, but the muscles describe. The fire burning in the words is an apparition, an amiable prodigality. The thunder feels like candy in the bones. It crackles and spits and sparks fly. It is luminous and jaunty. Congenial or indifferent. Unpredictable as a poem.

Granite speaks to us of duration. The sky struts across the water and coils around an idea. The idea of floating. The idea of wood. The idea of ballast and sail. The idea of eating. The idea of scale.

The world spins and the stars pulse explicit as time. There is always room for reflection. Volume employed to expand the music of mass.

A low murmur by the milk pail radiates purple haze. The intestines wobble by the wall. The universe is so big that we cannot see it. But it is there. It disturbs the surface of our coffee. Our faces. Our sugar. A buffalo stampede in 1850. Converging in a thought. The eye of a hawk.

Emphasis is the poet's best friend. Roar, shout, cry against injustice. There at the headland where the sea crashes. Address the world as you would a lover.

Sensation creates emotion emotion creates linen.

And indispensability.

A feeling glows and burns and circulates. You can hear it. Diving into books. Entertaining words. Pouncing on illusions. Eating them. Digesting them. Coughing up diversion. Squeezed rawhide. Punches and cogs.

This is a drug. A composite of thoughts and oceans and spoons.

I am bringing an ocean into your head. I am carrying it with my mind. I am spilling it in words.

ONTOLOGY 101 PART TWO

What is existence, i.e. what does it mean for a being to be?

Existence is a feeling. It is to be gallant as a whale, a dream hatching out of a paragraph, the incisions of surgery left in the skin as a mark of unction.

The hospitals are full of people injured in the course of existence. Existence isn't easy. It invites eloquence. It is a matter of fencing ghosts. Illusions. Folds of air.

Need begins us. Need is a staircase huddled against the wall, steps creaking as someone rises to tend the dying, or the agonies of birth.

Steel rails guide the locomotive. Attraction guides the heart. Attractions draw the escalator upward.

And downward.

Alpaca feels parenthetical against the skin.

History is the denim of consciousness. Mosquitoes plague the neck and arms. Incense swirls when the door opens. These are the rhythms of existence. These are the rhythms of being.

Imagine yourself as an extraterrestrial, deep in the quiet of reflection. You would look good in court in such manner, in a costume of wizardry, encrusted with jewels, as outside a rocket ship lands, bringing a wealth of information as you climb into yourself, and prepare to explain the paraphernalia of peacocks to a room of beings in a hive of honeyed thought.

Action is where we find the animal within. The brightness of Brighton, rocks and butter, the pigments of dawn breaking over the crest of a mountain. Waves slapping against riprap. The slop of elements. Images created by brush. A bowl of chowder blushing with butter.

Experience yourself as a living entity of bone and blood, muscle and skin. Propellers churn the water as lightning illumines the waves. The world is a ripe, resplendent logic of illogical buds and bubbles. Fire is a paradox. Quarks are quirks.

For example, birds.

Most things begin with an abstraction. An idea held in the hand like an eyeball. A late, midnight lyric squirting horses in pink anticipation of a light traveling through the nerves, an impulse dripping words of one's existence. Each word is a fist of thunder. If anything, for the sake of teasing gravity, which is the same as sweating as a feeling rises upward through the spine. For the mind is for thinking, and the throat is for sounding diversion.

Slow words lead to fast thoughts. Fast thoughts lead to slow words.

Opposites, expansive as a barn, generate the play of embryonic colors. Apparitions in the straw. Horns, powerfully kinetic and smooth. A philodendron on a neck of green. Elegance and sweat.

The horses gallop in panic as a form develops in the sky. The sky lowers and walks on the hills, singing. Its image excites the nerves. An old man plays an old guitar. Gravy flows over a mound of mashed potatoes. Mosquitoes brocade the air. The horses slow to a stop, and begin to graze. The sky combs through space leaving trails of orange and pink and gold.

Bolt this dream to the door in blots of damp thought.

The grapefruit merits attention. And the desk has a skull on it. The skull of a human, which now grins, its sockets hollow and dark.

Admire fingers. Admire thumbs. Admire everything that grows into maturity and labors and dies. Admire the cartilage in a spine as a body rolls into a somersault.

Syllables puddle into images. A pyramid under the stars. A destiny predestined in a tattoo. A cap on a bottle. The peristalsis of intestines. Cézanne working a texture into granite.

The mysteries of existence are opened by spirit.

Death is an insult.

And a balm.

The incongruity of it all tastes of peach and dough and rolling pin.

Wrinkles and cuts on an old man's face. A woman dancing on the wings of a biplane. The feeling of silk against the skin.

ONTOLOGY 101 PART THREE

Is existence a property?

If the existence of a thing is its sheer ontological presence, its *thatness,* then to ask what the properties of a thing are in order for it to exist is to ask about the *whatness* of this *thatness.* The *thatness* must have a *whatness.*

We are in the realm of *whatness.*

Existence exists by virtue of existence. The idea of existence comes into existence tangled and enthusiastic, like roots deep in a German forest. Flaming eyes in a fairy tale. It is partly imagined, partly constructed. Made of words, rags of dream. You break en egg and a hand comes out holding a giant atmosphere. Chaotic gases and lightning. The clash of titans. A conception of space and time boiling in the mind. Existence exists because pathos is piercing and there is an ox bearing a load of wood.

Can there be a pure existence stripped of all properties? Can there be a section of cheese without the things that make cheese, cheese? Cheese without smell, or shape, or density, or color? Without flavor? Without history? Without fatalism, or February?

Existence is a property because property itself has an existence. It is a presence felt as a vibration, or peculiarity.

Butterflies smell of words dipped in metaphor.

It is therefore marvelous to have access to drinkable water and electricity.

And cardboard. Cardboard is wonderful. But what is rattan?

A pretty abstraction, a prickly enigma. Rattan is rattan. A tautology of sticks. An object you can feel with your fingers. And the weight of your body. And the idea of existence. Which is sometimes a circus, sometimes an elegy.

As soon as a conception obtains purchase on a canvas, we begin to see war, and how it is magically ugly, and cold and brutal.

Language is language. Orange is orange.

This is why we are always busy embracing one another. The mystery of pain remains veiled. It is a form of fruit, a digestible meditation. Later analysis reveals how clumsy toys are. And sometimes I feel like drawing rattlesnake. Who knows why? I love diversions. Maybe that's it. There is a glittering presence in drops of rain. A palette larded with vibrant colors and a seminal snake tied to the Big Dipper. The sky, curiously alive, swallows itself. The pencil moves and a sphere appears. A skull. With two black sockets where a pair of eyes once moved, and blinked, and viewed the pageantry of existence.

There is always a fire burning somewhere.

Describe fire.

To an extraterrestrial.

Who has never seen fire.

And now you begin to see the problem of language. And existence.

This is a word, and it is on fire. Draw the flames naked and alone on a beach. A nearby sculpture begins to talk. A woman on a horse gallops by. There are paths leading nowhere and a fish that is orthogonal and wise. Like the Louvre at midnight. Or a passage through time.

Time is an existence. But what are its properties? An hour is round like a wheel but a minute is sharp like a knife. It is the same as a chisel. An instrument gouging shapes out of space. But by who? Who is it that gouges shapes out of space? What existence? What presence? Or is it all simply an accident of creation? Arbitrary as a bathing suit. An impairment, or hospital. May you enjoy this hat. I am giving it to you. It is shaped like a head full of eyes. Hundreds of eyes vulgar and round and misunderstood.

Consciousness splashes around in the head. A drug is a frequency, waves of energy. Most of the time I just look out of the window. Or slither across the floor bending time. Or float monstrosities in my mind, huge leviathans with diamond wings and blazing eyes.

Movement has existence, but does it have a property? And what about grace? Movement can exist as a mathematical modality. It can be measured, quantified. But grace is a quality. This raises another question. The question of quality. These are slippery rocks. The river is moving and it is graceful. Gracefully moving. Its grace alone has an existence but it is the river that brings the grace into meaning.

We are soothed by its water. We are carried by its being.

ONTOLOGY 101 PART FOUR

Is existence a genus or general class that is simply divided up by specific differences?

The answer, according to George Berkeley (1685–1753), is no.

Berkeley's argument offers phenomenological evidence (onions, French, mermaids), for the conclusion that an abstract general object is inherently predicationally incomplete. Thus, in A *Treatise on the Principles of Human Knowledge*, (1710), Berkeley states:

If any man has the faculty of framing in his mind such an idea of a triangle as is here described, it is in vain to pretend to dispute him out of it, nor would I go about it. All I desire is, that the reader would fully and certainly inform himself whether he has such an idea or no. And this, methinks, can be no hard task for anyone to perform. What more easy than for any one to look a little into his own thoughts, and there try whether he has, or can attain to have, an idea that shall correspond with the description that is here given of the general idea of a triangle, which is, neither oblique, nor rectangle, equilateral, equicrural, nor scalenon, but all and none of these at once?

In other words, "*esse est percipi,*" "to be is to be perceived."

Which means biology is everywhere and enthusiasm is holy.

Un coup de ton doigt sur le tambour décharge tous les sons et commence la nouvelle harmonie.

A communion of sand and salt water. Movement in silhouettes around a raging bonfire. This is where the story of each person on the freeway comes to reminisce and find themselves among specific steps in the mud.

The depth of water in a marsh. The acceptance of cloth, and what it means to wear clothes, and enjoy a sense of skin against silk, or water, or the warmth of another body.

Carve a face in a piece of wood: you will come to believe in the ardor of motion. Motion is sublime. Emissions of light sweeten the day, glance from the blade of the chisel. There are men who personify the sun and women who personify the moon.

The moon as its light strikes a wall of ice in Iceland. Fading of stars as daylight breaks. Compressions of night geyser into composition. Mud bubbles. Fumaroles vent. Fafnir stirs.

Puffins bob on emerald water. There is a shoulder of stone rising into a churning sky.

The diving of grebes. Raucous parliament of auks. Scree scree scree of glaucous gulls.

Language warms the air. We see it in steam. A meditation on the density and meaning of dreams. Bouillon in a black bowl of Zen pottery. Explorations of sound on a violin by a musician haunted by a life not yet lived but only dreamed.

Reflection of a mountain on a pond on a mountain.

Reflection of a mind in thought. In a hammerhead of green glass.

William Burroughs in Kansas. Plywood shot with a pattern of holes.

Predicaments awaken the mind. Magically pink. Naked and blue. Paint it whatever color you choose.

Or use words. Use words to describe what cannot be described.

Use words to describe a thought bouncing around the room.

Like an Earl. In amber and pearl.

Tubes of light in the solemn Kansas night.

Vacancy! Vacancy! Vacancy!

Spots of light, stains of abstraction. Sympathetic greens, noble reds. The loneliness of blue. Ginsberg's hydrogen jukebox in a bar in Abilene.

Record flops down, begins to spin: little scratchy sounds. Then *hello cowgirl in the sand. Is this place at your command? Can I stay here for a while?*

Name your tune.

Existence needs choice. Decision. Everyone is urged to confess their woes. Pressed against a rock. Apparitions of ourselves in a different history. In a song we didn't write. But sung. As if it were our song. Which in some way it is. And in some way it is not. But a song nevertheless. A sweet, ineffable tune. A sound consisting of silence. And later and never and soon.

Butter sliding down a mound of mashed potato. Blue flame from a canister of propane on a winter night. Bodies shadowed on the snow. Where the wind moves. You can see it in swirls. Spirals of white whirly snow. A trickle of icy wind down the back. Which feels like a kiss from the moon.

ONTOLOGY 101 PART FIVE

Which entities, if any, are fundamental? Are all entities objects?

The spoon is an admirable shape, especially when it holds a galaxy of sugar. I am stunned by the fullness of a full moon above the city hill and its twinkling lights. Further are the mountains. I grow into myself as I age, becoming fuller as I become less of myself. Nothingness is fertile. Ganglions wrestle the void. The circumference of the globe spins through space creating time, years, months, days. I am tickled by the ticking of the clock. And yet I cannot adjust to the imperial dictates of time.

An entity is a discrete phenomenon which makes itself available to consciousness as an abstraction or a perception. A hammer, a screwdriver, a column of water shooting up into the sky, a barking dog, a cat sleeping on the bed. Or a square or a rectangle or a circle. Or the idea of a circle. But how does an entity make itself available to the mind as an abstraction? That is to say, if there is nothing there to perceive? Is an idea an entity? If an idea is an entity, then anything the mind might conceive could be an entity. In which case, everything and anything is possible. There are no limits. And if there are no limits, then everything becomes a vast mental blur, a vast field of muzzy circumstantiality.

Where, then, is external reality to be found? If it is not already in the mind, then where is it?

The entity shatters unity. It becomes iron. It becomes a moon and the orbit of the moon. It owns itself by way of its determination. But what does it determine and who or what gives it determination? The mind stumbles through its language in quest of its being. How did it acquire being? The mind acquires being through an entity. The entity is compelling. It is a pocket. Leibnitz's monad. With loose change. It abhors nothing. Except a vacuum. And the vacuum itself is an entity. And so ascends the dawn of a new conception of language and perception.

A tree propels silk because it is aroused by jokes. Awed and held and gantry. The cloud ignites in incandescent report. A tonic accentuated loaf begun by vein.

The hirsute erects a paper. And the bikini becomes soft in that walnut. The fractions seethe like seminal morning. Spring pleads grease and there is a knot that whistles and a need that fumes. This pain is for the mouth and skull to articulate in a novel.

The punch bag is more than its cuticles. A Parisian orchard is more or less brindled among its hinges. The biography of a jerk is operated by dream. And the veins bloom amid their blood, even as a catfish is caressed by the river in which it lives and is carried to places where the water gurgles under the shadows of cottonwood and willow. Oats amplify the smell of this for a bug. Massive roots show what grace there is in bark.

The interior is illumined by pharmaceutical. A smooth redeeming jug imbues the meditation on lithography. I find bottles along the walk that cause necessity to flow into gravity. And forge cocoons that the unfettered churn of wind brings into being.

Each oddity bequeaths itself to the glorious fantasy of the sky. Purple is obscure at fibers in glue. A faucet tumbles through its water. A nimble Elizabethan pulls his rapier and floods this feeling with a sorcery of movement.

Bones crackle in Picasso. And in guns that the grammar of war garbles into a wicked symmetry of bark and cannon.

The charm of autumn unbinds us in its sculpture. Strength elevates our hunger above our handsprings. A tiger talks among rocks. Panic visits distance. The sticks sing. The paragraph obtrudes its images of heaven. An obscure injury forms a scar in the shape of a key.

An inflammation of the soul is hoisted by winch and slowly turns, exhibiting various sides of voice and spirit. The many emotions that fill a soul during the day and its slow accidents of tea and plug and cloud and beauty.

Poland is a rock. Experience comes in streams. Dissonance is good for garlic. It is sometimes enough to suppose that a cow has fireworks and that abstractions form between the threads of an embroidered romance. The larynx is neither a bag nor an olive but an intention of nerves and mucus and membrane that make a voice claim its penumbras. Even the calliope is unpredictable.

The trapeze is green. And the enigma of the entity is solved by wheels of the lotus. The things that make a flower spin into granite, creating fossils of expansion, peacocks at the fringe of our language. The seen and the unseen. Being and nothingness. Nothingness and being.

ONTOLOGY 101 PART SIX

How do the properties of an object relate to the object itself?

Fingers are fiercely particular. There are no universals for fingers, except fish, and planetary spheres, and doorknobs and handles on buckets that make a loud clattering sound when you set the bucket down.

I wonder if Aristotle ever carried a bucket and set the bucket down and found something embryonic in its declamation?

A subject (*hupokeimenon*) is what a statement is about.

A predicate (*katêgoroumenon*) is what a statement says about its subject.

Bacteria follow the hands. The pack mule follows her human. The sublime unpacks her suitcase at the top of the mountain.

Time is a universal ticking in lyrical hickory.

The night is anarchic and soft as moccasins. And long and forceful and the cocoons dangle from branches and inside them new life churns in squiggly metamorphosis. A congenial worm grows colorful wings.

My interpretation of universals is subjective and weird. That's because I have skin and weight and density and volume.

Perception is flimsy until it turns licorice.

The weight of a thought is shaped into hymns. And a refractory universal hungers for enhancement by the particular.

Contraption, conception, and butterflies.

Let me touch you.

Let me fill the air with the heat of my breath.

Let me fill the air with the taste of predication.

The properties of water, and things like skin. Beads of amber on an ebony belt. Kitchen drawer full of flashlight batteries. And beautiful spoons. And beautiful forks. Knives and pliers and postcards from North Dakota.

Pennies, keys, cellophane, bills.

Struts on a wing.

An ounce or two of Dr. Pepper left in the bottle I put in the frig three weeks ago after returning home from a session at Alliance française.

Muffins and Plato.

The photograph of an odor. A glass of water painted by Jean Baptiste Chardin. So beautiful it reminds me of your voice. And eyes. And a path surrounded by towering pines, garish and pink in the sparkling rain.

Steam rises from my body. Gold comes in flakes of supernatural beauty, the taste of predication. I am fascinated by sidewalks. The mountains speak to our hands and feet.

Represent yourself as you would a king. Or queen. Or orangutan.

Abstractions sleep among the adverbs. There are meanings harnessed to my words. Crustaceans. The mind boiling in indigo. Warm eggs warming the curl of our fingers. I fall through a hole in my personality.

The photograph of an odor. Jellyfish washing ashore. I hit the table with my fist and the cutlery jumps.

What is a moral? What is morality?

Let me watch you as I chew meat and crinkle potato chip bags.

Desire opens us to the world. I must rescue the cabbage from its intro-version.

Experience shapes perception. Perception shapes experience.

Or is it the other way around?

The hair on my head is wild. I rarely use a comb. I prefer to use a brush. And sometimes I drive to the end of the night in a Buick of prodigal fire. Grease envelops the axles. Morning is revelation. The birds are sweet to hear.

I swim among syllables dreaming of the chemistry of whales, outboard emotions, the hinge on the bathroom door bright in its metal.

There is no such thing as a subtle tattoo. Power comes to those who are drunk with ambition, and must be maintained by violence, and fear.

Power is a disease. The largest throat does not necessarily produce the deepest sound.

If my skin breaks, I discover an ocean of blood beneath it. The nostrils of my horse flare. My feelings explode into art. I forge words. I assemble fictions. My running shirt trembles above the baseboard heater. Heat fills it with life. Not my life. Another life.

I have a piece of string with which to operate my eyebrows.

The lake is crazy with diamonds. I hear someone walking upstairs. The spoon is a luminous milieu, a silk robe on a tin skeleton.

Do we have candles? I am amazed by light.

Skin is malleable. Fat on a globe named Falstaff.

Adjectives so burden the sentence that its weight causes it to sink and appear on the other side of the paper.

Someone, somewhere, is building a barn. Creating energy, thread, and DNA. The clouds are boiling with purple. Crickets pull our wagons, our words. A sweet blue exaltation of the sun at the end of the day.

It's curious the way rooms are connected, how one room leads to another room and in between is nothingness and motion and ghosts.

There is a ghost on the road carrying a gallon of gasoline to a car that no longer exists.

Ghosts are symptomatic of the failure to believe that there is an absolute end to existence. So that a glowing entity might implore a biography. Or the history of a knife. Or an animal chained to a crumbling wall.

The mind has neither shape nor substance. It is pure energy. And loves the verticality of things.

Water in a green jug on a blue table.

The universe crashes through the window, tasting of acceleration. And doughnuts. Mahogany in Madagascar. The weight of your voice. Tree branches clacking in the wind.

ONTOLOGY 101 PART SEVEN

What features are the essential, as opposed to merely accidental, attributes of a given object?

They're rioting in Cairo. But this is Nebraska. A giant eyeball floats over the prairie. Sunlight dazzles the terrain. Arapahoe and Pawnee. Wounds and feathers. Perpetual change. This is, after all, a prairie. The prairie cannot be reduced to an essence. The prairie murmurs the breath of angels. Odors are proposals. There is hunger in the wind. Wolves and abandoned farmhouses. The sky floats on purpletop. A flower yells back at the sun.

Do you own a hibachi? A sawmill in Alabama? Fill yourself with the world.

If I dangle a piece of space, gravity squeezes it together into a glocken-spiel, and flowers pop out of my mouth.

Sometimes a little propane goes a long way. You can push a thought through the loophole of a sentence, but a puddle of light forms on the wall, and the sky turns black.

Other things exemplify soup. The rants of a cynical wizard. Drugs on a hardwood floor.

If you can fill a paragraph with descriptions of raw sienna, you will be greeted by soft bare arms, golden women on a silver boat. And every-thing warm and gentle will counsel your heart.

Essence is insoluble. Life is insoluble. Life is an essence. It is viscous and smooth, a hand lotion.

It is rough and convulsive: a cowboy on a bucking Brahma bull.

Each thing has a presence. A thin yellow sun on a winter horizon. Everything implicit in blue. Everything revelatory in green. Onions. Ghosts. The art of translation. The heart of a lobster. The transcendence of eggs. Amber mounted on a copper ring. Clay and wood and chains and nails.

I have decided to shave. You can pull a language out of a thirst, but you cannot pull a thirst out of a fish. Sometimes you just have to accept the sawhorse as a demonstration of support. And the razor as a supplement of hygiene.

There is a dimension that eludes science. You can, for instance, bend a flashlight beam around a corner. But you can only do this on special holidays, or by further developing the autonomy of sleep, so that it resembles Portugal, and pulses with parables.

I have conducted experiments on language and discovered hysteria and ice cream. Brush your hair. Life is changeable. Write everything down. If a set of adjectives clash in a painting by Georges Braque, I ask you to consider the light and its full spectrum of colors. We express ourselves with napkins. There are bones buried beneath this sentence.

Try to find a little innocence. There are paths that lead deep into the forest. One is not required to be religious, but it helps to cultivate a sense of reverence. The process is blue, with nuances of red and white and green. There are almonds in the snow, and kumquat and milk. Boiling art. Auguries of spruce.

Marie Laurencin hides under the table, giving birth to strange ideas. Circles and waterfalls. Glens and neurons.

Sound waves create eyes in the air. What is visible is but the tip of the proverbial iceberg. A mouth moving on a canvas. Density, volume, weight. Color, design, texture.

Some things that are present to the mind do not have palpable form. Yet there is something essential about them. Intuition, premonition, perspicacity. A blowtorch made of thought. And blue flame. And metaphor and art.

A face falls out of a mirror, bitter and full of juice. Do not look at it, even as it tries to talk. Merely go on combing your hair. Listen to the sounds of the concertina someone is playing in the street. Assemble a sentence. Applaud vigorously when Polly Peachum finishes her song.

Since, therefore, of the things that are predicated some signify what a thing is, or quiddity, and others quality, and others quantity, and others relation, and others action or passion, and some the place where, and others the time when, to each of these the being of essence signifies the same thing. A shining incontrovertible whatness. A glowing. An aura. A saw blade gleaming in Alabama sunlight. The smell of sage. A Pawnee brave riding a roan stallion out onto the prairie.

Wrinkles tell stories. Realism is elementary. I remember the gunrack in my grandparent's farmhouse in North Dakota. The beauty of those rifles made you want to fire them. Load them. Shoot them. Fill yourself with the world. Hit the wall if you must. Contradictions can sometimes be more than you can bear.

It is a delicate situation. Colors persist after the sun goes down. There are a dizzying number of stars. Diesel locomotives. The scream of a butterfly. The ghost of Jim Morrison.

And Buffalo Bill. And Sitting Bull. And Aristotle.

What is emotion? The gleam of the sand when the surf recedes revealing a dead skate. The sound of the waves as they curl, tumble, hit the sand, or crash into rocks. How many adjectives do you need to describe an emotion? Construct an emotion? Purge an emotion? Hang an emotion? There is a stepladder in the closet. Form is something else. Form is a form of definition. Apollinaire walks by eating a sandwich. Cubism, he says. This sandwich is a perfect example of Cubism.

I call this mystery of being the noise of a café in the afternoon. Heat, attitude, clouds. A sack of potatoes. A plane taking off at noon. Divinations. Conjectures. Black feathers. Creak of a Salvation Army desk. A giant eyeball floating over the prairie.

VIOLET

I want to construct an emotion of such lucidity that it will mediate between the world at large and my own personal perspectives. The emotions I now have are murky and unserviceable. They obfuscate. They stretch out of shape and tear. They leave me feeling dark and unprecedented, like Baudelaire.

But this presents a philosophical problem. Feelings are a response to the world. How can I construct a feeling in advance of an experience? It's like trying to taste your food before eating it. Before putting it into your mouth and chewing it. Like laughing at a joke before you hear the joke.

A lit candle will paint the walls with a buttery light. That's the feeling I like. That's the feeling I want. That mellow, golden light. That's a feeling where I could linger and daydream. A feeling in which I could get along with the world and speak peaceably and tolerantly with people. A feeling in which I could accept all the burrs and injuries of human behavior. But one cannot ingest such a feeling like a food or a drug. I suppose codeine and Valium come closest to substituting for such a feeling, but they are, after all, synthetic and addictive, a false paradise.

And since feeling has neither form nor substance, the idea of constructing a feeling, as one might construct a birdhouse or violin, the problem walks a thin wire of flimsy conceit. Its being, its existence as a sensation is partly vibrational, partly neurochemical, and partly a manifestation of language. That is to say, it's a form of light sloshing around in the bucket of a sentence.

In the same manner that a certain arrangement of molecules will create a certain drug or chemical, a certain arrangement of words will create a particular image or idea, or a rearrangement of letters will create a different word.

The world is in continual flux. Language is a reflection of continual process and modulation. Emotion is an ocean caged behind the ribs. If the metaphor is mixed, it's because emotion makes a mess of everything, including T-shirts and planets.

There is the emotion of distance, which is an emotion of stratospheric calm and maneuverability. Radical emotions give steel. If I insult a pickle, the pickle will not explode, not because it's a pickle, but because it's not a hole. Holes explode because of the sticks of dynamite that have been placed there. In mining, this is called blast design and is a way to minimize ground damage.

The present tense is recommended for enduring pain. Do not put pain in the future. The ideal place for pain is in the past, where it can be forgotten, but this is hard to do without a sufficient quantity of garlic and opium.

Unfathomability can be achieved through the frottage of Max Jacob and eating lots of scallops.

If you slice a bean in half, you will discover a personality. It will help explain polygamy, and the structure of protein.

Grumbling is a good way to attach the truth to gravity.

Rage can be remedied with bromides, brochures, and the syntax of acceleration.

I will sometimes goad pronouns into action, or drift among the skeletons of shattered greed, reflecting on the futility of corduroy.

The circus will hurt your eyes if you break it into jokes. Rise peremptorily during a float. Milk opinion with whatever incentive urges, be it embodiment or infantry, truffles or ratiocination.

Language disintegrates when it eats itself.

Emotion is old and pressed into generation where it must visit cafés and grow thick with excuse. It is here that we must suppose diving into the bald powder of participles. For what paragraph floats unexamined beneath the world without a rudder or frequency? A wade through the small waves striking at our legs reveals the various flavors of consideration. Let us grip the handle and wheel our thought forward into further reflection. The zoom lens merges with the horizon and the emotion emerging in the distance is crumpled and ripped by a storm of livid violet.

FURTHER PROOF THAT THE UNIVERSE IS YARN

It begins with a bang. Then grows into mind and body and the singular beauty of clack valves. But it is the occurrence of nails in a birdhouse that crackles with an inner radical pleading.

We see it in our eyes. The need for fungus. The need for experience. For freshly dug earth. A thistle and a bag of nails.

The physicists arise at dawn. Failure luxuriates in bricks. Colors are unbridled and wet and clay. One needs all the proper drugs to experience animals.

I'm not necessarily recommending bric-a-brac, but it doesn't hurt to discuss irregularities of skin. If an idea is worth pursuing, wrap it in cellophane and put it on the black market as an appearance of something, meteorite, or pogo stick.

Wortaufschüttung, vulkanisch, meerüberrauscht, said Paul Celan.

We construct a car made of snow, and start it, and watch as it proceeds toward its shadow.

Otherwise we don't see what it is in its eternity. What we believe is shape and chrome exists to drive things forward until they become butter.

I was not present at the Big Bang. I was in Philadelphia, attending to some legal business, forming a constitution, signing documents, making speeches, and taking certain precautions so that no mildew formed in my wig, which had cost me a pretty penny, and was now so perfect in its waves and curls I had to stand backward in awe, and tripped over a shoe and fell to the floor. The carpet, I noticed, had a Persian design.

I want these words to keep moving until you find crisp red apples at the end of this sentence.

And the golden hunger of the mushroom.

The strange violence of webs and rust are unpacked in private rooms. If you punch the wall as hard as you can you can see a black dragon breathing crimson flames on the other side.

The truth is full of hallucination. There are alternate paradigms. Spurs and rubber. Daylight and cardboard.

This is why representation requires paper and metal. Tattoos are the colophons of the new century, emblems for the stain of experience. Snakes, scorpions, roses.

Mass is energy.

Now punch the wall. Punch it again. And again and again. Can you see it?

None of these words actually belong to me. They don't belong to anyone. They become the black heart of things.

Ghosts. The eternal reach of the real.

SUBLIME AND ODD IS MUTABLE

Now to lip the indulged feeling and gleefully hook grace to it. Grid a throat by stirring a bloom with lamp black. Pull a glow from phenomena.

Physiology begins jellyfish. Energy is pushed to parabolas to become paraphernalia. It might be sophisticated to bubble the scratch. Add fire to this chiaroscuro. Echo an anguish in consonants. The drive always explains the railroad.

The fantasy you hold is between ceremonies. When planets cause copper the coast will drip. Suppleness is the snow wherein a proverb oozes gantries. To assemble a passion requires more keys than stars. The garments cry nerve. The smears begin an erection. Words are packed in images because the energy is clean and wild.

Cubes do cartwheels. Source is a friendly inflammation. A love which is cracks. Strong coffee moistens the engine. The orchard moans in its heart with steam. Incision increases the chance of unraveling.

The luminous odor echoes from the bite in its personality. Circumference is what a metaphor does when its science is talking.

Grab vapor and consider wading through its inches. Add Max Jacob. Add seminal racks unearthed by lure and grasp.

The panic cracks syntax over mohair. Green brings food to a pulse, astronomy in a handstand. Put a zipper on the drizzle. Mortgage your confusion. Glue the rain with a tube of art. Necessity is often pharmaceutical. The opium sparkles in a corner of the photograph. The people are smiling with a rascally expectation, because the bug is an abstraction, and has 400 legs.

DEATH IS FONDLED LIKE A GUN

The circus is in town I wear a brass hat for doing the dishes my belt buckle shines I have punched a hole in the wall I need the lucidity of water I wonder what sort of fugue best supports this supposition there is more to Louisiana than you will ever know.

Perception is walking the twang of a guitar I dilate whenever I hear a book about goldfish and now a new noise convulses in the air but the telephone is silent.

The radio thunders in spectacular despair exhumed lines of poetry a tall man from Taiwan gives me a wide-eyed look because I wrote him a ten-page letter explaining trash bins I said please believe me when I say that I am trying to develop an improved rapport with ambiguity.

For example, last night an eternal life unequalled by worms swarmed below a surgical incision and was later glued to an armchair.

If any of this is a reflection I will fold it like a sweater and put it in a drawer. I will comb your hair I will do anything I will open your chest to a mongrel abstraction and give it wine for the eyes the armchair feels wonderful like a cracker.

There is nothing larger than denial an ecstasy raises a broom on the floor let yourself dissolve into eyeballs mass is a raw example of Africa everyone itches to see birds complex creatures acquire a curl of clouds while the sandman hammers a nest to the stepladder because I am too sensitive for technical details.

Have confidence in your hunger contemplate the fire while pressing the buttons in a bone of songs. A larynx is a guitar of the throat instinctive as furniture electricity imbues a handful of vowels and invites the metamorphosis of ducks.

Existence is a fluid Picasso painting a dog.

Anger swarms like punctuation a volcano bitter as grapefruit spitting leprechauns the clay is lyrical accept your giant but in a very eloquent manner express denim luminous balls loaded with parables descriptions without end act like a phonograph surrounded by beautiful planets.

Infinity crashes into a birthday cake the abalone is delicious stir yourself with a spoon a noise is a pink emotion anyone can arrange a black emotion if there is an incentive to see it happen drag some grammar into the light put a little plaster on it I prefer not to reveal my injury a ball of spun sugar can change your mind all life has the capacity to float there is a pulse in the wrist there are veins in the hand rivers of blood each is a surge of soft leather gloves the appetite sharpens support when death is fondled like a gun.

ALLEN GINSBERG PHONES ME FROM THE DEAD

Last night Allen Ginsberg phoned me from the dead.

How are you, I said.

I'm dead, he said.

What is it like being dead?

It's nice being free of the timeless sadness of existence. But I miss bon bons, the flowerness of any given moment, and Japanese lampshades. What's it like up there, in the world of the living?

Same old same old, I said. Endless war. Three wars, in fact. Afghanistan, Iraq, and Libya. Four, if you include Pakistan. Our roads are going to hell. The Pentagon sucks up trillions of American dollars and pours them down in the form of bombs. Shitty electrocuting showers. Feculent bottled water. Privately contracted thugs. People are hungry. There's an ad on the radio asking people to donate food. You never know, the family next door might be going hungry. Poverty is pandemic. 42 percent of financial wealth is controlled by the top 1 percent. 37 million Americans are on food stamps. I miss your voice, Allen. You were always a force for the good.

That's nice of you to say. I wish I could be there, too. But frankly, I like being dead. It's like being high on laughing gas. The universe is a void, in which there is a sweet dreamhole. It's the instant of going into or coming out of existence. But here, here among the permanently dead, the permanently non-existent, one is free of the sadness of birth, the sadness of changing from dream to dream. Can you dig this?

Yes, my time is coming. One thing though. If you no longer exist, who am I talking to?

You are talking to your imagination of me.

Oh yeah. That makes sense. I can dig that. Anything you miss about being alive? You know, like food, flowers, walking around in a body?

Well, sex obviously. The wiggle and play of my cock. Autumn gold. Wet glaze on an asphalt street. Holy sunlight. The great crystal door to the House of Night. Eyeball kicks on storefronts. The gaiety of tables in flirty restaurant rowdiness. The vast lamb of the middleclass. The crazy shepherds of rebellion. The rich rank smell of old apricots under October leaves. The breath in my nose. Auto lights in the rain. Frisco hilly tincan evening sitdown visions. My books piled up before me for my use. My texts, my manuscripts, my loves.

Have you seen Jack or Neal? Are they there? John Lennon? John Keats? Shelley? Janis Joplin? Shakespeare? Christ?

Yeah, yeah, yeah, we're all here. Everybody's here. But not in the way you think. The human personality is, after all, a very ephemeral thing at best. People die all the time and reinvent themselves. One way or another, dead or alive, it all comes down to yearning. There is yearning all over the universe. The universe is a universe of yearning. Not even the human imagination satisfies the endless emptiness of the soul.

So what is the difference between life and death?

Death is larger and larger loops. The dull sleep of idealistic brains. Life is work and frenzy. Insults and small talk. Threats and dollars. Thick men in dark hats. Wall Street cashmere hiding iron muscles of money.

That doesn't sound so good.

Well, money was always a problem. Even in death I still think about it. And remember. This is a me imagined by you. You are in the realm of money. Hairy buttocks and brainwaves. Abandoned buildings gutted and blackwindowed from old fires. And you're lifting lines of poetry from my big red book of Collected Poetry. Aren't you?

Yes, it's true. You got me. But tell me. What are ghosts?

Ghosts are animal trumpets below the abdomen. Visceral sensations of acute loss. Leaving us flying like birds into time. In and out of time. When you're dead, time ceases to exist. I miss the tick of clocks. The elegant joke of Swiss cuckoos poking out to tell you it's noon. Or three o'clock. Or the garbage truck at four backing up the driveway to take away crumpled plastic bottles and newspapers and pizza boxes with the cheese still stuck to the bottom. Ghosts are everywhere. They are the soot that falls on city vegetables. They are your own forlorn soul making itself at home in the void. They are your eyes weeping tears.

Kennedy throat brain bloodied in Texas. That's when the coup that took over America began you know.

Yes, I pretty much figured that was the case. Hey, guess what. Remember your pal Dylan? He's coming up on 70. Can you believe that? Dylan as an old man? It's a bit jarring to see that old jowly wrinkled face under a broadbrimmed cowboy hat. And those Texas swing jackets he's taken to wearing are weird too. He performed in China last Tuesday. Just before Chinese artist and activist Ai Weiwei was arrested.

That must have been awkward. Did Dylan say anything?

Not that I know of.

Mmmm. Well, Dylan was always hard to figure.

I remember a movie in which you showed Dylan the grave of Jack Kerouac and said that's where we all end up. Got any advice for me?

Sit down crosslegged and relax. Storm heaven with your mental guns. Don't abuse the planet. Enjoy life. Prepare for death. Pogo to garage bands. Make haiku of birds.

A BRAQUE AFTERNOON

Words carved out of air tickle the lucidity of mosquitoes during the revelation of pearl. Cylinders push the car. Space cures the gantries by duet. Limestone pipes heft the omen. Personification fantasizes a steam.

Brocaded proposals solicit tin zipper this. A Braque afternoon has energy. Anger stirs the train. Nimble dollops of brown put emotion in motion. Syllables house eyes.

Hirsute the may jar comb. Embody impulse wash the confusion with music. The sopranos jingle their processions behind the ink. Summer flows from the breath of spring. A box squeezed red until it rumors agitation.

This mutates into utility. Problems begin to stray into clarity. Moccasins enhance the talk of dinosaurs. We map the incense with bells and bamboo. Buffalo grab swimming and like it.

A cut in the car bleeds less than a carat. Oats are experience consonants are bowls. Humor description be an oval. Be a vague area in the Louvre yet serious as keys with a pungency of underworld Etruscans holding candles below the army of Philistines stirring our resilience. It ruminates Bach to a foot below me.

Excursion knots a despair when the swamp is privately painted. Languor has a spice that dazzles even the frogs. Touch personality with a decorated towel. The force of doctrine is rough on a puddle. Oblivion's lobsters burst out of a pronoun pinching the salt of stenography.

Wave the river scrupulously. Drag the paradigm out of the blob with a gargantuan yank. Birch and glue the skin. There is more theorem than kerosene in the meaning knob. Semantic trousers sewn with a walking eye.

The gift of fiction explains the bones of the cuckoo. Injury is more flower than wound. Navigation does not alter the sphere. Perception earns the treasure of your sun. Those who collide eventually take to flipping.

Clapping begins with the ravenous hands of a bemused public attention, and ends with the bottle of a hushed voice. Let's get our airplanes in order. Do nebulas in the flower parlor. Hum herds of meandering sound during a luminous cotton. Give hectic legs to a curious dance.

My chair is entirely metaphorical and upside down. If you find me sitting in it, you will find me upside down. Therefore is blossoming a suspension and suspension, however suspended, suspect in sustenance. The rascally gloves of time squirm in the fingers of bias. Erect a salon of wax then savor a vapor of wick and wicket.

Lure words to the brain absorption is hinged to mustard. Punish the tease of the fabric not the vividness of the skin. Montmartre bangs in its slants. Form heaves with simultaneity. Nothing succeeds like the coherence of wind.

RIVERS I HAVE KNOWN

You have to love the names of Washington's rivers: Yakima, Snoqual-
mie, Sauk, Cedar, Tolt, Wenatchee, Columbia, Snake, Satsop, Chehalis,
Nisqually, Duwamish, Cowlitz, Touchet, Tucannon, Cow, Crab,
Skookumchuk, Humptulips, Palouse, Skagit, Skykomish, Quinault,
Methow, Okanogan.

The Snoqualmie spurts out of the ground high in the Cascades in
three separate places then all three forks join near North Bend, the lit-
tle mountain community where David Lynch set Twin Peaks and all of
its weirdness and murder and strange mountain beauty.

The Sauk pops up somewhere in the Glacial Peak Wilderness and
forms its main stem at Bedal, flows northwest past Darrington (lots of
tarheels and blue grass music in Darrington), then north to join the
Skagit at Rockport.

I white-water rafted down the Wenatchee in April, 1985, by invita-
tion with a friend training to be a guide. Which meant I got to go for
free, and it being April, I also got to freeze. Even though I was wearing
a so-called wet suit. I found out that wet suits do not keep you dry.
They're just supposed to keep you warm. It didn't keep me warm,
though it may have kept me from freezing. I danced around in a park-
ing lot trying to get the suit off. I got in the car, turned the ignition on,
and when the engine got hot enough to put some real heat out, heat has
never felt so good.

The Duwamish empties into Puget Sound near downtown Seattle,
by Harbor Island, where a lot of ships get painted. Boeing has some
plants on its banks as well. When I worked at plant no 2 in the summer
of 1967 I used to take my sack lunch out onto the concrete dock by the
river's edge and stare at the water moving by and shiver to think of all
the industrial chemicals in it, arsenic, polychlorinated biphenyls, poly-
cyclic aromatic hydrocarbons, copper, lead, mercury.

I've never seen the Humptulips, which is over in the Olympic
Peninsula, flowing through the rainforests, which receive around 220
inches of rain annually. The Humptulips has gone by a variety of

names, including Hum-tu-lups, Humptolups, Humtutup, and Um-ta-lah. Humtutup sounds like the name of an Egyptian pharaoh, but all these names emanate from the Chehalis tribe, and either means "hard to pole," or "chilly region." The Humptulips empties into Grays Harbor, where the town of Hoquiam is located. Kurt Cobain was from Hoquiam, and I have two friends living there, Dan and Tammy, who owned the Jackson Street Bookstore which (sadly) has since closed. The name Hoquiam is derived from the Chehalis language, *ho-qui-umpts*, meaning "hungry for wood," because of all the loose timber floating into Grays Harbor.

The Cedar River is where Seattle gets its drinking water. It flows from the Cedar River watershed in the Cascades. Roberta and I went to the Renton Public Library once to kill some time before a wedding. On the way into the library, we crossed a bridge, which was lined with people, all gazing into the river as it slid over a bed of rocks shiny and clear as glass. We went to the edge and looked down and saw hundreds of salmon all seeming motionless as their bodies swayed ever so slightly as the current moved over and around their bodies, all heads pointed east, in the direction of the Cascades.

IT ALL COMES DOWN TO RAIN

I feel a comedy of feathers emerge from my skin. I become a bird. I become an inference. I become a direct object and an intermediary cabbage.

And I don't like cabbage. That's how serious I am. That's how ridiculous I am. I don't even know for sure what "I am" means. I is an overtone. A suggestion. A bird. A cabbage. A cabbage bird.

Identity spurts from the sternum and prickles with weird coordinates. Heaven sits cockeyed by the edge of a cliff. We must leap aboard when we get the chance. Meanwhile, there is soup, and litmus paper, and cloth. Cloth may refer to clothing, or it may just be cloth. Cloth.

We fold our desires and pack them into our hearts and head for Paris. We arrive in time to see Henri Poincaré ride a swan down the Champs-Élysées.

I like the thickness of syntax when it spins in the water and makes the sentence move forward through a cloud of midnight postage.

The fork is a utensil. The spoon is a postulate. But it is the knife that comes to a point.

I inflate my frustration until it reveals the muscular wallpaper of a meticulous opinion.

I explore the face of a genial distance. There's an elegy on the loose and I want to see it before it disappears into a good mood. The road is gravel, though I suspect you already knew that. You can hear it crunch under the tires of these words. Which aren't even round. They're oval. This causes the sentence to wobble, and go up and down, as if at sea.

I remember an old Swedish church on the prairie, with a foundation of stone. It had long ceased to function as a church, but its door continued to stay open. The wind flung it back and forth. It would creak open then slam shut as if invisible people were coming and going. Ghosts, I suppose. You could call them ghosts. Or conceits. Ideas. Dreams. An idea of invisible people in my head. An idea of invisible people in the invisible heads of invisible people.

The door of our apartment is a continual fascination. It has a little peephole in it. If somebody's making a bunch of racket in the hallway you can see who it is. Once I saw Abraham Lincoln doing his laundry. He looked abstracted, as always, and obsessed with holding the so-called union together. He wore boxer shorts: red hearts on a white background. On another occasion the Marquis de Lafayette paraded back and forth in a sugar of profligate oscillation.

I am surrounded by a mosaic of noise. There are sounds that are easily digested, and others that lead to dreaming. I'm not at all sure how to define music. Does anyone really know how to do that? Music is to sound what brass is to distillation. The drip of whiskey into a big oak barrel.

Think of steam. Now think of sarongs. And Malaysia. Time operates differently in different spaces. Different geographies will vary translations of time. Sometimes you will see it crawl over the knuckles of an arthritic hand, and on other occasions and in other circumstances it will slide under the bellies of fish in scintillations of light and shadow.

Why are spiders so difficult to coax out of a bathtub? You'd think they'd be anxious to ride a hand out of that porcelain into liberty. But they don't. They skedaddle at the least provocation.

If it's hot enough, I will put my running shirt on the porch railing to dry in the sun. Otherwise, I have to take it out back and shoot it. I have buried a lot of running shirts. One day their ghosts will arise from the drawer and dance in the darkness like one of those old-timey cartoons of skeletons and cats.

One afternoon after I hung my shirt on the railing I felt a young rain tree brush my skin.

Sensations are the pixies of our lives.

Is it wise to harbor so many generalities? Not when you're my age. Deductions become inductions. The redwood, bathed in light, touches the sky. A storm brews. Lightning stumbles on an electron. I stop to ponder an elephant. The elephant has been painted on the side of a barn, and is pink and happy with an upturned trunk. When you're young, everything is on arrival. When you're old, everything is on departure. The difference between them is not so large. The difference between them is that of a muscle on bone, camaraderie in an airplane factory.

Light survives the darkness. This is a daily occurrence. I get up, make the bed, go to the bathroom, take a piss, look at my face in the mirror. My face trickles down the mirror in beads of water. I remember looking younger. I remember that younger person I used to be. I remember the highways that were traveled. The cars driven and repaired. Gaskets replaced. Fan belts replaced. Too bad you can't replace a body so easily. Body work the mechanics call it. Medicine has a different name for it: abnormality. You have an abnormality. I've known this my whole life. Poetry is an abnormality. Poetry is a big abnormality. Poetry is a huge abnormality. For which there is no cure. Except more poetry. More abnormality.

Adjectives are the adipose tissue of the sentence. Fat. Adjectives can make a sentence fat. This, for instance, might be considered a big fat sentence, an abnormality beginning with a demonstrative pronoun and spitting blue fire from a mouth of ink and memory.

I feel the kiss of California. I speak to a canvas with a paintbrush dipped in a gob of blue. My feelings waltz when I cross the border. When I enter a state of abandon, the painting gets easier. The painting becomes goats. Cylinders. Forceps.

A willow grounds the elasticity of dirt. The stream urges conference with the hills. The hills confer with the sky. The sky argues back with rain.

THEY SAY TRUTH LIES THERE

It's 1:10 p.m. and someone coughed and a car started. Toby is finally sleeping after his tirade over the black cat from next door who walks by our ground-level window every day. I let Toby go into the hallway because sometimes that seems to appease him. Once he sees that the hallway is empty, he can imagine himself as the king of his realm, and all that he sees. But the ruse doesn't work. He stands by the door and wants to be let outside. We never let him outside. If we did, he would panic and disappear under a bush or up a tree the first time a car went by.

And so I lift him up and open the door. I worry that he'll jump from my arms so I try keep a firm grip. The black cat next door — a small female with a sweet and playful disposition — is just that moment scaling up the branch that leads to the above-ground patio of the house next door. I figure she'll be alarmed when she catches view of Toby in my arms and scamper through the little cat door provided for her. But she doesn't. She comes back down to our porch and looks up at me. She wants to meet Toby. Toby wants to meet her. It's tempting to put Toby down and let them sniff one another, but I can't take that chance. I bring Toby back in and put him down on the slate tile of the vestibule while I open the mailbox. It's the usual disappointing crap. A brochure from Trader Joe's featuring Halloween Joe's Scary Good Cookies, a bill from Birds & Blooms, a thank you receipt from Seattle's Union Gospel Mission, and a brochure announcing the ACLU of Washington's Bill of Rights Celebration Dinner.

Far away in the distance, to the east, over Snoqualmie Pass, awaits Roslyn. Roberta and I are going there November 3rd. I've been invited to do a reading for Oyez Roslyn.

The last time I was in Roslyn was 1993. I was with my father. He loved the TV show *Northern Lights* and Roslyn was the town featured in that series. We were doing a three-day road trip. We continued east to the Palouse country where the impeccable neatness of the German farms amazed me and the soft fine dirt, called loess, that comprises the gently rolling hills where a soft white wheat is grown.

Thoughts of dirt and Halloween remind me of the grisly description I came across last night concerning Shelley's exhumed remains in Edward John Trelawny's *Recollections*:

> The soldiers gathered fuel whilst I erected the furnace, and then the men of the Health Office set to work, shoveling away the sand which covered the body, while we gathered round, watching anxiously. The first indication of their having found the body, was the appearance of the end of a black silk handkerchief — I grubbed this out with a stick, for we were not allowed to touch anything with our hands — then some shreds of linen we met with, and a boot with the bone of the leg and the foot in it. On the removal of a layer of brush-wood, all that now remained of my lost friend was exposed — a shapeless mass of bones and flesh. The limbs separated from the trunk on being touched.
>
> "Is that a human body?" exclaimed Byron; "why it's more like the carcase of a sheep, or any other animal, than a man: this is a satire on our pride and folly."

I remember trick or treating at age nine in Minneapolis. This would have been 1956. There were no discussions of serial killers or pedophiles. People could walk freely at night without worry. Kids could go door to door unaccompanied by a parent.

I wore a Frankenstein mask. It smelled of rubber, and I had a difficult time seeing through the slits that served as eyes.

Frankenstein was, of course, the creation of Shelley's wife, Mary Shelley. Nice to think that at age nine I already had a connection with the Romantics.

I think, too, of Trelawny's account of Percy Shelley learning to swim:

> I was bathing one day in a deep pool in the Arno, and astonished the Poet by performing a series of aquatic gymnastics, which I had learnt from the natives of the South Seas. On my coming out, whilst dressing, Shelley said, mournfully: "Why can't I swim, it seems so very easy?" I answered, "Because you think you can't. If you determine, you will: take a header off this bank, and when you rise turn on your back, you will float like a duck; but you must reverse the arch in your spine, for it's now bent the wrong way."

> He doffed his jacket and trowsers, kicked off his shoes and socks, and plunged in, and there he lay stretched out on the bottom like a conger eel, not making the least effort or struggle to save himself. He would have been drowned if I had not instantly fished him out. When he recovered his breath, he said: "I always find the bottom of the well, and they say Truth lies there. In another minute I should have found it, and you would have found an empty shell. It is an easy way of getting rid of the body."

> "What would Mrs. Shelley have said to me if I had gone back with your empty cage?"

> "Don't tell Mary — not a word!" he rejoined, and then continued, "It's a great temptation; in another minute I might have been in another planet."

"But as you always find the bottom," I observed, "you might have sunk 'deeper than did ever plummet sound.'"

"I am quite easy on that subject," said the Bard. "Death is the veil, which those who live call life: they sleep, and it is lifted. Intelligence should be imperishable; the art of printing has made it so in this planet."

THE OCCURRENCE OF SADNESS AND GLASS

Whatever phantom slides through you pay it no mind. The dead are everywhere. It takes effort to fully occupy a living body. Each experience is an egg to break, the glop of its yolk spilling out as one glistening nucleus. It's finding that nucleus that's difficult.

Age is a thorny plant. Look for a hiatus, a rupture in the fabric of time, and occupy that. It's easiest to find those places in art. Places which are non-places because they don't exist in linear time or three-dimensional space.

If you fold a piece of tin into a placenta you will acquire a Technicolor hammer. It won't be a real hammer, a hammer that you can use to pound nails. It will be a metaphorical hammer, a hammer that you can use to build similes. A house like a grape. A hat like an artichoke.

I see two eyes in the rain. Later, I see the sky lying on the ground. I pick it up. I tie it into three hundred knots and exchange it for a pair of boots and a birch canoe. This is the sort of thing you can do in language that you cannot do in normal life.

Falling down is a maniacally brilliant sensation if it's done correctly. Of course, it has to be a complete accident. How do you plan an accident? You don't. Accidents plan you.

If writing happens by accident the words will overflow their margins and tumble over the rocks of an imagined envy. For example, how old is Robert Redford? Sip the elegance of cider from a crystal glass and answer quickly. The answer is a red dream with a savory tang crawling across a piece of paper weeping tears of iron. This has nothing whatever to do with Robert Redford and so it is correct.

If I'm being excessively resplendent it's because life is full of headlights and syllables. Life cries effervescence at the disciplinarians. We bring our more serene behavior to the bank and feed it money. The walls echo with my criticism. Money is too complex, too sentimental. Money should be serious, like dereliction.

Cézanne stirs a lot of emotion. I throb like a monster to see such color, such shape. I dream of a museum full of steam and sorcery. I see a Blob with a voice and meanings which froth into Kuiper belts of astronomical vertebrae. I have a neck full of light and an arm full of circulation. Each time something sublime happens I glitter like an area code.

Large ambiguities rescue us from idealism. It feels pervasive, like a pumpkin. I walk down the road looking for a job. I specialize in irritation. I wear gloves of oak and an alternating current. I get a job folding napkins into whispers. I stumble over a sentence teeming with words and fold it into a beautiful collision. This involves tuna, honeysuckle, and a tiny fork. My lobster eyes pull a world of color out of a solitary potato. This is how things are done around here. Circularly. There are things that cry for diameter and circumference and a little cherry pi.

Emotion is a cherry whose charm murmurs sociability. That's what emotion is for, largely. The sky hammers the ground with rain and thunder. And at the end of the day, the sky drags the night over the mountains, the train starts to roll, and social instincts awaken the occurrence of sadness and glass.

BEFORE THE SHIP LEAVES

Before the ship leaves the port I want to buy a few trinkets. I have a
pretty good grip on things. I know the streets. I know the museums. I
know the pharmacies and dead ends. I wear a thick green wool sweater
and a pair of cotton pants but I feel naked underneath and my neck
hurts. It is a species of pain I call Chuck the Imponderable. I see the
spars of a ship named Delectation out on the horizon. I stretch. I spin.
I pray. I go to plays. I go to pieces. I round the corner and find a boat
calling me to go on a journey. Instead I buy a canvas and slide around
on it dribbling a world of paint with my elbows and crocodile slither.
I have scales and feathers. I am a monster gardenia. A beautiful ghost
haunts the incision on my chest. I wash it with goat blood. I practice
Hinduism and ambiguity. It occurs to me that the curve of a boat pro-
peller is precisely the kind of acceleration I admire. I also admire the
air. And the garish abandonment of echoes. A batch of lightning shoots
out of my enthusiasm. I feel parallel to an emotion propelled by an en-
gine of birds. A 10 pound thought enriches the bone black antiquity of
my Metro ticket. It was supposedly in the possession of a pharaoh visit-
ing Manhattan 3,000 years before the birth of Christ. Before there was
a subway. Or shoe stores. A massive pink cloud tumbles through the
brocade of a burning filmstrip. A sideboard screams mahogany. I open
a bottle of root beer and begin to paint. Delectation is coming into
port. I paint the bow blue. I paint the sails white. I paint the eulogy
puce and the slobber Sicilian umber. It all congeals. It weighs a thou-
sand tons. It is an entire world. A world of paint. A world of pain. I title
it "Poetry Of The Stove" and buy a sack of pancake dough. I head for
the dock, and brush my fedora with a wad of Pythagorean moss. The
captain is a clumsy angel with a stethoscope and a bowl of bouillon.
Three months later we arrive in Cartagena. I have a headache the size
of China. But the pain in my neck is gone and I have a trunk full of
paintings. Watercolor. Oil. Pencil sketches. I am greeted by a lime green
crab. I shout take me to the finest hotel. I need a bath. He shouts get a

cab. I'm a crab. The cab is mandarin orange. The driver is hellebore red. We arrive at the hotel at sunset, which is old gold and opera pink. My ganglions are celadon and I like my whisky neat. Let it be remarked that practical medicine takes this shape from its own necessity. No voyage is whole without a piano. And the first condition of playing it successfully is to know that it is incomplete.

THE SHAPE OF YEARNING

Running has the shape of yearning. It's seminal to the production of movement.

The breath stirs explorations of Paris. The visceral heat of a social component. The colors and glow of a jukebox. Life on the farm. Sweat.

It's a joy to consider the breath of another person, the heat of a barn, slats of old wood, rusted nails, blocks of straw.

Autumn has opium eyes. The amniotic fluid of a quiet moment. The perfect unavailability of a woman's gaze.

Swallows carrying the wind across the spine of a river.

There is a spider building a web. It urges reverence.

The Queen of Hearts wanders through her words wearing alligator earrings and a sparkling, crackling protoplasm.

She will produce a dead morality in a mound of snow. She will break the light with her beauty. She will shine into the bruise of our wounded existence.

In our wrinkles are our histories.

The overly-concerned concierge knocks on the door and asks if there is a problem. No, you say, *tout va bien*. Meanwhile planets circle your thumbs. A shadow snaps a phonograph on.

The glow of a brass eyelid summons the candy of sleep. Montmartre is obscured by fog.

Sometimes a feeling will harden into words and cut the air with its grammar. When it reaches its destination it will assume the shape of Prague.

THE BEAUTIFUL WEATHER OF GERUNDS

What physical presence does not taste of heat? I think of pipes in basements, dripping and cold, and don't really mean to derive energy from that. I prefer to catch a taxi. All the hardening I've been learning to medicate may now retire on its own terms and have a blast representing envy. I'm done with embarrassment. That's for youth. What I want is solitude. Maybe a walk would do me some good. My blood is stirring. Powwows and popcorn exist without approval. You know? Some things just are. Others are propelled by a mood of yearning, treading architectures of hope and filigree. Not many people read these days, I mean really read, you know? The kind of reading that results in canvas, paint, ruffled necks and big hats with silver buckles. I'm often entranced by the postcards one sees displayed on drugstore racks. This kind of reading requires the tools of chronology and a head like a world. It isn't difficult to find continents of thought in your head or kings sculpted in granite if you provide yourself with a little time and a rawhide vest. There's a parable of value in each and every eye. Mirrors are even wilder. The reflections are elusive, difficult to hug, but grapple with consciousness like the rest of us, those of us still flesh and blood, getting wrinkled, bald, but knowing just how to set up a stepladder and paint a ceiling without getting paint everywhere. That takes a certain skill. The journey doesn't end with a dock and a group of people greeting you as you remove your life jacket. It makes a segue into another thousand themes of dogs and engravings. There's no way you can expand a circle without spreading your wings and dropping a regret or two on somebody's head. The elegance of maturity begins with a monstrous recognition of mud, what it is, how it congeals, how much of it there is, how it never ends, but sticks to the shoes and is left with imprints, the tread of tires, the patterns on the bottoms of running shoes, which become a text. Heraclitus was right about change. It's swollen and textured, incongruous and unpredictable. Hence, poetry. Burning and migration, intestines and leaves. Paper existed long before the computer, and is best savored in a spirit of resistance. Whatever else you think about potato chips, the friction of life is what cultures pearls. Every time I crack an egg I feel sublime. Though it's mostly when I'm thirsty, and there's plenty of juice in the refrigerator, and none of my opinions matter anymore. Just the screws I've written into a sentence to hold everything together, the rain against the window, the keys on the table, the mercury in the thermometer serving us conversation and numbers, as if a religion crawled out to be born, inspiring architecture and plays, oblivion and self-effacement. Puddles. Bob Dylan. Beggars and groans. The beautiful weather of gerunds, brimming with imagery and voyage. Why, I continually ask, is there something instead of nothing? Nothing pleases or puzzles me more than life. Just don't ask me to fix anything electrical. It's enough that I shave, get dressed, and occasionally offer my friends something stereophonic. Life is a tale of dusky migration. Ask anyone. They will tell you what a gerund is. That it turns brown with age, and will attract a great many words, describing coffee, describing romance, describing blue.

BREATH AND SHADOW

I respect trees. They purify the air and shade the ground. I respect their silence and mosaic of leaves and squirrels, their peculiarities and sprawl. They attain spectacular heights and bend with the wind like shadows. They exude nobility. It is a privilege to wander among them and follow the curves of their crazy branches. I stray from the path and slip in the mud. I see something gleaming among the trees and assume it is a river. I go to the river and unfurl my being. I open inside. Something in me feels damaged and needs healing. I imagine the pain as a rag of blood and squeeze it and the blood drips on the rocks giving them the appearance of speckled gray eggs. I appeal to the wind. I appeal to the water. I grab a walnut and watch the ground teeming with ants. I take out my gun and shoot a cloud. Rain comes spilling from the cloud. The cloud disappears. The sunlight returns. Coins of sunlight dapple the ground. Steam rises, sweetening the air with the fragrance of rot. I fish, and furnish myself a dinner. Slabs of pink meat sizzle in a frying pan of thick black iron. I wallow in rumination. I dig a hole and bury thirteen dollars and a spool of red thread. I break the eye of a fish against a tree and stomp on it until it is nothing and the fish cannot see me anymore. I do not like it when the dead look back at me. I grab a rock and throw it at the sun. Shadows of sound spill out of my mouth. I shout. I whistle. I fulminate. I scream. It is broad daylight but I can see the moon. The moon is full. The moon is the cadaver of a beautiful woman floating in the sky. By the time the sheriff and his posse arrive I am ready for them. They see a naked man arise from the earth. They see a naked man approach them with his arms outstretched and blood running from his eyes.

HA HA HA HA

Hit the burn with plaster. Conceive a helter-skelter cat sweat. Roughen it with strong adjectives. The pain expands its parameter. And a bicycle pleads rain.

I manipulate the massive wash. This exemplifies a boiling nerve. My gargle smacks this pound. Send the shaken thought flap. Horses galloping through a compulsion smash.

We push our kaolin hands. Your empty block convulses bulbs. The image sparkles a mirror. It assembles by gratifying brains. An immediate crack cures trickling.

What is action ocher decorations. Arrange behavior beneath your breath. The squashed mode succeeds at wheels. Ha ha ha ha it accentuated my ocean. Ha ha ha ha it oiled the sorcery.

Ha ha ha ha it continued in fire. Ha ha ha ha it pounced the leaves. Ha ha ha ha the stilts drooled existence. Ha ha ha ha mimicry dwells in eating. Ha ha ha ha flaps boils nibbles.

It fires your sparrow propeller. Toss the paraffin to bitumen. Build the charcoal sympathetically structured. Writing flourishes in the past. Memory ignites on the face.

The asphalt explains its connectedness. It does this by segments. The highway juts this opinion. I feel it disturb Milwaukee. The spirit nominates its rivers.

Experience ruptures the abstract furniture. Experience is velvet to cake. Experience brings meaning to anxiety. Gargoyles supply the other sounds.

Touch your skin at war. You will feel ghosts dance. Proposals embedded in secret money. Green buttons murder the horizon. Bacteria feather amid the tears.

I trap the hissing emotion. It feels like Hindu algebra. Ultramarine ripples aloud like wheat. Life absorbs its flopped contraptions. The emotions bark around plums.

The stethoscope endures its hearing. I have formulas for sophistry. Grammar pinned to the air. Hospital Cubism in joyful bedlam. Tug propelled by scorching endeavor.

Incandescent bathers tickle a definition. For what for cooking principles. Ha ha ha ha flipped in a bag. Ha ha ha ha inflated by limestone money. Ha ha ha ha hurrying a chiseled light.

NOCTURNAL BYPASS

I tend to bump into things a lot. The bookcase between the bedroom and bathroom. The coffee table. The ghost of my father. The refrigerator and filing cabinet. I construct maps from whistles and distillations of fire escape shadows. I hear the night squeeze a window and extend itself into a worm and drift through the universe writing alphabets with its body and clutching planets with exhilarating dexterity. But then, where isn't it night? Isn't it always night in the universe? Cold black endless void. Never hug an image. Especially one of your own invention. Just jabber. Jabber away ploughing the air with your words and mouth dropping names and hints and insinuations. You might groan a little from time to time. It lends sincerity to your discourse. Crackle with inner fire. Clasp your friends and tell them you love them. Then skidoodle. The last thing you want is to get invited to their next poetry reading. Chat with a cat. Thicken yourself with occurrence and coughing. Smack your lips when you eat. Twitch and convulse when you drive then dig the expressions of your passengers. It will freak you out. Me I like to gnaw on deep philosophical subjects. Especially those that are related to conceptions of paradise. Sometimes I imagine pain as a landscape and I am in a hot air balloon drifting overhead and see its shadow on the ground. It looks like a giant round head. It moves over a hillock and distorts. I release more flame. The balloon rises. I reach for a cloud and fall out of the basket. As I fall to the ground I realize that in a few moments I will be experiencing a new kind of pain. The last pain. The last pain I will ever feel. And then I twitch and kick and awaken just before I hit the ground. And consciousness floods my head and my eyes open and there I am. A man in bed. No balloon. Thank god. I think. I'm not sure. That taste of oblivion was so near. So sweet. Such a tasty morsel of nothingness. An ache that follows at my heels throughout the day. Into the operating room. As I make incisions, and study the pumping of somebody's heart.

A PROPOSITION

A proposition possesses essential and accidental characteristics. Neon, stupefaction, and leather. Words meander. Description unzips. Helicopters survey the traffic. A joyride accords occasions for expression and perhaps a little redemption. One of these days the windows will strangle their mass and yield profusions of milk. Who would prefer the clacking of jade pendants if she heard the stone grow in the cliff? Definitions are formed by canvas and metaphor. Waterfalls clothe the air with energy. Poetry, on the other hand, does not wish to fall into theory, but pullulate with words in the margins of society, wheeling round and round like a mad mechanical wart. What else would you expect language to do? It begins in a placenta of sound, develops syllable by syllable into hue and heart, opens its eyes, thrills with life, steadies its wings, catches a stirring of air and drifts into reverie.

A LITTLE LOAD OF PAINT

Cézanne sags during a moment of paint. There is an umbrella in the room whose surface collects his thoughts. Outside in the rain the grass and garden smell strongly of spring. Fruit litters the table. Light through the window writhes in conversation with shape and color. There are elevations beyond the mind. There are nerves that will bring the world closer. There are nerves that bring the universe to our tongues and ears. Some shapes demand red. Some green. Some yellow. A few blue or black. Black is the ocean that guzzles us when we open to its possibilities. The road is wife to the husband horizon. You cannot muzzle a color with shape. Shape is to color what rock is to dirt. Clay imparts a stunning vindication of resilience. The eyes find their syntax in tears. Consciousness is malleable. You can put the universe in a jar if it rolls by your feet. Later, toward evening, it will glow. It will swallow you whole. It will collide with everything you think you know. Everything you think you think you know. Then press your hand to your forehead and feel that weariness turn to straw. The lightness of a thread blown upward with the breath. In thought. In reverie. In linear intricacies and a crisp blue line bringing contour to a jug. Volumes anchored to a surface of linen. Lines on linen in which the essence of seeing is itself a theater, a stunning echo of consciousness in pigment and space.

RUMINATION

Let me tell you about my appetite. It is enormous. How enormous you ask. Let me put it this way: I have just eaten you. You were my sandwich. You were delicious. Now I'm going to eat a railroad. I'm going to spread it with butter and put it in my mouth and chew it until it is gone. I'm going to eat an orchard of apples, an orchard of pears, an orchard of peaches and a grove of olives. Why, you might ask, are you so hungry? Well it is this way. My appetite is a fiction. I'm not hungry at all. And this frightens me a little because it makes me feel a little separate from life. Thus, I created an appetite of fiction. For fiction, one might say. Of fiction. For fiction. I am cultivating a willingness to devour anything. I will eat a chemistry lab. I will eat a perturbation if I can figure out how to cook a perturbation. Things perceived in the abstract are difficult to cook. It's better to stick to protein. I don't want to become diabetic. Not in the service of fiction. I want to grow strong. I want to eat my fill of bread and honey. I want to fulfill the wildest dreams of my stomach in its ambitions to digest the world. When I'm finished writing this paragraph I will eat it. I will crumple it up and stick it in my mouth and eat it. I will eat whole chimeras of food. The food of utopian kitchens. The food of reverie. The food of the written word, which is a digestion of the mind rather than the stomach. This is the chewing of the mind. This is the rumination of the distant and ultramarine. Far horizons. Where the food arrives in a basket of clouds and is served on forks of lightning.

WIND BAG

Last night I decided to go through my bag of wind and sort things out. I'm a hoarder, and wind is no exception. I collect winds.

I found two siroccos, five simooms, three foehns, eight Chinooks, ninety gales, thirty zephyrs, two nor'westers, a monsoon, a harmattan, one hundred flurries, two tornados, a Kabibonokka, a Wabun, a Shawndasee and three Mudjekeewis's, a packet of eight hundred squalls (they were on sale), a pair of gusts, a used but mint condition sirocco, and a mistral still soughing in the reeds of the Camargue (but without the actual Camargue). I got them all out on the floor where they growled and whistled and sighed and roared, puffed and huffed and bellowed and blew. It was hard keeping them separate. I wouldn't put it in a category with herding cats, but close. In the ballpark. Definitely in the ballpark.

I've never seen so many wafts. What was I doing with all these wafts? When I was I going to use a waft? Or a suspiration? Or a bluster? I do all my blustering myself. Was there an organization to which I could donate some of these puffs and whiffets?

Too bad the days of the clipper are gone. I still have some yachtsmen for clients, but mostly I keep the collection for my own enjoyment. My own private afflatus, as it were.

I attend conventions occasionally. Have you ever tried to pack a white squall with your T-shirts and underwear? It's not easy. I envy the bubble and foam crowd. But then, everything is always wet. You never find a nice dry pair of pants.

People call us wayward. We are. I freely admit it. We're a wayward bunch. It's the nature of the medium. If it doesn't blow your mind, it will blow you away. And if it doesn't do either, you're just not a wind person. Not a wind bag.

The Hindu say that Vayu, the Lord of the Winds and Deity of Life, is a deity of exceptional beauty and moves loudly and lordly in his shining coach, which is driven by two or forty-nine or one-thousand white and purple horses, and carries a white banner.

This wind is not in my collection. You cannot possess Vayu. You can only breathe Vayu. Inhale and exhale Vayu. It is not a collection. It is a rhythm.

STROLLING IS TROLLING

This is an exercise based on the "I remember" (Je me souviens) writing prompt developed by Georges Perec. I used the same subject/predicate structure, but wondered what might ensue if I used different verbs. I chose verbs at random and took it from there, using the verb to produce a reflection, generally something personal. The first verb was 'stir.' The final verb was 'inspire.'

* * * * * * * *

I like stirring sugar into my tea. I use a chopstick. The restaurant where we usually go for Chinese food never provides spoons. But they do offer chopsticks. I use the chopstick. It doesn't do the job as effectively as a spoon, but it works. The sugar dissolves into the tea instead of lying on the bottom.

Whenever I hear the word 'tumble,' I think of the Beatles. I had a tumbling class in high school in 1963, when the Beatles were first heard on U.S. radio. We used to mock them. Their sound was so girlish and effervescent. The Beatles committed the cardinal sin of rock 'n roll: they were cheerful. There is simply no such thing as cheerful rock 'n roll. But I could be wrong. I was wrong. It wasn't much longer that I fully embraced the Beatles. But by then they had come out with Rubber Soul and had ceased sounding so cheerful. In fact, a lot of their songs were tinged with malaise. "Nowhere Man." "Norwegian Wood." "Help."

That scene of Tom Cruise climbing the Burj Khalifa building in Dubai is enthralling.

Who doesn't love splashing water? Several days ago, when Roberta and I were out running on the asphalt paved path at Myrtle Edwards Park on the shore of Elliott Bay, it was extremely windy. Waves were being buffeted against the rocks and a flock of seagulls hovered over them in a state of evident excitement. I assumed there must be a school of smelt or salmon beneath the waves. We stopped to watch them and noticed the heads of a number of seals emerge and disappear. The sound of the water is lovely. So quiet. It contrasted wonderfully with the screech of the seagulls, which sounded like insane laughter.

I have never once greased a wheel or an axle in my life. I am simply not given to mechanical things. I chose writing as a profession because it's relatively clean.

I have never stolen anything from anyone, although I could confess to time theft. There have been many occasions in the past when I shirked work at a job, hung out in a basement reading a book or enjoyed a long, vigorous conversation with a fellow employee instead of doing some actual work.

I have a huge respect for fellow poets. There are so few rewards when it comes to writing poetry. People generally regard you as a fool. Though as anyone who has attempted to write a poem knows, it's hard. It's really hard to write a good poem. One of those poems that hits the brain like a line of Merck cocaine. Ignites a firework display in your neurons. That's a lot easier to do with an electric guitar and a good drummer than a handful of words, let me tell you.

I dislike bending over to pick something up. I have to do a lot of bending when I visit Suzzallo library at the University of Washington because in order to pay the guard at the underground parking lot I have to open the door of our Subaru so that I can lean out far enough to get my hand into my back pocket to pull out my wallet. This process must be repeated when I put my wallet back into my back pocket. That constitutes a lot of bending for me.

Hanging from anything is fun. Unless you're hanging from a rope all night on the side of a cliff. Though I suppose the rigors of the sport would be fun for you in a deeper sense. The thrill of imminent death. The adversities of the weather. The novelty of your position.

There are so many needs in life: food, shelter, sex, companionship. I frequently wonder if art is a need. I know a lot of people who would instantly and vigorously argue yes, of course, art is a need. It's a spiritual need. It is the need for transcendence. But I'm not so sure. One of the things I like best about art is that it's not needed. It's superfluous. It really doesn't serve any purpose. That appeals to me because, deep down, I'm pissed off at the whole set up. And art is seditious. It says, fuck you forces that be. Fuck you forces that brought me into this life. I'm going to enjoy something that has nothing whatever to do with my survival. Something that is simply exciting. Sensual. Uplifting in a goofy, inexplicable way.

The word 'progress' doesn't do much for me. Either as a noun or a verb. I prefer to say move rather than say progress. I don't say: I'm progress-ing to the store to get some crackers. I say I'm going to the store to get some crackers. Progress has a clunky feeling because of all those dry, textbook articles about so-called human progress. Human progress is destroying the planet.

I love strolling. Just aimlessly ambling along. Looking at things in a detached but absorbed kind of way. Taking the world in at my leisure. Strolling is trolling for abalones of pure amusement.

How often do I feel the need to clutch something? I don't remember that last time I clutched something. Did I clutch my mug of coffee this morning? I'm not sure that's clutching. Not clutching in the proper sense of clutching. I held it carefully but not firmly. Firm enough to keep it in my hand, but not so firm that I could say I was clutching it. I've never, for instance, clutched a gun. If I had need of a gun, if I was in that sort of situation, I would definitely be clutching it.

I've never punched anyone. I've been punched, but never even punched back. I blame movies for this. I have the fear that if I ever punched anyone, they would fall and hit their head on a rock or andiron and die. Then I'd be up for murder. One minute you're pissed, the next minute you're on trial. For fucking murder.

I do a lot of sifting, but this is not the sifting of a gold miner . This is the sifting of research and writing. Sifting details. Sifting words.

I'm fascinated by heat, the way it quickens things, makes them sizzle and bounce, turn brown or black, makes them churn or bubble, boil or simmer. And yet I am not really into cooking. I guess I could be. But I'm not. Couldn't say why. I'm just not into it.

I am insufficiently inspired. What inspires me is the desire to get high. Stimulated. My mood altered. Euphoria. Buoyancy. Thrills. This is what makes me want to write. Put words by words and see what happens. It's a great kind of chemistry. The explosions are intellectual. No hands are burned, no glasses broken. Yet control is illusory. There is no actual control. And that's what makes it so wonderful. You never know what's going to happen. You don't even know what's possible. Or impossible. All the perturbations are glorious.

A TRAGIC VEGETABLE

The onion is a tragic vegetable. It has all those layers, the outer ones brittle as ancient medieval parchment, as if to say "the one who writes here must use a pen as delicate as air, for life is ephemeral, and the life of the onion evolves in darkness, in dirt, and grows into a globe that is acrid and sour and so compact in its bitterness that it can only be opened by knife."

When the onion is chopped and sliced its cells are damaged, which produces a volatile gas known as the onion lachrymatory factor, which is the cause of its notorious stinging sensation. The onion is bitter and wants us to cry, to share in the acuity of existence, the exquisitely intricate contrarieties of existence, which are sharp with sensation, and binding in their constancy.

The onion repulses as it draws us to it. We must back away, then return to its rings, if we want to add the onion to our broth of cloves and sausage.

We must chop the onion into bits. We must cry. We must endure. We must protect ourselves as the onion does, in layers and rings and sour emanations.

The tear itself is a sign of capitulation. It grows in weight and trickles from the orbit of the eye in a slow irregular path. Weeping has a formal weight, a gravitas. It is different than sweat. Sweat is more acrid and covers the entire body with a sheen of salty moisture, a residual luster of healthful endeavor. It is the result of exertion, not strong emotion. Sweat lacks the sympathy of tears because its origin is mechanical rather than emotional. Sweat attends the drama of bodies in intense motion. It is the juice of aggression. War and sports. Vigorous sex. Hot summer days and long summer nights in voluptuous ceiling fan abandon. It is the stuff of Hemmingway novels and bar bells. Tears are the emblems of romantics and Pre-Raphaelites. Tears are Dante Gabriel Rossetti. Sweat is Arnold Schwarzenegger.

Blood is the opposite of sweat. The object of blood is to stay within the body and bring oxygen to the cells. You don't want to see blood outside of the body. That's not where it's supposed to be. You don't want to see blood at all. Unless you're a surgeon doing heart surgery and your attention is focused on the rhythmic diastole and systole of the heart. Pumping blood in, pumping blood out. Or giving blood in a bloodmobile, the dark fluid of your body moving through a transparent tube into a plastic bag.

The adult human heart has a mass between 250 and 350 grams. It is about the size of a fist. It is located between the vertebral column to the rear and sternum in the front. Symbolically, it is the seat of all emotion, all feeling. If we say someone has a lot of heart it means they have a lot of feeling, a certain gallantry of generous being. If we say a prostitute has a heart of gold it means that her rough mercenary exterior belies an inner warmth and generosity.

Shakespeare makes frequent reference to the heart: My heart is heavy and mine age is weak; if my heart were great, 'twould burst at this; there were a heart in Egypt; the heart of brothers govern in our loves and sway our great designs; my heart was to thy rudder tied by strings; throw my heart against the flint and hardness of my fault; O that your Highness knew my heart in this; now I do frown on thee with all my heart; warr'st thou with a woman's heart; their very heart of hope; the head is not more native to the heart; a heart unfortified, a mind impatient; but break my heart for I must hold my tongue; for my manly heart doth yearn; he'll drop his heart in the sink of fear; the king's a bawcock, and a heart of gold; come, here's my heart; I shall be out of heart shortly, and then have no strength to repent.

The heart of a matter is its very core, its essence. Its most enduring part. Here in the realm of metaphor, a heart could feasibly be anything, except a diesel locomotive or a tulip. Which is grossly off-target. It can be those things, too, if you can massage the language into accommodating the chatter of humpbacked toads, or the language itself assumes a more leading role and simmers in its own casserole, concocts scarlet antennas, mechanical beards and splashes of apparitional splendor. Metaphors never die. Metaphors metamorphose. Metaphors metastasize into larger and larger metaphors until at last a dream of life seeks the warmth of the soil, turns toward the sun, and a phenomenal flux occurs, generating thousands of leaves and winds, lavender on the hills of Provence, secret metals in sparkling parables, onions in rows in the fields of eastern Idaho, a heart beating fast in a fight in Tallahassee.

Silverware gleams on the beautiful white tablecloth. A waiter appears, bringing plates of onion quiche. Hearts beat, wine flows. The waiter has been working hard. There is a sheen on his brow as he leans forward, gently putting a plate on the table.

BLOOD

Every day approximately 1.5 gallons of blood circulate through the veins and arteries and capillaries of my body.

Fine.

But what does it do?

Lub dub, lub dub, lub dub, lub dub.

Blood brings oxygen and iron to the places where oxygen and iron are needed. My brain. My lungs. My muscles. My kidneys, pancreas, intestines. My fantasies of life in Fiji. My opacity and optic nerves. My flaws and flirtations. My trajectories and disappointments. My hopes and illusions. My thoughts and cynicism. My appeasements and caprices. All washed by blood. Imbued with blood. Blood blood blood. Blood everywhere pumping and pushing and pulsing.

The scene in *Limitless* after Eddie Mora stabs Gennady and Gennady falls dead to the floor and his blood starts oozing out from under his body onto the hardwood floor of Eddie Mora's super-expensive Manhattan penthouse and Eddie, who is lying next to Gennady in a state of exhaustion, gets the idea of drinking Gennady's blood because it contains the drug that makes you super smart and able to make connections at lightning speed and get yourself out of dangerous situations by quickly reading all the available possibilities, is a graphic illustration.

Blood is cinematic. There are, not surprisingly, many movies with blood in the title. *Blood Alley. Blood Beach. Blood Brothers. Blood Castle. Blood Dolls. Blood Frenzy. Blood Money. Blood Moon. Blood of a Poet. Blood of the Innocent. Blood Relations. Blood Simple.*

All beauty comes from beautiful blood and a beautiful brain, says Walt Whitman.

It inspires me to think of ink as blood. Ink is the blood making Walt Whitman's words have life in them. Though they could exist as pixels on a computer screen. In which case the metaphor could be transferred to electricity instead of ink. But it's so much easier to think of ink as blood.

Computers have circuits, not blood. When discussions of artificial intelligence come up I have to laugh. Consciousness without blood is not consciousness. You need the crimson of blood to have real consciousness. The blood of the raspberry. The blood of prayer. The blood of war. The blood of form and vision. Blood without precedent. The vowels of the night slapped into blood.

BOX SET

I live in a box. I think I'm a shoe. Though I may be a pen. I don't know. Identity is hard. Hard to figure out what one is. What one might be. May be. Easy to laugh, though. And cry. Crying and laughing. That would argue against my being a shoe. Shoes don't laugh, or cry. Nor do pens. Or do they? Writing is a form of weeping. Tears from the tip of the pen form images, stars, moons, the interior of a planetarium, that broad sweep of stars above one's head as someone stands at a podium identifying the constellations, Andromeda, Draco, Cassiopeia, Ursa Major, Ursa Minor, and so on, the infinite of the infinite, which cannot be imagined, particularly if you live in a box. My box is located on the border of time. There is also a lake and an alpine village and a hardware store where you can find light switches, pliers, hammers, glue, everything one needs to repair things, everything, that is, except what goes on inside one's being. What is it that repairs Being? Being with a capital B. Being. Pure Being. Being in a box. Being in a circle. Being in a pickle. Grammar isn't being. Grammar is a form of wardrobe. It is how we dress our thoughts. Our thoughts of Being.

Did I mention the ant? I have an inflatable ant. It decorates a corner. The furniture is high density foam and kiln-dried hardwood. Brass studs, paisley prints. I have a philosophy of furniture and it is this: furniture should thrill consciousness. I believe that there should be a separate form corresponding to every predicate and separate forms for hair, mud, and dirt. I believe that a table should differ from bees and that a bed is essential for sleep. Apart from that, furniture should just be furniture, and provide comfort for our aching bones.

I keep several brooms in the closet, one for the porch, one for the floor.

I also have a vacuum. It plugs into the wall. It makes a sound like humming, but it is not humming, it is something else. It is the whir of a vacuum as it might sound if it were written in words on paper. A swarm of words congealing to make a vacuum.

A light veil keeps the mosquitoes out.

Silverware jingles in a drawer by the refrigerator.

When I open the door and step into the world, I feel the spin of the planet in our ride around the sun. The planet wobbles and creates seasons. Right now the season is approaching that of winter. There is the tincture of snow in the air, just a suggestion, a whisper, a proposal, an intimation. The wind stirs in dry old leaves. If you pick one up you can feel how dry and crinkly it is. The life has gone out of it. The sun has gone out of it. What is left is a dry parchment. What is left is a chapter from the story of a tree.

Puddles indicate the passage of a storm during the night. Signs of distress litter the ground. Branches, some of them fairly large, lie strewn on the ground.

Isn't it funny how a mosaic of neurons in our heads receives sensations from the outer world and grows into postulates and letters? Toads, eggs, claws. Umbrellas, apparitions, forests. A cat walking across a keyboard. A paragraph presented in the form of a box. A leaf. A being. A power stirring in the air.

THE PUSH-UP RANCH

There is a push-up on the ceiling. I don't know how to get it down. I've tried hitting it with a broom. That just made it blow steam. I asked my wife, did you do push-ups on the ceiling? She did. Why? It's easier up there. The cat doesn't bother me. Well, you left one up there. We called in a specialist from Dallas, Texas. He brought a special kind of vacuum. He lifted the hose attachment and nozzle and asked me to flip the switch. As soon as I flipped the switch, the machine began to hum, the cat hid under the bed, and I heard something that sounded like a herd of rogue capillaries get sucked into the belly of the push-up vacuum. We paid the specialist his usual fee of $500 dollars and he left. Guess I'll have to go back to doing my push-ups on the floor, my wife said sadly. I wonder what that guy does with all the push-ups he collects in his vacuum. I forgot to ask. I don't know, said my wife, I'll look it up on Google. Turns out there is a ranch in Texas for herds of push-ups. Cartwheels, somersaults, and jumping jacks as well. It's called Voltereta Rancho. People go there to exercise and improve their health. They pay a Little extra because the excercises have already been done for them. They just sit around drinking margaritas and fix their eyes on the surrounding vista for various cartwheels and push-ups to come and graze on the barren hills of mesquite and sage. Sometimes a colorful excercise boy in chaps and blazing bandana will ride out on a horse and rope a push-up to bring in if someone actually feels like doing one.

METAMORPHOSIS REVISITED

When I met Gregor Samsa he was still a cockroach, erratic and skittish whenever the light came on. We often spoke in the dark. I empathized. But I gave him credit where credit is due. He was self-sufficient. He survived. He went about his business without injury to other people.

Identity is always unclear. It's a proposal at the very start. The very first breath.

My visits with Gregor were brief. His body repulsed me. It saddens me to admit that, but it's true. Nobody likes hanging out with a cockroach for very long. One is never quite sure which of the legs to shake in greeting. Or what exactly to serve for refreshment. Crumbs? Something gone bad in the refrigerator?

Gregor had a fascination for socks and shoes. That's mainly what he saw most of the time. His judgments of the world and its people were based on socks and shoes. Shoe sizes. Shoe soles. Shoe tongues. Shoe laces.

We would often talk until midnight. He was especially fond of Vincent Price. He liked those scary late night movies of vampires and mummies.

I think to this day he is still a cockroach. I was never sure if this metamorphosis to which he referred had been a matter of accident or intention. But who am I to probe into such matters? My antennas are not as sharp as they used to be.

CATHEDRAL OF AIR

What is an emotion? An emotion is a cathedral of air. It is forest and rocks. A simmering thirsty bone. An old TV shouting the sky into space.

Faucets are different. Faucets are particular and chrome.

I heard the door slam, yet no one came in. This happens a lot.

There is no way to map an emotion. Emotions are vague. Mercurial. What you can do is rip the night into shreds and ache for the essence of things.

Cause and effect are a smell.

Each day is a voyage whose destination is sleep. The shell is full of subtleties, like the lips of a young woman.

No one really knows what true beauty is. It arrives in the rain when we least expect it.

Willpower is an internal phenomenon involving five large emotions and a spine.

Cherubs kiss in the shrubbery. The black back of a snake slithers into a hole. You can see a personality shine in someone's eyes and believe beauty is not distinct from the Jardin de Luxembourg. You can follow the bells of Saint Sulpice to a stairwell and find beauty in the eye of a woman falling out of a clock.

My interior reposes in an operating room with a sewing machine and an umbrella.

The meeting of diagonal ribs in the vault of a cathedral is powerful and gray.

Attach a thought to a sentence and watch it fly to the pommel of a saddle and ride away.

The cliffs of Norway are cathedrals of rock. A Viking sleeps in thick furs at the stern of the boat. He dreams that each word is a shape like a knife. When he reaches Torgar, he will carve the air. He will carve it into gods and dragons. He will carve it into silence and gold.

DIVERSIFICATION

I like money. I always have. Money is the reason I don't have to sharpen a stick and go kill something. But what fascinates me about money isn't merely its buying power but the concept that gives it meaning and value. Money is a form of language. Of substitution.

Money and language are hallucinations. Who doesn't like hallucinations? They're images with no power to hurt us.

Or do they?

Money has become phantasmal because when Bill Clinton signed away the Glass-Steagall Act in 1999 he created a situation in which commercial bank affiliates were permitted to gamble with their depositors' money. The Glass-Steagall Act separated commercial banking from investment banking. Once you get into investment banking, and do it on computers that flash algorithms in a split-second, you've got a situation in which money begins to lose meaning. Wealth, hosted on computer-based electronic trading systems, deal in debt or equity-backed securities. These phantasms of wealth assume the form of pension funds, hedge funds, or sovereign wealth funds. The word 'fund' makes it sound real. But it's not. None of it is real.

Why does a dollar still mean dollar to the guy at the 7-11 or barbershop or law office? Why does a thousand dollars still mean a thousand dollars to the hospital administrator or electrician or casino cashier?

I have no idea. It amazes me that money still has meaning.

The dynamic that is money is based on the mystery of the zero. This is where concrete reality ends and the world of the algorithm begins. Where wealth assumes dizzying magnitudes of irreality.

Zero, which is a sign for nothing, allows for the multiplication of numbers into larger and larger sums. It is the blood of the algorithm. It is what brings oxygen to the tissue of finance. It is to mercantile capitalism what the blood of young maidens is to the fangs of Count Dracula.

Zero is sexy. It is the very stuff of poetry. It is the very essence of the meta-sign, the first non-real thing to assume a conceptual existence in thought. No ideas but in things, said Williams. But what about zero? Is zero a thing? Can a no-thing be a thing? Can the no-thing-ness of zero be a thing-ness in the sense of being a sign? Can a representation of nothingness be a radical semiotic goldmine of chandeliers, magic potions, and Gilgamesh?

Yes. In the realm of the zero, assent and credence have no limit.

From that point of view, the point of view of zero, money is pretty interesting stuff. It can also do a lot of harm. Money, when it goes wild, destroys empires. Implodes. Collapses on itself.

When the paper in my wallet has less value than the pixels on a computer screen, it's time to learn how to boil water and make soup out of dandelions.

When the coins in my pocket cease their meaningful clatter on the drugstore counter and become the dead metal they truly are, our routines will end and we will all have nothing but time on our hands.

DADA BUDAPEST

Infinity solicits our ears to assist in the worship of latex. We walk in exhibition of ourselves, comfortable in our structures of sound, living in the full evidence of our fingers, coaxing meaning out of mud and interacting with the sirens as they lure us further into the poem of life. The journey begins with a hot wet kiss and ends with a defiant hoop skirt. The miles in between are long and argumentative but the darkness stirs the blood and the stripes in the center lane are a confection of pigments and synthetic resin. The gravel at the side of the road is more like crockery than fruit, but tastes of science, a multitude of atoms fused into one dominating impression of words and whispers of rain. It is why I must consider the heat of this moment as a flame bundled together to make a cloth. It is obvious that physical science is an abstraction, but to say this and nothing more would be a confession of philosophic failure which I, for one, am not prepared to make. If you think how you fold things you will see what I mean. Abstractions smell of consciousness, especially at these higher elevations, where the wildflowers shout their names. The truck is old but runs like a top. We enter Dada Budapest moistened by paraffin. It isn't Nebraska. It's more like navigating a bubbly ear with a beautiful finger. There are feathers in the toolbox, and themes of redemption, which are good for hanging curtains. If I strain to describe my belt I discover a form of geometry crawling over itself in reckless abandon. I'm held together by shoes, like most people, but sound like a piano if someone gets too close to my paddle. Let's face it, art isn't always as hospitable as you might think. Have you ever tried buying a bathtub at Home Depot? How did that enterprise get started, anyway? And when did Dada become so emphatic as to deserve an entire city? This is how I've learned to bare myself upon impact. When endurance meets popcorn the result is a stepladder. I've been pregnant before, but not with a paragraph. Unfolding it has been surprisingly round, like the dome of a skull reposing on a block of ice. I feel the friction of life during the intuition of screws. This happened in a crustacean, once, and the result was wood. Everything velvet stands erect. I salute the presumption. There is this silk to wear, have you heard of it? It gets hazy when you pull it over your head and then stimulates conversation as it unites with the bed linen. Somebody said that's a symptom of depression and I opened it and found a horse. I clasped the wind to my breast and crushed a nearby sob with a flick of my gland. Which gland, I'm not saying. Let's just say it has something to do with propulsion. Who doesn't like the west coast of Ireland? Is that all you can say? Retire on your own terms. Periodically, I like to sparkle when no one is expecting it, and the hit songs that once made life squirt with stereophonic glee are now all understood as knobs, or Indian paintbrush.

THE PROBABILITIES OF GRAY

Who doesn't like silk? I like silk. Do you like silk? I climbed out of a deluge yesterday and the first thing I saw was a consonant groaning under the weight of a drumstick. Some of my emotions are tilted and full of ostentation but most of them hide under the bed when the light is turned on. Money is only a rumor. Time is a mildly personal cart-wheel. And so I got a job photographing gargoyles in the wild. This required oranges, sedatives, and whistles. I parked my clothes in the garage and went swimming.

Sooner or later a dream of death will blend with enough syntax to become orthogonal. If this happens, assemble a thyroid. It helps to hop into a little cotton and apply some gravity to a predisposed weight. If the weight isn't heavy it's probably an eye. All the flowers cry "hinge." What is meant by "hinge"?

Everything in life is a door. The rain is a door and the reflections in the puddles are doors. Even the doors of perception are doors. They were the first doors I remembering opening. I must've been young when that happened. Quite possibly before I was born. I was dead before I was born. I must've been, because I don't remember being alive. At some point I must've opened a door and crawled into life.

Warts aren't doors but they do make good windows.

I need a good generality to wire a resumé so that it lights up and gets me the kind of job I want. Which is what? Geez, I don't know. I do enjoy sweeping. The broom and I get into a rhythm I can only describe as a gravitational wave. It feels a little like giving benediction to a participle.

Everything has a structure. Even a puddle has a structure. If it drops below zero your average puddle will succeed easily at becoming ice. If stepped on, it will crack. Things with structure generally crack. But don't try experimenting with a pillow. You'll only wind up frustrated and begin writing poetry.

I see most things as a tendency. According to quantum theory, matter doesn't exist at the subatomic level with any degree of certainty.

Rather, it shows tendencies to exist. These tendencies are expressed as probabilities, shoehorns, and cats.

Or waves. Almost everything is a wave of some sort. An energy moving through the water that is the fluidity of our lives causing perceptions to roll and swell and flop down on a rock or a stretch of sand, preferably the nice white sand at Carmel, California, where tendencies to do anything or create anything are immense probabilities regaling the mind with regenerative power.

Of course, the probabilities of quantum theory are purely mathematical. These probabilities make waves that oscillate in time and space like the vague uncertainties of hotel accommodations before we arrive at our destination and enter the lobby in our fatigue and rumpled clothing after our ride from the airport in heavy traffic in a foreign city.

Probability waves aren't like the waves in the ocean on a windy day but are abstract mathematical patterns.

I think of myself as a consortium of waves. Cells and waves. Cells in waves. Events rippling through me creating attitudes and opinions, appetites and tempests.

Tendency is what permits the waterfront to become a semantic vehicle of treasured moments. Quiet, sad, reflective moments. This makes walking, which is a simultaneity of legs in movement, wander into thought and invite itself to get written down.

As I am now doing. If I rub the cement a certain way it becomes provocatively indefinite. It begins to boil and transmit meanings that I can wrestle into grammar and allow myself to dilate and blast into parallels and comparisons, weighing and distilling, searching for meaning in an aquarium or T-shirt. If I can infringe on the veracity of fingernails for a moment, I would like to offer a murmur of optimism to the absent-mindedness of wool. People call this "wool-gathering." I see it as a tribute to the color gray. Perhaps I can one day forge a chariot of sparks and withdraw into privacy to enjoy the probabilities of gray. Meanwhile, I'll just sit and watch the sun as it moves through the sky flattering the trees and feeding their leaves a salad of nuclear fusion.

DAY OF THE PRUNE

I like to gather delicate things. Anything. So long as it's delicate, symbolic, and glass. Perception is a process so strangely is there something behaving until it becomes a bakery. I walked through postulation lifted and here I am. I'm the weather. Snow falls on my hand and the afternoon threads a shiny pain until it knocks on the door. What do you do when reality is injured? Distance does currents and dots drip on a map of my heart. Movement is the fertility of experience creeping slowly across the ooze of learning. People are irritating. I think of kelp. It helps. Appeal appeals and is appealing. That, too, and the bakery causes itself by rubber. Writing is always a warrior yelling in battle. Cement is worship. If we reflect on glowing we are a people of ink. I suckle a headlight in the greenhouse and cage a little alligator in my prophecy. I feel most palpable when a cloth enhances hope, which is to say coffee squeezing a moon with my subtleties contoured to look like syntax. And we all know what a push up is. Scatter these words in your mind and wave to me from a farm. I will coagulate. I am stretched into you like a long abalone on a lone night in Tuscaloosa. I am a color walking in bones. I will sell you an odor for one dollar but you must choose the scent. I will start this sexual incense notwithstanding. I am not with standing I am pulling a dream out of the taste of hail. I come to compose this despite the power to chirp, which is easier, but less effective. If I fill a suitcase with enough injuries I can get dressed in a hothouse Picasso and feel its rags sag into air. And so my statements are not the same as strolling, I know this, it's riveted to a big construction, gnarled as an oak and wet as veins. So this makes it that a ship is rope and not as disturbing as lightning shooting from the mouth of the dishwasher. His name is Walt and he likes science, Arizona, and towels. I've said this before and I'll say it again. Consciousness is exhausting. It's really so much easier to bless one's shoes with quietude and go swimming anyway. I think of music and don't really mean a house. I'm just energy, you know? I do like immediacy and ghosts and antiques. I like willow and exploration. Writing is better when it's catching a taxi then when it's remembering miniskirts. But that's just a useless generality. Don't listen to me. I smell like an ice cube. I float in my head like a world and hope someday to whistle. But really, when you think about it, frogs are as stunning as dumbbells, and I'm an eel like anyone else, a phoneme languishing in prunes.

JOHN OLSON has published nine collections of prose poetry. He is also the author of four novels, including *Souls of Wind*, which was shortlisted for a *Believer* Book Award in 2008, *The Seeing Machine, The Nothing That Is*, and (most recently) *In Advance of the Broken Justy*. In 2004, Seattle's popular weekly *The Stranger* awarded Olson its annual Genius Award for literature and in 2012 he was one of eight finalists for Washington State's Arts Innovator Award.

TITLES FROM BLACK WIDOW PRESS
TRANSLATION SERIES

A Life of Poems, Poems of a Life by Anna de Noailles. Translated by Norman R. Shapiro. Introduction by Catherine Perry.

Approximate Man and Other Writings by Tristan Tzara. Translated and edited by Mary Ann Caws.

Art Poétique by Guillevic. Translated by Maureen Smith.

The Big Game by Benjamin Péret. Translated with an introduction by Marilyn Kallet.

Boris Vian Invents Boris Vian: A Boris Vian Reader. Edited and translated by Julia Older.

Capital of Pain by Paul Eluard. Translated by Mary Ann Caws, Patricia Terry, and Nancy Kline.

Chanson Dada: Selected Poems by Tristan Tzara. Translated with an introduction and essay by Lee Harwood.

Creole Echoes: The Francophone Poetry of Nineteenth-Century Louisiana. Translated by Norman R. Shapiro. Introduction and notes by M. Lynn Weiss.

Earthlight (Clair de Terre) by André Breton. Translated by Bill Zavatsky and Zack Rogrow. (New and revised edition.)

Essential Poems and Writings of Joyce Mansour: A Bilingual Anthology. Translated with an introduction by Serge Gavronsky.

Essential Poems and Prose of Jules Laforgue. Translated and edited by Patricia Terry.

Essential Poems and Writings of Robert Desnos: A Bilingual Anthology. Edited with an introduction and essay by Mary Ann Caws.

EyeSeas (Les Ziaux) by Raymond Queneau. Translated with an introduction by Daniela Hurezanu and Stephen Kessler.

Fables in a Modern Key by Pierre Coran. Translated by Norman R. Shapiro. Full-color illustrations by Olga Pastuchiv.

Forbidden Pleasures: New Selected Poems 1924–1949 by Luis Cernuda. Translated by Stephen Kessler.

Furor and Mystery & Other Writings by René Char. Edited and translated by Mary Ann Caws and Nancy Kline.

The Gentle Genius of Cécile Périn: Selected Poems (1906–1956). Edited and translated by Norman R. Shapiro.

Guarding the Air: Selected Poems of Gunnar Harding. Translated and edited by Roger Greenwald.

The Inventor of Love & Other Writings by Gherasim Luca. Translated by Julian & Laura Semilian. Introduction by Andrei Codrescu. Essay by Petre Răileanu.

Jules Supervielle: Selected Prose and Poetry. Translated by Nancy Kline & Patricia Terry.

La Fontaine's Bawdy by Jean de La Fontaine. Translated with an introduction by Norman R. Shapiro.

Last Love Poems of Paul Eluard. Translated with an introduction by Marilyn Kallet.

Love, Poetry (L'amour la poésie) by Paul Eluard. Translated with an essay by Stuart Kendall.

Pierre Reverdy: Poems, Early to Late. Translated by Mary Ann Caws and Patricia Terry.

Poems of André Breton: A Bilingual Anthology. Translated with essays by Jean-Pierre Cauvin and Mary Ann Caws.

Poems of A.O. Barnabooth by Valery Larbaud. Translated by Ron Padgett and Bill Zavatsky.

Poems of Consummation by Vicente Aleixandre. Translated by Stephen Kessler.

Préversities: A Jacques Prévert Sampler. Translated and edited by Norman R. Shapiro.

The Sea and Other Poems by Guillevic. Translated by Patricia Terry. Introduction by Monique Chefdor.

To Speak, to Tell You? Poems by Sabine Sicaud. Translated by Norman R. Shapiro. Introduction and notes by Odile Ayral-Clause.

Forthcoming Translations

Fables of Town & Country by Pierre Coran. Translated by Norman R. Shapiro. Full-color illustrations by Olga Pastuchiv.

MODERN POETRY SERIES

ABC of Translation by Willis Barnstone

An Alchemist with One Eye on Fire
by Clayton Eshleman

An American Unconscious by Mebane Robertson

Anticline by Clayton Eshleman

Archaic Design by Clayton Eshleman

Backscatter: New and Selected Poems by John Olson

Barzakh (Poems 2000–2012) by Pierre Joris

The Caveat Onus by Dave Brinks

City Without People: The Katrina Poems
by Niyi Osundare

Clayton Eshleman/The Essential Poetry: 1960–2015

Concealments and Caprichos by Jerome Rothenberg

Crusader-Woman by Ruxandra Cesereanu.
Translated by Adam J. Sorkin. Introduction by
Andrei Codrescu.

Curdled Skulls: Poems of Bernard Bador.
Translated by Bernard Bador with Clayton Eshleman.

Dada Budapest by John Olson

Disenchanted City (La ville désenchantée)
by Chantal Bizzini. Translated by J. Bradford
Anderson, Darren Jackson, and Marilyn Kallet.

Endure: Poems by Bei Dao.
Translated by Clayton Eshleman and Lucas Klein.

Exile Is My Trade: A Habib Tengour Reader.
Translated by Pierre Joris.

Eye of Witness: A Jerome Rothenberg Reader.
Edited with commentaries by Heriberto Yepez &
Jerome Rothenberg.

Fire Exit by Robert Kelly

Forgiven Submarine
by Ruxandra Cesereanu and Andrei Codrescu

Fractal Song by Jerry W. Ward, Jr.

from stone this running by Heller Levinson

Grindstone of Rapport: A Clayton Eshleman Reader

The Hexagon by Robert Kelly

Larynx Galaxy by John Olson

The Love That Moves Me by Marilyn Kallet

Memory Wing by Bill Lavender

Packing Light: New and Selected Poems
by Marilyn Kallet

Penetralia by Clayton Eshleman

The Present Tense of the World: Poems 2000–2009
by Amina Saïd. Translated with an introduction by
Marilyn Hacker.

The Price of Experience by Clayton Eshleman

The Secret Brain: Selected Poems 1995–2012
by Dave Brinks

Signal from Draco: New and Selected Poems
by Mebane Robertson

Soraya (Sonnets) by Anis Shivani

Tenebraed by Heller Levinson

Wrack Lariat by Heller Levinson

Forthcoming Modern Poetry Titles

Funny Way of Staying Alive by Willis Barnstone

Geometry of Sound by Dave Brinks

Memory by Bernadette Mayer

LITERARY THEORY /
BIOGRAPHY SERIES

*Barbaric Vast & Wild: A Gathering of Outside and
Subterranean Poetry (Poems for the Millennium*, vol. 5).
Eds: Jerome Rothenberg and John Bloomberg-Rissman

Clayton Eshleman: The Whole Art by Stuart Kendall

Revolution of the Mind: The Life of André Breton
by Mark Polizzotti

WWW.BLACKWIDOWPRESS.COM